Praise for JOHN FULLERTON
and *Regenerative Economics*

Sooner or later we will cease our tinkering and realize that heading north is much more than adjusting our path south. But, the new path to economic rules and institutions in line with a living Earth "must be beaten while we walk it." For ex-banker John Fullerton, 20 years of walking has led to a radical rethinking of how technology and finance would need to change fundamentally in order to create healthy commons rather than continued private gain and collective collapse.

—PETER SENGE, MIT Systems Awareness Lab
and author of *The Fifth Discipline*

John Fullerton perfectly captures a seminal moment in our economic history with this astoundingly articulate, profound, and hopeful book. In recent years, it has become clear to many working on sustainability across the whole of society that many of the solutions are failing to deliver a sustainable economy. This book offers a perspective as to why, and also offers a deeply intelligent worldview as a genuine pathway to true long-term permeance for our economy.

Regenerative Economics explores how our deepest liminal assumptions inform our worldview and how our current economy—driven by a mechanistic, reductionist set of mental models—is essentially misaligned with how life and nature really work. This separation from reality has led to the myriad of issues encompassed in the polycrisis that continue to get worse. John's brilliance—borne out of many years of pioneering leadership in this field—is in exposing us to ourselves. He reveals many of the false assumptions on which our current economy has been built, and why we are collectively destroying life rather than enhancing it. Importantly, the book offers a hopeful, truly credible path forward. By aligning our economy to how life really works, to nature's true nature, we can build a new system that is regenerative and life enhancing.

Please read this important book; it will change your life and by extension change our system for the benefit of all Life that will come after us.

—COLIN LE DUC, founding partner of
Generation Investment Management

In a profound breakthrough, *Regenerative Economics* is the way-shower we need to urge our collective agency from separation to wholeness, domination to partnership, and conflict toward our evolutionary potential for planetary peace.

—DR. JUDE CURRIVAN, cosmologist, author,
and co-founder of WholeWorld-View

Having experienced the 9/11 attacks full-on, John Fullerton knows a "disturbance in the force" when he sees one. Increasingly, he senses wider, systemic disturbances looming over today's taken-for-granted market realities. A 20-year Wall Street veteran, he warns of accelerating "elite decay," a standard precursor of societal collapse. But instead of covering his head in ashes, he outlines a systemic remedy: regenerative economics. This book should be on the desk of every politician, CEO, CFO, and investor, worldwide.

—JOHN ELKINGTON, sustainability pioneer and author of 21 books, including
Tickling Sharks: How We Sold Business on Sustainability

These are crucial reflections for an overheating and chaotic world.
—BILL MCKIBBEN, author of *Here Comes the Sun*

Exactly as predicted by Donella Meadows and colleagues a half century ago in the Club of Rome's seminal report, *Limits to Growth*, humanity has not only hit planetary limits, but human progress is moving backwards. The good news is that there are no limits to learning. With *Regenerative Economics*, Fullerton shows us a fresh pathway forward. The time has come to honor the wisdom of *Limits to Growth* by applying what we know and building an alternative future that makes us proud! This book and its thinking contributes to that edifice.
—SANDRINE DIXSON-DECLÈVE, global ambassador for the Club of Rome and co-author of *Earth for All*

Regenerative: everyone's using the word these days. You owe it to yourself to enjoy this deep dive from the man who made the term popular. More importantly, he had the vision and audacity to apply its meaning to the entire economic system. When I first encountered John's work a decade ago, I told him, "Wow, John, in 50 years of doing this work, this is the best I've ever found. I could quibble with this and that, but, full stop, this is the best framing of how we need to go forward that I have found." It still is.
—HUNTER LOVINS, president of Natural Capitalism Solutions, author of 17 books including *Natural Capitalism*, and winner of the Right Livelihood Award

John's book is a compass. It reminds us that our current maps, rooted in separation and machine metaphors, cannot guide us through the polycrisis we face. Here, he develops the dimensions of a new story: an economy that behaves more like a forest than a factory, a system that regenerates instead of depletes. It is an economy grounded in genuine wealth—the vitality of people, communities, and ecosystems—not the abstractions of financial capital alone. We might think of it as a wayfinder's journal, written by someone who walked out of Wall Street and into the wider world, returning with patterns that can help us re-remember how life works.
—BILL REED, principal at Regenesis Group

As someone whose training in economics began in high school and culminated years later in a doctorate, and who has struggled in different ways to go beyond the boundaries of the discipline, it is sobering, comforting, and disturbing all at the same time to encounter and digest John Fullerton's ideas about regenerative economics. John comes at economics as an outsider, aware of but not captured by its teachings, especially those of the dominant neoclassical school, and finds them wanting. In this thought-provoking book, he urges us to take a more holistic approach to understanding the economy, ourselves, and the environment, and to base that understanding on the regenerative process common to all life. More than that, he points the way.
—PETER A. VICTOR, professor emeritus at York University and author of *Escape from Overshoot* and *Herman Daly's Economics for a Full World*

This is one of the most important books on economics in our times. Fullerton understands clearly that our human economy is a subset of nature's economy. But he goes further. In aligning our economic systems with nature's generative processes, he points us toward creating a flourishing Earth community. This perspective echoes the wisdom found in many ancient teachings, offering a pathway to transcend our separation and join together as an interdependent planetary species. *Regenerative Economics* is an indispensable beacon shining the way to our shared planetary future.

—Mary Evelyn Tucker, co-founder and co-director of the Yale Forum on Religion and Ecology and co-author of *Journey of the Universe*

Here we go, double clutching our way through a paradigm shift. John Fullerton is that rare individual who left Wall Street to embrace whole systems economics. Perhaps helped along by a whale who broke the rudder on his sailboat crossing the Atlantic while he was reading *Moby-Dick*? Nature calls. And "Nature States" as distinct from "Nation States" may be the frame we need to respond to Oren Lyons' call, and John's appeal: "Value change for survival."

—Spencer B. Beebe, managing partner of Salmon Nation, founder of Ecotrust, and author of *Cache*

John Fullerton's new book, *Regenerative Economics*, is a light for dark times, offering a new lens for us to reconsider livelihood and how we live in community with ourselves and the natural world. Those who have been waiting for a rigorous yet soulful definition of regeneration and regenerative principles will find Fullerton's approach refreshing, coherent, and comprehensive.

—Vincent Stanley, Director of Philosophy, Patagonia

We need to rethink everything–our economics, finance, culture, politics– if we are to meet the great challenges of our times. Let's begin with this powerful and timely book.

—Rebecca Henderson, John & Natty University Professor, Harvard University

This remarkable book is a compass for navigating through difficult and mysterious times. John Fullerton is a visionary awakened by discomfort on his own journey. Drawing on the wisdom of courageous thinkers, he explores the many aspects of mind, the yearning for relief that makes us prone to misunderstanding and false resolution, and the limits of left-brain false certainty and the dangers it creates.

In the large, this book teaches two particularly important lessons. First is how to see the world and why fear in uncertain times makes many of us cling to a false certainty. And secondly, we learn through Fullerton's example how each of us could channel the experiences, particularly those that are painful, into a new soulful mission and a constructive contribution to the well-being of ourselves and society. John is a beautiful example of that mission and striving.

The beacon of John Fullerton and his book *Regenerative Economics* is a new North Star. It's just what the doctor ordered in these turbulent times.

—Rob Johnson, president of the Institute for New Economic Thinking

In a world with multiple cascading crises, our leaders across society are failing to lead. This is a failure of character, but also a failure of vision. What we face is a crisis of imagination in the age of technology. Fullerton's book is radical, as in getting to the root of the matter. It offers the kind of imaginative thinking our leaders urgently need to transcend our differences and align around the vital challenge of our time: economic system transformation. *Regenerative Economics* offers an inspirational and credible pathway forward; it stirs our souls with well-founded hope.

—Sam Pitroda, innovator, entrepreneur,
author of *Redesign the World*, artist, and
former advisor to two prime ministers of India

Too often we treat our economic system as a given, rather than a human construct that can be changed. And based on its recent track record, it should be. But how? Drawing from the latest systems science and an ecological understanding of how living systems really work, John Fullerton's *Regenerative Economics* brilliantly explores the extraordinary opportunity to design an economic system that supports a more environmentally and socially just world. It's an essential pathway of wisdom, possibility, and hope.

—Jonathan Rose, co-founder of the Garrison Institute
and author of *The Well-Tempered City*

Our project of civilization has reached a crossroads, and the decisions we make now will shape our collective future. The time has passed to wonder if something should be done. For those who remain lost, Fullerton's eye-opening, wise, and highly readable book is a must. His main premise sets the tone: the old paradigm of the economy as a money-making machine is bankrupt and outright dangerous. Instead, Fullerton argues that the economy is a living entity, as profoundly connected with our planetary ecology as we are. This book is an urgent manifesto for the new world we need to build now.

—Marcelo Gleiser, physicist, best-selling author of
The Dawn of a Mindful Universe, Templeton Prize laureate

The world's polycrisis is tearing apart the social and ecological systems vital to our well-being. How can we reduce these terrible risks? John Fullerton guides us to an essential answer. We must shift from the reductionist thinking, institutions, and practices driving the polycrisis and instead reimagine—and then reconfigure—our economies as complex living systems. Lucid, impassioned, and entertaining, *Regenerative Economics* offers a master plan to arrest our collective slide towards disaster.

—Thomas Homer-Dixon, PhD, executive director, Cascade Institute
and author of *Commanding Hope*

For 4 billion years, evolving life has tinkered ever-novel ways of making our livings with one another. *Regenerative Economics* powerfully reminds us that our tasks are to sustain functional integration of the global economy as we flow into the Adjacent Possible we create. GDP, a mismeasure of Man, does not measure functional integration.

—Stuart Kauffman, MacArthur Fellow, Fellow of the
Royal Society of Canada, and author of *Reinventing the Sacred*

REGENERATIVE ECONOMICS

REGENERATIVE ECONOMICS
REVOLUTIONARY THINKING
FOR A WORLD IN CRISIS

JOHN B. FULLERTON

Copyright © 2025 by John B. Fullerton
All rights reserved.

Cover design: by Diane McIntosh. Cover Graphics © iStock
Book Designer: Terri Wright | Book Lotus Productions | booklotus.com
Editors: Beret Olson and Paula Dragosh
Part and chapter opener images: Adobe Stock/ Fernando Batista

Printed in Canada. First printing September, 2025.

This book is intended to be educational and informative.
It is not intended to serve as a guide. The author and publisher disclaim
all responsibility for any liability, loss, or risk that may be associated
with the application of any of the contents of this book.

Inquiries regarding requests to reprint all or part of *Regenerative Economics* should
be addressed to New Society Publishers at the address below. To order directly from
the publishers, please call 250--247-9737 or order online at www.newsociety.com.

Any other inquiries can be directed by mail to:
New Society Publishers
P.O. Box 189, Gabriola Island, BC V0R 1X0, Canada
(250) 247--9737

New Society Publishers is EU Compliant. See newsociety.com for more information.

LIBRARY AND ARCHIVES CANADA CATALOGUING IN PUBLICATION

Title: Regenerative economics :
revolutionary thinking for a world in crisis / John Fullerton.

Other titles: Regenerative capitalism

Names: Fullerton, John (John B.), author

Description: Second edition. | First edition published as a booklet under title:
Regenerative capitalism: how universal patterns and principles will shape the new
economy. Stonington, Connecticut: Capital Institute, April 2015. | Includes
bibliographical references.

Identifiers: Canadiana (print) 20250263033 | Canadiana (ebook) 20250263041 |
ISBN 9781774060360 (softcover) | ISBN 9781550928280 (PDF) |
ISBN 9781771424240 (EPUB)

Subjects: LCSH: Economics. | LCSH: Sustainable development.

Classification: LCC HD75.6 .F85 2025 | DDC 338.9—dc23

Funded by the Government of Canada
Financé par le gouvernement du Canada

New Society Publishers' mission is to publish books that contribute in
fundamental ways to building an ecologically sustainable and just society, and
to do so with the least possible impact on the environment, in a manner
that models this vision.

To Dana Meadows,
for her vision, courage, intellect, and beautiful humanity.
I regret learning of her work only after her untimely death.
It changed my life.

And to Emma, Grace, and Jack,
whom I hope and pray will see the emergence of
regenerative culture in their lifetimes.

Every idea, sentence, word, and image
contained within is 100% Human Intelligence,
no artificial additives of the machine.
Inspired through synchronicity, curiosity, and intuition,
with an expanded view atop the shoulders of discovered giants,
and woven together through the author's imagination,
intuition, scholarship, lived experience,
and grit.

Without doubt, there is unconscious theft involved.
Or perhaps not theft at all, but the timeless pulse of "one mind."
Meaning, this book is also your book. May it resonate accordingly.

"The total number of minds in the universe is one. In fact,
consciousness is a singularity phasing within all beings."

—ERWIN SCHRÖDINGER,
who predicted quantum entanglement

CONTENTS

Foreword, xvii

Preface to the Second Edition, xxi

PART ONE   1

CHAPTER ONE: INTRODUCTION 3
   What Comes Next? 7
   The Regenerative Hypothesis 10
   Today's Copernican Shift 13
   Second Edition Reflection 14

**CHAPTER TWO: FROM A MECHANISTIC TO A
HOLISTIC WORLDVIEW** 17
   Separate Parts Versus Dynamic Wholes 18
   Beyond Mere Metaphor: The Empirical Science of Flow 22
   Creating Regenerative Economies Using the Laws
      of a Holistic Universe 24
   Second Edition Reflection 29

**CHAPTER THREE: EIGHT PRINCIPLES OF
REGENERATIVE VITALITY** 39
   What Is a Regenerative Economy? 40
   How Do You Build Regenerative Vitality? Eight Key Principles ... 45
   Rethinking Capitalism 85
   Second Edition Reflection 88

CHAPTER FOUR: REGENERATIVE ECONOMIES EMERGING IN THE REAL WORLD 93
Regenerative Movements in Action 94
Creative Regenerative Projects and Enterprises of the *Field Guide* 99
Implications for Politics and Public Policy 104
Implications for Finance 106
Measuring and Managing Systemic Health in Complex Webs ... 111
Second Edition Reflection 117

CHAPTER FIVE: CREATING A REGENERATIVE CIVILIZATION 121
Changing the Dream 125

PART TWO 127

CHAPTER SIX: INTRODUCTION TO PART II—A Decade of Learnings and a Theory of Change 129
Theory of Change 133

CHAPTER SEVEN: MISUNDERSTANDINGS ABOUT REGENERATION 137
The Science of Regeneration 138
The Implication for Economics 141
On First Principles 147
Rethink Everything: More Than an Environmental or Agricultural Idea 149

CHAPTER EIGHT: THE REGENERATIVE PARADIGM 155
Two Fences and Two Leaps 156

CHAPTER NINE: EPIPHANY—THE MISSING INSTITUTION OF THE COMMONS 167
Historical Context 170
Universal Property Rights 172
Biosphere and Technosphere 173
A Thought Experiment 178
Two Epiphanies 183
Commons Sector Architecture 186

CONTENTS

CHAPTER TEN: REGENERATIVE TECHNOLOGY—AN OXYMORON? 195
    Can the Master Resume the Throne? 199

CHAPTER ELEVEN: THE FINANCE ALGORITHM 203
    Metamorphosis 210
    Immune System 211

CHAPTER TWELVE: REIMAGINING PUBLIC POLICY 221
    Ten-Point Regenerative Policy Proposal 227

EPILOGUE 237
    A Call to Action 243

Acknowledgments, 249
Endnotes, 253
About the Author, 265
About New Society Publishers, 266

FOREWORD
by Nora Bateson

I HAVE OFTEN MARVELED at how difficult it can be to explain the importance of understanding the vast and complex interdependency of life. Often the reality of this complexity gets brushed off as "abstract" and "impossible to contend with"—while the whirling blades of reductionism that deconstruct the necessary interbeing of life into bits and pieces to be controlled are hailed as "practical." It seems to me the exact opposite should be the case. Life, and the living world within which we all exist, is moving through relationship and communication. Break the relationships, and you break life. Control is an illusion.

John Fullerton and I have been in conversation for more than a decade now. Our inquiry has been a reaching for language, stretching rigid agendas of conferences around the world to accommodate the blurry, messy vitality of life. We have been trying to let the depth of the practice—of seeing the complexity of life—seep into conversations that might otherwise be forced into seductive models of linear solutions to the world's problems, including its obvious and accelerating economic issues.

John has been eager, and wise—he has held open the gates of learning when those around him assigned him with expertise. He is an expert, and his experience is profound—precisely because he continues to go deeper. Beyond the questions of economy, beyond the questions of climate disaster, beyond the issues of runaway technology and cultural polarization, there is something more to study. That something is life.

In these pages, John does not shy from dilemma. The difficulty of reshaping economies is not only an economic issue. The dilemmas and double binds run through culture, education, notions of identity, history, and law—all of which reflect onto ecologies and families—becoming the pathways of tomorrow's global crises, embodied in the most banal tasks of our daily lives.

Breakfast holds the whole story: the agriculture of the grains, the soil, the treatment of dairy animals, the distribution and marketing of foods, the ideas of health shaped by medical studies and amplified by journalists, as well as farming technology and media around fitness. Breakfast illustrates the murky choreography by which a family gets out the door in the morning demarking intergenerational habits, traumas, and ideals. Each moment in a day holds expressions of multiple contexts at play—shaping what people do, think, eat, love, hope for, and fear.

The economy is not only the movement of money, but rather it rides a wild wind of intangibles, pushed and pulled by countless invisible pressures of past and future. This is what makes it so painfully difficult to change an economic system that is so obviously destroying life. It is truly baffling that, despite so many brilliant people having long known the need for change in economic practices, the situation seems only to worsen.

Ancient peoples around the world once lived in rhythm with their environments, but today, our environments have been altered by a rapidly changing climate, and the cultures of desire and success have shifted dramatically. We can't simply "go back," but there is so much to be learned from the wisdom of cultures that were not driven by the mishaps of overvalued individual wealth.

Objectification is a slicing that can be enacted upon a person, a society, an ocean, a mineral. The initial violence lies in the severing from the necessary interrelational contexts of relationships that give life. This is precisely what our economics does with its abstraction and reductionist metrics, which have taken control of our every institution, our markets, and with them distorted our ability to perceive complexity. Over generations, the cut is forgotten, and the fragmentation has become home. This haunted home is a horror story, and yet it is home.

For many, this fragmentation has obscured and atrophied the ability to perceive life-lifing. Some few have gained or inherited luxury in the deal, most others have lived in suffering. Decorated with the histories of ancestors who have done what they had to do to feed the children, to achieve success, to be relevant in this distorted world of valuation, this distorted home is wound into a transcontextual knot of systemic issues. I deeply respect and commend John's tender and serious care in addressing so many issues that, if actually acted upon, would upturn the apple carts of established markets. For some, John's work is a relief, and a sanctuary of reason. For others, it may present dissonance that is irreconcilable with current practices. For me these are one and the same.

As the lioness hunts in the savannah, she is likely not thinking about the antelope population needing to be kept in check, so as to protect the grasses that, in turn, protect the soil where the bacteria that provide the basis of life in the savannah allow for the ongoing survival of future generations of entire ecosystems of organisms—including lions. Yet the hunger that drives her is informed and formed into a vastness of multicausal processes, reaching both forward into futures and backward into evolutionary interbeing. Her fur is the color of the grass, her gait is rhythmed into the blowing gusts of wind, her eyes are honed to see the nuanced differences between the shadows and the glare, her claws are long. Where is the edge of the lion?

In hopes of bringing a sense of personal experience to the rather overwhelming notion of complexity, I often encourage people to ask the question, "Where is the edge of me?" It is a provocative question, intended to push perception of the self beyond the habits of individualism inculcated by modern, industrial thinking, the same kind of thinking that drives decision-making in our broken economic system. Is the edge of you your name? Your skin? Nationality? Ancestry? Future generations? Is the edge of you your microbiome? Your culture? Ideas? Bank account? Legacy? Loves?

Very quickly, it becomes obvious that defining the boundaries of a living system—such as you are, and I am, and a forest is, and an ocean is—is not so simple. Where do I end? Where does an ocean begin?

Where is the edge of responsibility?

That is the difficult and vital question this book invites us to explore—dissolving the "arbitrary lines" we have drawn under the illusion of control and inviting the unseen, interwoven relationships within the vast interdependency of life to be revealed and honored.

Thank you, John.

PREFACE
to the Second Edition

WHEN I RESIGNED FROM JPMORGAN in the spring of 2001 after a nearly twenty-year career, I didn't know what my future would hold. What I did know was that after the merger with Chase Manhattan Bank, I no longer recognized the Morgan culture I had once cherished. In truth, I had become restless over the previous years, feeling that my career had lost any purpose beyond achieving "success" as defined by Wall Street.

The culture I had so valued had been defined by J. P. Morgan Jr. in his testimony to a Senate subcommittee following the Great Crash of 1929. There Morgan spoke of the banker's "code of professional ethics and customs." He concluded by saying that, while the Morgan Bank had made mistakes, those mistakes had been "errors of judgment, and not of principle."

To be fair, this principled approach to banking had been in decline for years—some historians would question Morgan's assertions in the first place, a perspective I'm now quite sympathetic to. Regardless, such principles that we believed in became a victim of the fierce pressure of competitive global capital markets in a deregulated world, where economic brawn increasingly trumped civility. The takeover by the muscular Chase merely put the final nail in the coffin. Now, my future would require answering to new bosses flexing their power. I was unhappy, restless, and now in hostile territory. So I walked away with no plans other than to decompress after a twenty-year sprint.

Turns out, the universe had other plans for me.

Unemployed and without an excuse to say no, I joined some friends sailing across the Atlantic that summer in a fifty-foot sailboat. One week into the voyage, we got hit—hard—by a humpback whale that came up from the deep and destroyed our rudder so that we could not continue. Unfortunately, the whale would not continue very long either. To say that it was freak accident would be an understatement. After a period of chaos, the Canadian Coast Guard arrived and towed us north to St. John's, Newfoundland. And this part I could not make up. I had decided what better time to read *Moby-Dick* than while crossing the Atlantic! A coincidence? Perhaps. But now a quarter century later, the meaning and the message only continue to deepen, and they are directly connected to the story awaiting you.

But my little decompress phase wasn't over yet. My first day back in New York City, I was to meet a charter school CEO for an exploratory conversation. I had made what we now call an "impact investment" (seeking both social and financial returns) into charter school company Edison Schools while I was at JPMorgan and was contemplating setting up a nonprofit charter school company to tackle the education crisis in America. The meeting was downtown at 9:30 in the morning. At 9:10, my train stopped at City Hall, about five blocks north of my destination. The doors remained open, and we waited. Then a man came in and announced three feet from my face, "They just flew a plane into the Trade Center." I headed for the stairs. As I got to the street, I watched the enormous fireball as the second plane exploded. Far enough away that I was safe, close enough that it made an indelible mark on my soul. Career disillusionment now seared into despair, and utter confusion. What did it all mean?

What followed were years of searching. I was searching for how to make sense of a world that I could no longer explain to my children. At some level, I was also searching for my own purpose in it all, and the meaning of my encounter with the great whale.

This search first opened my eyes to what we now call the polycrisis, the profound, interlocking crises—ecological, economic, social, and now political—including the shocking prospect that we are destroying the planet's ability to support life as we know it. I read books bankers don't read. *Limits to Growth*, the controversial but now remarkably prescient Report to the Club of Rome by lead author Donella ("Dana") Meadows, rocked me to the core. Exponential growth on a finite planet—the premise of economics and the very design of the global economy and the source of our presumed prosperity—was in conflict with the laws—not theories—of physics. My most startling discovery, however, was that the modern scheme of economics and finance—what Wall Street "geniuses" (like me) practiced so well—was ground zero for these systemic crises. The "finance algorithm" was the structure that kept the entire exponential-growth-based economic system locked in place. It was doing exactly what it was designed to do: optimize return on capital (at basically any cost). To be clear, this has nothing to do with capitalism versus socialism. Both are predicated upon undifferentiated exponential growth in the material throughput of the economic system. This means more matter, more energy, indefinitely, and exponentially. The problems we recognized, such as climate change, were in fact mere symptoms of the flawed system design. But even most who were aware of the looming crisis were just focused on problem-solving rather than the unimaginable: We were facing profound system change, either by design or by disaster.

This realization occurred before the 2008 financial crisis and exists independently from it. However, that egregious display of irresponsibility, fraud, and greed further confirmed the reality that Wall Street had lost its way. Worse, it was unwilling and seemingly unable to see what I was beginning to see. My questions were a threat to Wall Street's very identity. I found its leaders remarkably uncurious, even when the stakes were everything we hold dear.

I went to school, so to speak. But what I needed to learn was not being taught even in the best universities where scientific materialism, the Newtonian "clockwork universe" worldview, is the unquestioned reality. Newton was, of course, a genius. As complexity scientist Dr. Stuart Kauffman likes to say, Newton taught us (in the West) how to think. Mechanistic reductionism, reducing what's complicated down to its parts to understand it, has given Western science tremendous explanatory power. But this very success has inadvertently created intellectual gaps, depriving us of our ability to perceive the essential emergent, self-organizing properties of complex living systems that can be understood only through the interdependent relationships of the whole, not their parts.

What I discovered is that there is a long list of thinkers who have known this for a long time, but who all struggled to be understood and have failed to shift our worldview. Names include Goethe, Leonardo da Vinci, Einstein, and Bohm; Whitehead, Smuts, von Bertalanffy, and Schumacher; Fuller, Bateson, Maturana, and Varela; Capra, Meadows, and Senge; Prigogine, T. Berry, Currivan, Swimme, and Faggin, the man who invented the microprocessor. Of course, the world's leading wisdom traditions and indigenous cultures have all understood this for eons. But for reasons I still struggle to understand, Western thinking remains largely trapped in the "clockwork universe" worldview, treating organizations and the entire economic system as if they were merely complicated machines that can be modeled and forecast with accuracy, and optimized to our desires using left-brain-centered reductionist thinking.

Critically, my "school" included practical experience through my impact investment projects and a tireless curiosity. Standing on a ridge in Montana with holistic grazing pioneer Allan Savory looking over a sea of grasslands, it hit me like a bolt of lightning. He was explaining the principles of holistic planned grazing to me, and about the whole under management. The context, this "whole under management," was the complex living system of two hundred thousand acres of prairie. If this holistic approach to decision-making worked to manage the health of the whole in this context, why shouldn't the same approach apply to all living systems contexts? Of course it should, and it must. We see it emerging everywhere, from regenerative agriculture to integrated or "functional" medicine, to the built environment, to product and materials design using biomimicry by biologists like Janine Benyus, even to business leadership with early pioneers W. Edwards Deming, Peter Senge, and Arie de Geus, and now my partners at nRhythm and many others. And it turned out, early visionaries such as Jane Jacobs, Buckminster Fuller, Hazel Henderson, Sally Goerner, Fritjof Capra, and Stuart Kauffman had begun to explore how to apply this living systems approach explicitly to entire economies. But it was all quite exploratory. There was no theory of Regenerative Economics, an economics reimagined from the ground up through the lens of living systems science.

I had found my purpose.

We needed an entire new theory of economics, and its offshoot, finance, aligned with this living systems reality of how life actually works. It will be based on the premise that the economy is a living system, subject to its principles and patterns of vitality, which our latest science broadly understands yet continues to learn more about all the time. Therefore, if our economy is to be sustainable, much less evolve and thrive in the long run, it, too, will need to follow these same patterns and principles. By analogy, if you desire a flying machine, your design had better obey Newton's law of gravity. The logic is self-evident to me.

Why a new theory when the world is on fire? one might reasonably ask. I'll defer to Einstein, who is widely believed to have observed, "It is the theory that determines what we are able to see."

In other words, it is of course true that seeing is believing. We need new practical models that work in the real world. But it is equally true, and far more profound, that believing is seeing. Our worldview colors what we are even able to see, much less imagine. A technologist sees the internet as part of the tech stack infrastructure, which it is. But I see it as the emergence of the regenerative economy, exponentially expanding relationships of connection and the circulation of information and even empathy with emojis, but only if we have the wisdom and will to govern it for the health of the whole. Today, we are often ignorant of the limitations of Newton's clockwork universe or even aware that there are alternative forms of perception. This is the core premise of Regenerative Economics.

The first edition of this book was launched as a booklet with a lecture to students in Yale University's joint graduate degree program between the School of Management and the School of the Environment in April 2015. Two months later, Pope Francis released his masterful encyclical, *Laudato Si': On Care for Our Common Home*. In it, he emphasized the interconnectedness of all life, human and nonhuman alike, and made an urgent plea to protect our planet. He referenced regeneration and called for an "integral ecology," an integrated approach to address our social and climate crises. "We urgently need a humanism capable of bringing together the different fields of knowledge, including economics, in the service of a more integral and integrating vision."[1] It almost felt like a divine endorsement for a holistic approach to Regenerative Economics!

Later that same year, world leaders gathered in Paris at COP 21, the UN Climate Conference, and negotiated the historic Paris Agreement. My first and only COP, I had the opportunity to attend a small workshop with a group of climate luminaries, including climate scientist James Hansen and writer/activist Bill McKibben, as well as a delegation from the Vatican. The agenda was to discuss *Laudato Si'* and how it could be leveraged to drive systemic change. I felt that this was my opening to introduce Regenerative Economics into the serious policy discussions about to take place at COP.

As the meeting began, we went around the table to each offer a three-minute summary of what we were working on and how *Laudato Si'* could be used to increase its impact. I quoted the sentence above calling for an integral and integrating vision and explained how my work was exactly such an "integral" theory of economics that aligned with the regenerative process common to all life. I asserted with conviction that it was the key to seriously addressing the root causes of what we would later call the polycrisis. I urged that we needed to get past problem-solving and goal setting, as important as these activities were. We needed to address the system design that was manifesting the problems in the first place. Understanding the regenerative process was at the core, as was the related shift in consciousness.

At about the two-minute mark of my intervention, I could tell that no one had any idea what I was talking about. I paused. After a moment to take a breath, in deep frustration I simply concluded my remarks. "Let me put it this way. I am working on what the world will only become interested in when they realize what they are working on is not working."

A lot has happened in a decade—and sadly, not much has changed. But the idea of Regenerative Economics has begun to gain some purchase, at least within the sustainability bubble. Of course, political divisiveness has generated blowback to the entire sustainability agenda, particularly in the United States. I consider this a self-inflicted yet probably necessary pause, not a reversal. We must get serious and move beyond the sustainability approach of incremental change, as important as that is to buy us more time as Hunter Lovins likes to say. We must let go of our "clockwork universe" and embrace an entirely new paradigm.

Into this void and tumultuous time, I'm pleased to release this ten-year-anniversary second edition of *Regenerative Economics: Rev-*

olutionary Thinking for a World in Crisis. The core idea of my work remains the same ten years later.

New scientific affirmations during the ensuing decade have done nothing but reinforce my confidence in this idea. The explosion of interest and practitioners in the space from around the globe is heartening. We now see the topic of regeneration appear on stages of sustainability and impact investment conferences, in corporate and consulting firm brochures, and even at the World Economic Forum (although often without an understanding of the paradigm shift it suggests).

Even the sustainability experts who initially saw this idea as just another name for sustainability are recognizing that our well-intended problem-solving approaches such as embracing circularity and the United Nations' Sustainable Development Goals (SDGs), and using environmental, social, and governance factors (ESG) to complement financial metrics—while useful and even essential—are by themselves not up to the task. Cascading social, ecological, political, and economic crises in the real world leave us feeling afraid and unable to cope. We now characterize this as the polycrisis. It is beginning to open the mind to the more profound paradigm shift that is already underway. I feel certain this will only accelerate in the years to come, although no doubt in ways that will surprise us.

If we think deeply, we find a single root cause sitting underneath the multiple crises we face—the myth of separation, just as it was described by Pope Francis a decade earlier. It is the same wisdom that sits often unrecognized in all the world's great religions: oneness. We grip tightly onto a confused and dangerous belief that we are independent, separate from each other, and separate from what we call the environment or nature. Evidence-based science now tells us this is profoundly wrong, remarkably aligning with the intuitive understanding of our indigenous elders. We are a part of nature, not apart from nature. Our task is to literally "re-member" ourselves with nature, to participate productively in the process of life.

I find this convergence of our latest, twenty-first-century Western science with many of the intuitive insights of the world's ancient wisdom traditions awe-inspiring and simply breathtaking to contemplate. I invite you to pause here for a moment and ponder that fact, and the importance of its revelation at this time. Science is reconnecting with spirit after a four-hundred-year separation in the West. It must carry profound meaning for us all at this moment of crisis. I am convinced it will usher in a new way to see the world, and with that, humanity's unique place in it. We may even discover for the first time our true purpose and be able to answer the age-old question: "Why are we here?"

> *We are not living in an era of change.*
> *We are living in a change in era.*

With only a few exceptions and deletions, the text in part 1 of this second edition has not been changed, but a ten-year reflection is added at the end of each chapter. I have updated several of the graphics, added the graphic of the eight principles of regenerative vitality that I created after the first edition was released on the good advice of visual genius Kate Raworth. Otherwise, the text has been preserved essentially intact, now in a proper book as my colleague and regenerative scholar/practitioner Daniel Christian Wahl recommended, "for posterity's sake." I have put important clarifications and fresh, provocative material in part 2, based on learnings with colleagues over the decade. It also contains my working theory of change, a ten-point policy plan, and a call to action for your consideration. It is clear to me that the scale and scope of change we face remains under-appreciated. My intention is to expand our imaginations and invite collaboration in constructing viable and practical action plans. This book is only a beginning; there is much more work to do.

My quest to give birth to an initial theory of Regenerative Economics ended up answering the question of why I left JPMorgan now over two decades ago with no knowledge of what my future might hold. It also gave new meaning to my twenty-year experience participating in high finance's spectacular rise during my career and then witnessing from the outside its subsequent alarming descent. It even has helped me grapple with the meaning of my encounter with the great whale. Yet my appreciation of how purpose enables us to rise to the occasion, transcend our differences, and find true meaning in our lives came most directly from my father.

A few years before he passed away, we took a three-day trip together along the coast of New England. The longest one-on-one experience I can recall with my dad, it was a unique opportunity for me to hear him reflect on his life. What struck me was that he kept coming back to the war. My dad had served in the navy during World War II, took part in the Normandy invasion, and later captained a sub-chaser in the Pacific. The glimmer in his eye as he spoke revealed that the war, despite the fear, loss, and horror it had brought, had given his life meaning. What became clear to me listening over those three precious days was that it was certainly not his career, nor even family, despite our being close, that defined his life. It was the shared, noble purpose of the war—sacrifices included—that had come to define his life. He was, after all, part of the Greatest Generation.

Our generation's challenges and threats are different. We, too, must overcome our fears. But we must also transcend our ideological divides and our false separation from one another and from our environment. Climate change, grotesque and ever-rising inequality, insecurity, rightful anger and resentment, and violence and cruelty of all kinds, all are symptoms more than we realize of a deeply flawed economic system based on a Newtonian economics foundation of separation and scarcity. A systemic shift awaits. Again, I'm not talking about capitalism versus socialism. This is way bigger than that. And it most certainly includes the transformation of the financial system to embrace a meaningful purpose in service of a regenerative world. Granted, watching the crypto fiascos unfolding in broad daylight makes me wonder. But this, too, shall pass.

We face an unprecedented challenge that holds the possibility of uniting our generation in a shared purpose. But make no mistake, we are on a knife's edge, as Bucky Fuller warned a half century ago. We now have a more rigorous understanding of how to create the conditions for healthy human networks—this alone constitutes an amazing opportunity. It is time to learn new ways of seeing and dancing with complexity, and to act. Our actions, now, will most certainly define the nobility of our lives and our legacy. This is the Great Work of our time.

And miles to go before I sleep.

—ROBERT FROST

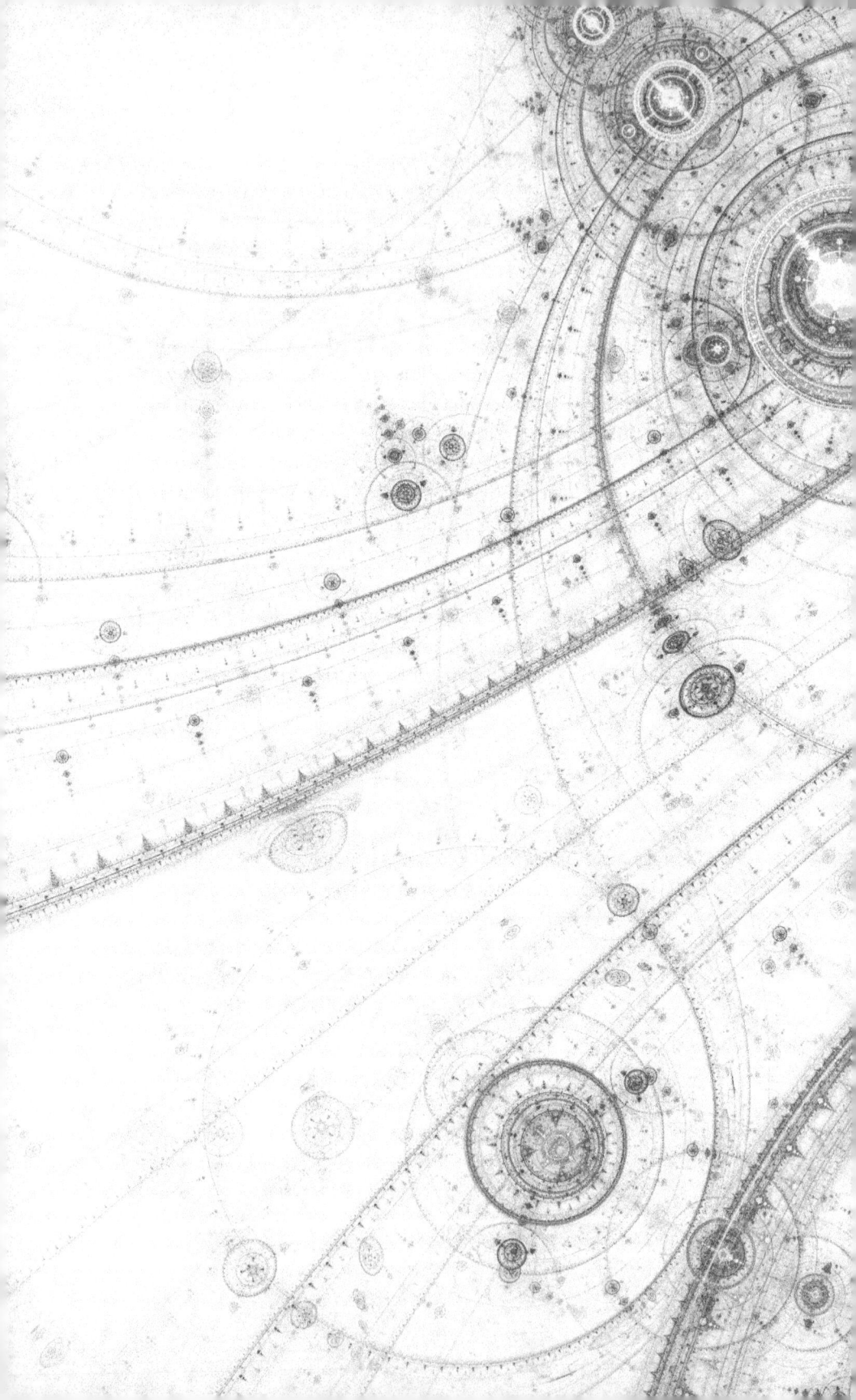

PART ONE

The occasion is piled high with difficulty, and we must rise with the occasion. As our case is new, so we must think anew, and act anew.

—ABRAHAM LINCOLN

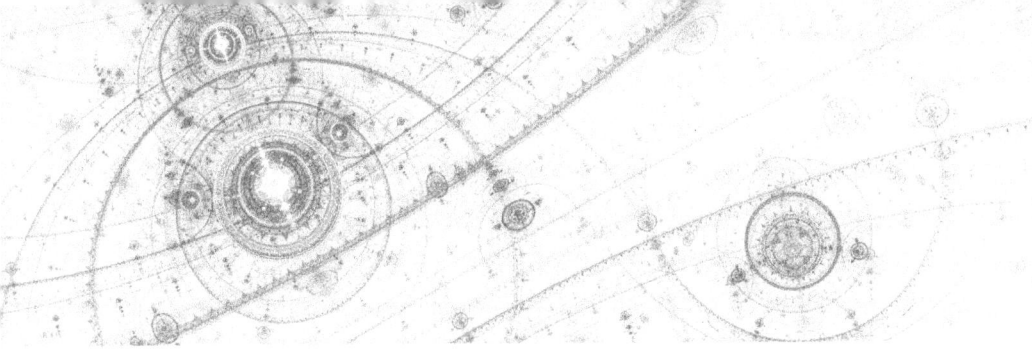

CHAPTER ONE

INTRODUCTION

In the years since our most recent finance-induced Great Recession, a growing number of thoughtful people are concluding that the modern global economy may be incapable of providing for the well-being of the majority of humanity. At the same time, its systemic "take, make, waste" design has left in its wake a crescendo of interconnected environmental crises that threaten to undermine the very foundation of the economic system itself. And, I will argue, it is the exponential function embedded in the DNA of finance that is at the root of this systemic crisis, setting aside the financial sector's many other shortcomings—intellectual, analytical, and ethical.

The indications are everywhere. There remains intractable poverty facing nearly half the world's human population, and unconscionable and still-rising inequality of income and wealth in the world's leading economies. There are troubling statistics on structural unemployment in developed economies, accompanied by institutional failures of government, business, and particularly finance, but also of education and religion. Global terrorism finds sympathizers, at least in part, among those who have been brutalized by the indignities of impoverishment and hopelessness.

Despite its many achievements, including a dramatic rise in the material well-being of a small minority of today's growing global population, science tells us that our current economic system, fueled by a single-minded growth imperative, is fundamentally at odds with the finite boundaries of the biosphere and the laws (not theories) of physics.[2] Similarly, climate change and, more broadly, the degradation of the life-supporting functions of a healthy ecosystem threaten life as we know it, presenting an existential threat that has no parallel in human history. We are destroying the planet because there is a profit in it.[3]

Clearly, what cannot go on forever will eventually stop. In 2015, global economic activity was already breaching four of seven critical "planetary boundaries"[4]—atmospheric carbon, nitrogen, and phosphorous flows from agriculture dumped into our river systems, land use changes, and the rate of biodiversity loss. Freshwater stress in specific locations was on the rise. In the process, we have compromised the Earth's interconnected life-support systems. These boundaries are depicted individually in the graphic in figure 1.1, but it is important to realize that since everything is connected to everything else, any one breach of a critical scientific boundary is enough to shift the entire system into destabilizing collapse. Note, in this second edition, we have updated the charts in figure 1.1 to reflect the 2023 research depicting now nine boundaries, of which six have been crossed. In short, we are playing with fire.

Symptoms of this truth abound, most notably the extreme weather events accompanying recent reports that we have exceeded 422 parts per million of atmospheric carbon (up from 400 a decade ago), when science tells us that we must rapidly reduce that level to 350 if we are to preserve life as we know it on the planet.

We live in a time of reckoning.[5] Although perpetual expansion of material throughput in the economy—ever more resources extracted, ever more waste dumped into the biosphere—clearly cannot go on forever, both sides of today's ideological divide continue to accept the notion that our economic system's primary purpose is to foster perpetual, exponential, and undifferentiated economic growth.

Lulled into complacency by a misunderstanding of Darwin that leads us to hold to the belief that the "fittest" are the ones that survive in a competitive marketplace,[6] we have failed to arrest the rise of an amoral plutocracy that is taking hold of the global economy and destroying democracy and human health, dignity, and civility—as

Introduction 5

OVERSHOOT: PLANETARY BOUNDARIES FRAMEWORK

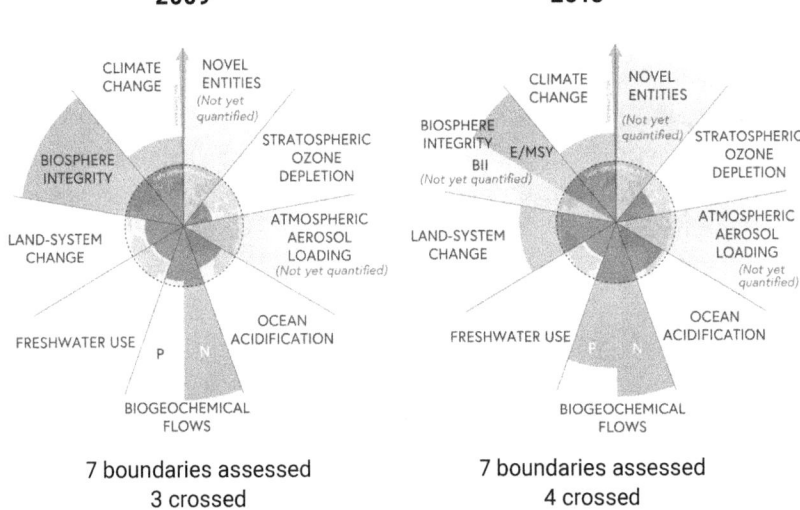

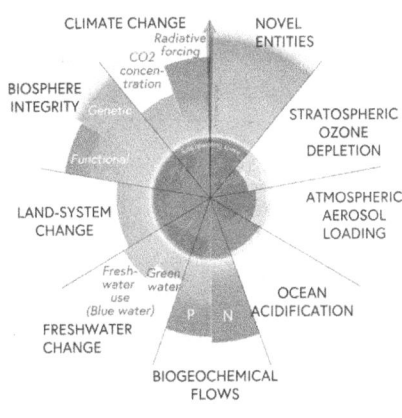

■ **Figure 1.1 Six of Nine Boundaries Now Breached.** *Credit: Azote for Stockholm Resilience Centre, based on analysis in Richardson et al. (2023), Steffen et al. (2015), and Rockström et al. (2009).*

well as the planet. Plutocratic propaganda combined with blind faith in GDP growth, the naive belief that markets always know best, and the discounting function at the heart of finance that flat out ignores the devastating and logically expected costs associated with our single-minded pursuit of near-term profit have hijacked the human value system enshrined in our Declaration of Independence.[7] Our government, once created to protect the "unalienable rights" to "Life, Liberty, and the Pursuit of Happiness," has been suckered, bought and sold, and is now failing in this primary duty. Unfortunately, because America is the largest economy and dominant superpower on Earth, nations all over the world seek to emulate prosperity in the narrow way we have come to define it, counting money as the sole measure of success, regardless of how that money is made or how much harm it does to people, civilization (now and in the future), and the planet.

These mounting social, ethical, economic, financial, and environmental crises, connected in an incomprehensibly complex web, are converging into a global emergency that even the most entrenched denialists will soon be unable to ignore. It is now critical that our modern economic system evolve past today's immoral "rationalism" to address both the environmental crisis and the growing list of societal challenges, most notably chronic unemployment, the grotesquely inequitable distribution of wealth, and the oppressive poverty of nearly half of the world's population.

In short, we are in trouble—systemic trouble, the kind that can be addressed only with systemic solutions, not more point-focused problem-solving.

Yet, despite a growing chorus of demands to rethink our economic assumptions—beginning with Robert Kennedy in his famous 1968 speech[8]—most people continue to stick their head in the sand. Many believe that we will be able to innovate our way out of impending disaster at the eleventh hour without challenging the core assumptions of the system. Others have succumbed to fatalism. If civilization is headed for collapse, as many great societies before us have done, we might as well absolve ourselves of any responsibility and dance while the music still plays.[9]

Here we offer a third alternative. Against all the odds, let us rise to the challenge, working collectively to effect systems transformation—a paradigm shift—in response to the reality we understand. Let us invoke our uniquely empowering human agency to decide upon a better future for our children and endeavor to accomplish that dream.

WHAT COMES NEXT?

The dominant economic model of the developed world is unsustainable.[10] The consequences of that unsustainability are unacceptable and raise ethical questions that society can no longer avoid. In fact, capitalism as we know it is now in question.[11]

Extrapolation of current trends—high structural unemployment, particularly among youth; persistent poverty even in the richest countries; widening inequality within countries and regions; and now for the first time on a global scale (which is why this time is different) cascading environmental crises, most notably climate change, desertification, and biodiversity loss—leads ultimately to system collapse, with the weakest among us the first to be affected.[12]

This systemic crisis is well understood in sustainability circles and is slowly being recognized inside mainstream institutions and among policymakers. By and large, however, it remains heresy among both liberal and conservative mainstream economists whose thinking dominates policy debates. When it comes to sustainability, our leading business schools are primarily engaged in furthering the technology-enabled resource productivity opportunity, just as they earlier focused on the labor productivity opportunity. The current business school mantra goes something like this: Business will innovate as they always have done. They can become more profitable through innovation that reduces costs through better resource efficiencies. Fine, as far as it goes.

Individual firms are attempting to decouple their growth from material throughput through critical energy and material efficiency gains (offshoring manufacturing simply shifts the problem elsewhere). Utilizing strategies such as "Factor Five" resource productivity improvements[13] and circular economy business models,[14] the potential exists (theoretically) to achieve up to 80 percent improvements in resource productivity profitably, extending the runway for the transition to truly regenerative business models in the process. But decoupling material throughput from economic growth for the entire system, indefinitely into the future—that is, continuous economic growth while continuously reducing absolute material throughput of the economy—is quite a different matter.

As sustainability expert Hunter Lovins suggests, we must urgently focus on efficiency gains to buy time. But at the same time, we must also look ahead and envision a truly regenerative system design. That is something entirely new, requiring fresh imagination, not just incremental tweaking around the edges.

In simple language, we need a new story to believe in—one that rings true and captures our hopes and aspirations for a prosperous future. Applied to our economic system, this new story must credibly address the growing systemic inequality and related oppression we know will ultimately undermine civil society if left unchecked. This story must be socially and ecologically just, and credibly shift us away from systematically destroying the planet, the health of which we know is the source of our true wealth and upon which our very survival depends.

Fortunately, a growing interdisciplinary movement is beginning to understand the systemic nature of the challenges we face and that systems change is not only inevitable, it is already underway. It turns out, in fact, that the study of systems is a robust and growing field of inquiry, and beginning to penetrate the minds of politicians, financiers, and the corporate elite, that is, the people who run the world.

Of particular importance to us is preeminent system scientist Jay Forrester's disciple,[15] the late Dana Meadows, coauthor of *Limits to Growth*, commissioned by the Club of Rome, and published in 1972.[16] Meadows explained that the most important leverage point to change a system is to reimagine the paradigm, or belief system, out of which the system arises.[17] The challenge is to imagine a new story with not only new goals but a new way to perceive reality that is able to transcend the dominant story when it no longer works.

There is also now a rich literature explaining why business as usual is a sure path to collapse.[18] Pioneers such as ecological economist Herman Daly, formerly of the World Bank, and his many colleagues and disciples, as well as progressive academic institutions such as the Bainbridge Graduate Institute, Presidio Graduate School, and Bard's MBA in Sustainability program, are probing the deep and difficult conundrums of modern capitalism. Yet few in the mainstream dare question the accepted paradigm, the story that money buys happiness, that optimizing shareholder value is ordained truth and is our fiduciary duty, that fair and transparent markets will magically guide our decisions to optimal outcomes, that there are limitless physical possibilities of growth, that there are unlimited possibilities for substitution of inputs through innovation, and that undifferentiated economic growth is the answer to our problems and the source of our prosperity.

But as we have seen, that story no longer holds up to careful scrutiny, for if it did, we would not be on a collision course with systemic collapse. Increasingly, it seems, we have lost touch with what it means to be human.[19] What we need now is a story that ties all these pieces together in a way that provides a positive path to the future.

I propose that our new story will be built on an intellectual and emotional understanding of the regenerative process that enables all life in the world.

I need to be very clear up front about the source of my proposal. While this book offers a theoretical framework for regenerative economies and has been deeply informed by my readings and the influences of many thought leaders, in particular by those listed in the acknowledgments, my conviction arises first and foremost through experiential knowledge.

I have seen this understanding successfully applied to land management practice on large landscapes,[20] and in the built environment,[21] unlocking unimaginable potential leading to true regenerative wealth—social, ecological, and economic. I have seen it further demonstrated in the real world in each of the now twenty-five stories of our *Field Guide to a Regenerative Economy*.[22] In other words, the theory I present is firmly grounded in the concrete particulars of practice in the real world.

I now believe that this conceptual framework can also be used to create a model of multilevel economic health that ranges from the level of firms and place-based networks of firms in value-adding relationship with one another, to the global economy itself.

In this way, the regenerative paradigm has the potential to evolve our present unsustainable capitalism to a higher level of complexity,[23] in keeping with the evolutionary process in which the human economy takes part.

THE REGENERATIVE HYPOTHESIS

The regenerative story starts with a single core idea:

> We can use the universal principles and patterns underlying stable, healthy, and sustainable living systems, including insights from nonliving systems throughout the real world, as a model for economic-system design.

A regenerative economy also requires a clear statement of purpose. A regenerative system is self-organizing and self-sustaining. It does not "kick the can down the road" as our modern political economy does with respect to inequality, poverty, natural resource limits, pollution, health, deficits, pension plans, retirement, education, and regulatory reform. Instead:

> The purpose of a Regenerative Economy is to promote and sustain human prosperity and wellbeing in an "economy of permanence."[24]

To achieve sustained human well-being in an economy of permanence, we must first study the laws and patterns that the cosmos uses to build healthy networks that actually exist all around us. If the global economy is to become sustainable, we must not simply measure the outputs we desire; we must learn to identify the underlying factors that generate lasting systemic health. We must then design the economy—and the financial system that serves it—to embody those principles.

What qualities make an economy healthy and sustainable? Following the lead of sustainability experts, the first requirement of permanence is to maintain reliable inputs and healthy outputs. Ecologist, and co-creator of the "ecological footprint" concept, Bill Rees explains, "A regenerative system is one that does not deplete or pollute its host and, at best, facilitates its host's thriving. In other words, consumption by the system must not exceed production by its host; waste production by the system must not exceed the assimilative/recycling capacity of its host." Therefore, a regenerative economy maintains reliable inputs and healthy outputs by not exhausting critical inputs or harming other parts of the broader societal and environmental systems upon which it depends.

The next most critical characteristic of health lies in being self-nourishing and self-regulating. So, while many systems, such as tornadoes and lightning bolts, rise up only briefly to diffuse an energy buildup, the systems we care most about—living organisms, ecosystems, and societies—are designed to constantly channel energy into nourishing their internal workings. Living organisms, for example, are designed to turn the food they eat into the energy they need to maintain their own existence. If we are to build healthy human economies, this idea must be applied to human networks.

Just as living systems are sustainable because they are characterized by self-nourishing processes, so must a regenerative economy nourish the human networks upon which its vitality depends.

Yet regeneration also defines the evolutionary process itself. Little known in the West today due to his association with apartheid, Jan Smuts, the South African general and prime minister who later founded the League of Nations, and pen pal of Einstein, was wise beyond his time. He observed that it was the regenerative nature of life itself to evolve into higher levels of complexity in the face of the powerful degenerating law of entropy.[25] Here the term *regeneration* implies a "continuous process of becoming"—including human and societal potential. This broad form of regeneration implies an indivisible connection among humanity's physical, psychological, and spiritual dimensions, as well as with the entirety of the energetic whole we call the universe. It is this deep interconnectedness that Smuts referred to when he described holism as the universal principle that defines matter, energy, and spirit.[26]

Can we not, then, view the emergent regenerative economy as a more highly evolved response to the extractive economy it will replace?

Regenerative economies must embrace the continuous process of becoming necessary to sustain life in the natural world.

Critically, however, our understanding of the operating principles common to all natural systems must be informed by an appreciation of the unique qualities that collectively offer insight into what it means to be human. These qualities include higher cognitive function, analytic reasoning, the dexterity of opposable thumbs, morality, a higher potential for conscious awareness, and even the possibility of spiritual enlightenment. And critically, we must integrate the clear reality of the power of human agency itself to affect the outcome of the system. We are not simply passive passengers in the evolution of the human economy. Certainly, these qualities collectively create the potential for highly intricate systems of economy characterized by higher levels of complexity and therefore more advanced function than achievable without the human species.

Some environmentalists claim that the Earth would be fine without human beings. But we must also remember the vast regenerative potential that exists solely because of humanity's unique qualities.[27]

Can we not see that the potential for life on Earth is richer because of the human species, and that it is our purpose to co-create the healthy manifestation of that potential?

Looked at in this light, the great progress that industrialism has brought to the human project is the unfinished business of self-organizing human creativity rather than merely the misguided arrogance and greed that have led to the destruction of the natural world. Rather than leave us trapped in a flawed and outdated ideology, our very unique human qualities must enable us to learn and improve based on the new knowledge we acquire of the nature of economies as healthy human networks.

It is our task, now, to bring our economic system into alignment with the regenerative process. When we do, like turning a canoe downstream after a long struggle against the current, our journey will be lightened, our destination assured.

TODAY'S COPERNICAN SHIFT

> The first Copernicans had experienced a kind of inner conversion. Their epiphany was at once intellectual and spiritual, psychological and cosmological. . . . Their intuition ran ahead far in advance of all the theoretical and empirical work that had to be done.
>
> —RICHARD TARNAS

Changing a society's root paradigm is an enormous undertaking. Copernicus and Galileo spent uncomfortable lives trying to replace the notion that the Sun revolved around the Earth because the medieval church had used the indisputable perfection of the Earth-centered model to buttress the idea that aristocratic rule centered on the church was God's immutable plan, regardless of how abusive and dysfunctional such elite rule might be. Yet today we happily accept the idea that the Earth revolves around the Sun, and that democracy is a better form of government than plutocracy.

Now, we are the new Copernicans. We find ourselves in the early years of a new millennium at a critical inflexion point in the history of civilization. What are the odds that ours is really a pivotal moment in time? I would suggest that the evidence is all around us, if only we have eyes to see. The difference is that this time the belief system we must overcome is the idea that perpetual, undifferentiated economic growth is the key to prosperity—or even physically possible.

Our challenge is to illuminate this integrated story and to craft a coherent narrative around the evidence that supports it. Our goal is to use this now empirically grounded and integrated new story to catalyze the already emerging paradigm shift from today's oligarchic and increasingly parasitic brand of capitalism to a pluralistic system of regenerative economies. This requires the birth of a new discipline: Regenerative Economics.

Still, we should also tread carefully, remembering, as Meadows instructed, that no paradigm will ever represent ultimate "truth." Regenerative economies are about learning, adaptive change, and the continual evolution of systems. Regenerative Economics, a call for regenerative multicapitalism, is a paradigm that addresses the monumental challenges we face at this moment in time as we participate in the ongoing evolution of the human project.

Having absorbed Dana Meadows's wisdom and been deeply inspired by such great storytellers as mythologist Joseph Campbell, I have come to believe that it is only with a new, shared belief system, a shared story, all enabled by a shift in collective consciousness, that we can tackle the immense political, social, and economic challenges we face as we race against time to find our way to the regenerative economies awaiting to unfold. It is my hope that this preliminary theory of Regenerative Economics contributes to that emerging story.

At this time, as we shift from the ten-thousand-year-old and stable Holocene to the human-controlled and volatile Anthropocene,[28] it is the logical evolutionary path of our economic system and the creative challenge of our age to usher in regenerative economies, bringing the human economy into holistic balance with nature and ourselves.

A work in progress . . .

> It always seems impossible, until it is done.
>
> —NELSON MANDELA

SECOND EDITION REFLECTION

This introduction has held up reasonably well with the passage of a decade. I offer an admission of some unpleasant factual updates, and a reaffirmation.

The admission is that my language about the nature of the crisis was reserved when I wrote ten years ago. I was worried about sounding overly strident or even apocalyptic to what I perceived as my more mainstream audience. I knew then, and it is obvious now, that the situation we face is far more dire. And that's not counting the rise of extremism, authoritarianism, wars of aggression, and of course the new unknowns of artificial intelligence. I'm just talking about what we have come to call the polycrisis: the interconnected social, political, economic, and ecological crises spinning out of control.

My optimistic words for the possibility of 80 percent resource productivity improvements from concepts like circular economy were a mistake. I didn't fully believe them at the time I wrote the words. But notions of a circular economy were all the rage at the moment, promoted as a win-win by most of its naive even if well-intended popularizers. I didn't want to appear overly critical at the time. The exceptions to this euphoric embrace of circular economy I found were the entrepreneurs who ran recycling businesses and knew the challenges. One told me that the only "R" that matters in the Reduce, Reuse, Recycle mantra was the first one. The recent *Circularity Gap Report* makes the stark facts clear: Circularity is, in fact, still moving in the wrong direction. Despite a tripling of articles and discussions, "the share of secondary materials consumed by the global economy has decreased from 9.1% in 2018 to 7.2% in 2023—a 21% drop over the course of five years."[29] At the same time, consumption of materials has continued its upward trajectory, just like CO_2. Hmm . . . As I said in my opening, what we are working on is not working.

The factual updates are not good news, but this is no surprise. The Stockholm Resilience Centre updated its planetary boundaries research in 2023, as mentioned above, expanding from the seven boundaries assessed in 2015. The news is sobering: Six of the nine boundaries assessed have been crossed. And we continue to move in the wrong direction. In other words, ten years on and God knows how many PowerPoints and pledges, goals and reports, we have failed to even begin to turn the ship around. It is no doubt fair to say that it would have been worse without our efforts.

The reaffirmation is simple. While suggesting that we are in a change in era and not merely an era of change might have seemed a provocation in 2015, it is now crystal clear to me ten years later. I have no doubt that we are in the business of paradigm shift, a literal metamorphosis. Dana Meadows's words were indeed prescient. And profound. Paradigm shift means that we must ask better questions and accept hard truths. Rather than, "What's the business case for sustainability?" we must ask, "What's the sustainability case for your business?" Rather than think that better measures and reporting alone will allow us to "manage what we measure" and thus manage change, we need to rethink what we even can manage. And as we will discover, rather than rely on our well-honed reductionist problem-solving method, we had better invoke our imaginations and live up to the promise of what it means to be human.

> We need to replace the industrial mind with the ecological mind.
>
> —WES JACKSON

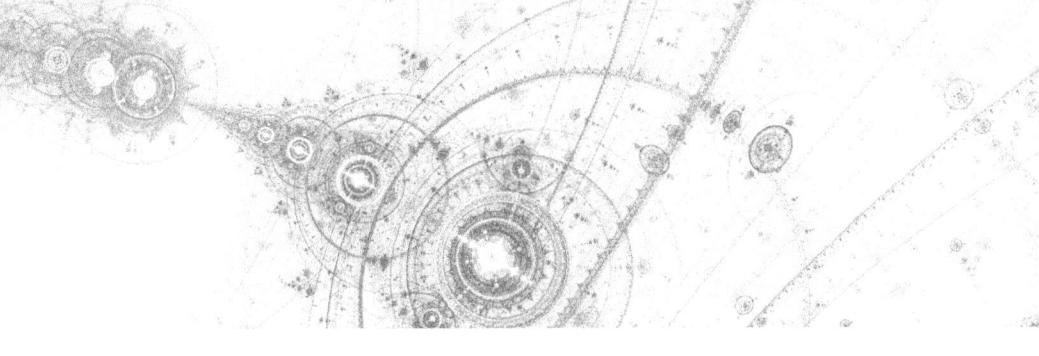

CHAPTER TWO

FROM A MECHANISTIC TO A HOLISTIC WORLDVIEW

The predominant free market economic system today is built around a narrow interpretation of Adam Smith's metaphor of the "invisible hand." The acts of individuals and firms in a market economy, it is assumed, miraculously self-direct toward an optimal allocation of resources and therefore the highest level of well-being for society. That's the premise.

Yet we forget that Adam Smith set the operation of the invisible hand in a moral context of "sympathy" toward one's fellow man, as he described earlier in *The Theory of Moral Sentiments* (1759). My reading suggests that Smith uses the word *sympathy* the way today we would use the word *empathy*, defined as "the ability to understand and share the feelings of another." This is not Gordon Gekko's invisible hand as portrayed in the 1987 film *Wall Street*.

Furthermore, no thinking person in the twenty-first century would credibly suggest that an "invisible hand" alone can solve the crisis of climate change, despite the important role that fair and transparent markets can play as a tool to address it. Nor is it any longer a defensible intellectual stance that the invisible hand will take care of chronic unemployment or contain exploding inequality.

At the same time, conventional thinking on the left would suggest that when markets fail to solve problems, the government must step in and act on society's behalf. Many government programs and regulations have achieved remarkable success in this regard. Yet again, no thinking person in the twenty-first century can deny that government solutions often come with excessive bureaucracy, waste, and too often ineffectiveness as well. This is not to suggest that more effective government involvement in the economy, addressing needs that the private sector alone is incapable of handling, should not be a priority.

We are left with the reality that in the current market system context, we are trapped in an ongoing debate—more government to constrain markets and fill the needs that are not being met, or less government with the inefficiency and unintended consequences that come with it. Is it possible that both sides have a point?

Our premise here is that the free market versus government intervention debate is a classic divergent problem, as E. F. Schumacher called them. The world is full of such problems, like freedom versus order, justice versus mercy, or discipline versus creativity. Unlike simple convergent problems such as those found in basic mathematics, the more one wrestles with complex, divergent questions, the more the answers diverge. The only solution is to transcend the problem through cognitive processes that go beyond the reductionist logic that has informed the way we have seen the world ever since the Enlightenment. This new way of reasoning requires us to step back and think in systems to understand what determines system health. It requires an inquiry into complexity science and holistic decision-making in order to grapple effectively with the wicked problems of the age.

SEPARATE PARTS VERSUS DYNAMIC WHOLES

We are in trouble because modern economic theory and the practice of finance especially, now the dominant global frameworks around which modern civilization is organized, remain dangerously grounded in an outdated mechanistic worldview that fails to reflect the reality of the more accurate living-systems worldview.

Capitalism as practiced today is in question for good reason.[30] Neoclassical economics—the mechanistic, equilibrium-based theoretical construct for today's dominant form of capitalism—is built on several false assumptions that will never be addressed by contemporary political debates about how to rein in the irresponsible financial sector or how to address inequality.[31]

Neoliberal economics, the conservative version of neoclassical economics pushing for a smaller public role in the economy and less regulation, along with globalization and privatization, assumes the primacy of the individual and that broad-based prosperity can be achieved through the operations of unfettered, free markets that efficiently allocate resources, presumably maximizing what economists call the "utility" of the participants in the system. But it's important to understand that both the right-leaning neoliberalism variety of neoclassical economics and the more left-leaning neoclassical economics that envisions a larger role for the state to soften the free market's rough edges—"neoclassical economics with a heart"—are expressions of neoclassical economics, two denominations of the same faith. Both contain a number of common assumptions that are, in fact, all fatally flawed. These unquestioned beliefs include that the economy is separate from the biosphere and the environment, and that maximizing profits for shareholders, growing GDP, and optimizing consumer material utility (more stuff) all lead to prosperity and happiness. Another assumption is that when markets are fair and transparent, they will efficiently allocate scarce resources, irrespective of temporal considerations.

Each of these core assumptions is grounded in an outdated mechanistic worldview that is at odds with today's scientific understanding of the world. Today, most researchers realize that, as John Muir said, "When we try to pick out anything by itself, we find it hitched to everything else in the Universe." Unfortunately, one of mechanism's core tenets is that everything in the world can be broken into separate parts with little or no reference to the patterns of relation among those parts. French philosopher René Descartes, for example, maintained that to understand a complex phenomenon, you need to break it down to its component parts (reductionism).

Mechanism's dangerously reductionist way of viewing the world is so deeply entrenched, however, that most scientists and laypeople alike—including many politicians and economists—equate scientific thinking with analytic, reductionist methods.[32]

People who see economies as separate from other parts of society and the biosphere often ignore (or address separately) the harm done to other parts of society and the biosphere. Most leading business schools, for example, still teach the mechanistic idea that optimizing near-term "shareholder value" should be a firm's primary goal. This idea poses a clear and present danger to the health of human communities and all life on Earth because it assumes that the firm is separate from the greater whole of society, as well as from the biosphere upon whose life-supporting functions the firm, its employees, and its customers depend. No amount of precision in reductionist thought can ever remedy the harm done by ignoring such critical relationships. Instead, a first crucial step must be to shed light on the problem by putting honest prices (to the extent possible) on wastes that harm other parts of the system, as well as the inputs and services they provide.

Consequently, mechanism's simplistic approach inhibits our ability to grasp the meaning of the whole in all its complexity. Even more critically, human agency and creativity have no place in this framework whose metaphor is a machine, impervious to change triggered by the participants of the system's collective actions.

In contrast, an emerging scientific worldview emerging today takes up Muir's perspective and extends it rigorously into the human world. Originally called holism, it is now referred to under titles ranging from systems theory, cybernetics, and complexity to the ecological or living systems worldview. The fundamental tenet of this newer and more sophisticated science is that whole systems can be understood only through the dynamic relationships among all parts. In fact, the whole emerges out of the dynamic relationships of the parts, but cannot be understood through an examination of the parts alone. Reductionism is not compatible with a true understanding of life.

This brings us to another regenerative hypothesis: The principles of holism, which underlie a systems worldview and drive the co-evolutionary process in living systems and nonliving flow networks alike, must be extended to our understanding of the human economy, replacing the flawed, reductionist, mechanistic, and destructive logic of so-called industrial efficiency.

Jan Smuts introduced the idea of holism in his 1926 book *Holism and Evolution*. He defined it as "the tendency in nature to form wholes that are greater than the sum of the parts through creative evolution."[33] For example, two molecules of hydrogen and one molecule of oxygen when joined chemically create water, a new "whole." Similarly, the human body, including the human mind, is far greater than the sum of its cellular and functional parts.

Smuts observed that this quality is constant throughout the natural world (living and nonliving), and importantly, the tendency toward the creation of wholes drives the creative evolutionary process. "Holism, as the operative factor in the evolution of wholes, is the ultimate principle of the universe."[34]

How different holism is from the reductionism that informs our current mindset and upon which our Newtonian, mechanistic worldview is based! A holistic or systems worldview challenges much conventional religious thinking by placing humans within nature,[35] not separate from or above it. We are participants in the biosphere and the evolutionary process itself. In such a worldview, the environment is not an "issue" or a "special interest." The environment is us, or more accurately, we are a part of the greater whole that is the environment and beyond, just as an organ of our body is made up of cells. We are part of One Whole, embedded in and inseparable from civilization and the environment.

The words *economy* and *ecology* both come from the Greek *oikos* meaning "household," which applies equally at all scales from individual households all the way up to planet Earth itself, literally our home in the universe. So economy, literally the "management of the household," is inseparable from "ecology," which means "the study of the household."[36]

Critically, regenerative principles will demand that we shift from a competitive, mechanistic worldview to a more cooperative and collaborative, ecological worldview. Regeneration demands that we acquire a sophisticated understanding and comfort with complexity, in turn a demand to discover our humility as a species.

To be clear, when we invoke the evolutionary model and metaphor, we are not alluding to the common misinterpretation of the Darwinian notion of "survival of the fittest" (actually a term coined not by Darwin but by the English philosopher Herbert Spencer). Nor are we referring to Darwin's theory of evolution by natural selection. Evolutionary biologists now understand the process is far more interesting than simply random, although randomness plays a role. Social Darwinists have often willfully misconstrued these terms to justify the most hypercompetitive and antisocial behaviors of capitalism. Darwin would not have agreed with these interpretations, which are inconsistent with modern biology's understanding of the role that competition and cooperation play in nature. As we shall see, when Darwin used the word *fittest*, he was referring to a species that "best fit" into its particular environment.

Biologist and biomimicry expert Janine Benyus further emphasizes that "life is a team sport!" As she says, it is "collaboration rather than competition that is the survival mechanism in natural systems." Organisms evolve out of competition as quickly as possible because it is bad for all parties. Thus, the giraffe evolved with a long neck in order to eat from the top of trees, so as not to compete with the zebra.[37] Weeds compete, grow fast, and die. Life in mature and sustainable forests is collaborative at its core.

BEYOND MERE METAPHOR: THE EMPIRICAL SCIENCE OF FLOW

Today, the scientific study of self-organizing flow systems is turning this general holistic worldview into precise, empirical understandings of health, growth, and development.[38] This rigorous research means that Regenerative Economics need not be based merely on loose ecological metaphors; rather, it has empirical substance grounded in the science of energy flow networks. In my 2015 booklet *Regenerative Capitalism*, there is an appendix, "The Science of Energy Flow Networks," authored by Dr. Sally Goerner, science adviser to Capital Institute in our early years. In it, Dr. Goerner provides an overview of some of the hard science underpinning Regenerative Economics. I excerpt only a few key insights from the appendix here, but strongly encourage readers to take a detour to it if you are curious.[39]

The big discovery here is that many of the same physical laws that govern health and development in ecosystems and living systems are common to all flow networks—and therefore apply equally to human networks such as economies and societies.

In her 2000 book *The Nature of Economies*, Jane Jacobs suggested that economies are governed by the same rules as nature itself. Her actual hypothesis, however, was that living organisms, ecosystems, and economies are all types of flow networks, and that similar principles of growth and development apply to them all.

The study of flow simplifies the study of systemic health by providing a logical basis for systemic behavior that holds regardless of whether the network under study is a single living organism, a nonliving network such as the Internet, an ecosystem, or the entire economy itself. This simplification is a result of the fact that the basic dynamics of flow are universal. . . .

The existence of universal patterns then provides precise targets for systemic health and development that take us far beyond metaphor. Geometrically precise patterns—that play out in every kind of system at every level of our world—have been the object of both awe and science since the ancient Greeks labeled them "sacred geometries" over 2,500 years ago. Today most researchers believe such patterns exist because they support some aspect of systemic health. The study of fractals provides a modern example of how universal patterns provide precise, measurable targets for optimal systemic health.

This combination of universal principles and measurable targets of systemic health provides a truly powerful framework for rethinking capitalism, and the public policy agenda that will support long-term economic health. Fractals, for example, provide a measurable understanding of healthy hierarchies. The combination of universal principles and measurable targets also confirms growing suspicions that imbalances, such as the shrinking middle class and domination by "too big to fail" organizations, are dangerous to systemic health—while at the same time providing precise explanations and targets for what constitutes too big, or too few.

The next section outlines some of the implications that this rigorous and scientifically grounded form of holism holds for business, finance, and economics.

CREATING REGENERATIVE ECONOMIES USING THE LAWS OF A HOLISTIC UNIVERSE

Our latest scientific understanding tells us that, notwithstanding its many achievements, today's form of capitalism rests upon outdated reductionist thinking that is fundamentally at odds with both the finite boundaries of the biosphere and the laws of systemic health in an interconnected world.[40] Despite lifetimes of admirable struggle and superficial signposts of progress, our effort to address symptoms instead of causes is a losing battle that has blocked us from seeing the underlying decay in our economic fabric. It is now clear that those leaders of commerce and governance who seek to support the transition to a regenerative economy must discard the outdated intellectual maps that created today's crises, and instead help chart a new course using a new intellectual map.

As we work to craft our new road map, the imperative is to begin at the beginning, rather than add patches to a failed design. We must ground Regenerative Economics in the solid empirical understandings of the laws and patterns of systemic health. We will find this latest scientific understanding is remarkably aligned with our many ancient wisdom traditions that have stood the test of time, and with indigenous values and ways of seeing our place in the world.[41] Instead of the self-serving, command-and-control methods we so often use today, we must seek to align our planning and policy interventions with the self-organizing, self-nourishing, self-regulating characteristics of healthy systems in nature.

We are just now beginning to realize how profound this Copernican shift will be. For instance, because the science of flow is about networks, its big realization is that the only way to build a vibrant economy is to build ecosystems of healthy human networks. This focus on human networks brings a new vision of the relationships and values needed to build vibrant economies. Because it is a (relatively) exact science, it provides the solid foundation and effective measurement tools we need to build a healthy regenerative economy.

This Copernican shift in vision changes the context of economic discussion by showing that:

- Small, medium, and large are all necessary. The trick is to avoid excesses, to maintain a proper balance of constructive competitors at every scale, and to keep members at all levels serving the health of the whole and not just their narrow self-interest. Easier said than done, but we know empirically now what is required for health.
- Some inequality is to be expected in a market economy based on differing skills and how they relate to the imperatives of commerce and differing personal choices. But too much inequality (as we will see in the next chapter) is deadly for economies and societies.
- Powerful elites have a special responsibility not to use their power for self-serving ends but to practice restraint. Society must have a mechanism to ensure that this vital component of systemic health is upheld. Greek democracy to Athenian hegemony, Roman Republic to Roman Empire, American free enterprise democracy to modern corporate oligarchy—history shows again and again that we have not perfected this requirement yet.
- Robust cross-scale circulation of information/money and matter/energy is critical. Excessive concentrations of financial wealth and excessive draining of lower levels can destroy an economy by stifling circulation.
- Both systemic efficiency and resilience are necessary, and too much or too little of either one causes problems. These problems can be catastrophic, as we have seen from finance's relentless pursuit of "shareholder value" in the name of "capital efficiency"—when what is needed is a more integral understanding of stakeholder value and the multiple forms of capital that must be in balance.

We will expand on these ideas in chapter 3. What is critical here is to understand that the new hard science of whole systems brings a new level of rigor to our practice of business and governance while also providing an empirical foundation for our abiding belief in the need for justice, integrity, and ethics in business, finance, and economics at large. Where we previously had only a vague idea of how human economies should mirror nature's design for vitality, we now also know that regenerative economies should follow fractal patterns that integrate the contributions from a diverse array of unique individual households, communities, and bioregional networks to the global-scale economy.[42] We also now see that this unified global perspective stands atop and provides coherence for the infinite unique contexts of specific local cultures, places, and bioregions, at all scales.[43]

Instead of merely being connected to all things, we also now know that all things on Earth and even in the cosmos at large co-evolve—a fact solidly grounded in the physical and mathematical study of flow networks and central to Smuts's theory of holism. Consequently, as preeminent systems scientist Stuart Kauffman explains, "We live in a universe, biosphere, and human culture (including economy) that are not only emergent, but radically creative. This is a central part of the new scientific worldview." Consequently, Kauffman continues, "like the biosphere, the global economy is a self-consistently, co-constructing, ever-evolving, emergent whole."[44]

The hard science of holism even helps us debunk some of the unexamined assumptions mentioned at the beginning of this chapter. We now know, for example, the following:

- The economy is not separate from the biosphere or the society in which the economy is embedded. A vast literature largely ignored by mainstream economists on both the left and the right methodically critiques modern economic theory to show that the economic system is in fact embedded in the biosphere, not separate from it.[45] The failure of modern economic theory to acknowledge this reality has had profound consequences, not the least of which is global climate change, which Sir Nicholas Stern called "the greatest market failure ever."[46] I would say it is more than a market failure; it is a profound and deadly fundamental error in the theoretical framework upon which we run the modern world.
- Maximizing profits for corporate shareholders, optimizing "consumer material utility" for the self-interest of a so-called "rational economic man," and growing GDP for nation-states do not automatically lead to prosperity—at least not stable, widely shared prosperity. For example, research using the Genuine Progress Indicator suggests that genuine progress decoupled from GDP growth in the U.S. around 1980.[47] Not only do human, community, and environmental well-being often go down when shareholder profits and GDP go up, but a growing mountain of

evidence—and the common sense of a child—suggests that people care about much more than simply "maximizing material utility." Indeed, a vast cohort of researchers is now documenting the richness and depth of values that contribute to human prosperity beyond material wealth. This work generally shows that once a certain threshold of material wealth is secured, more material goods become increasingly less important to our well-being.[48] These truths, of course, underlie all the world's great religions and are well-established in modern psychology by work such as Abraham Maslow's "hierarchy of needs."[49]

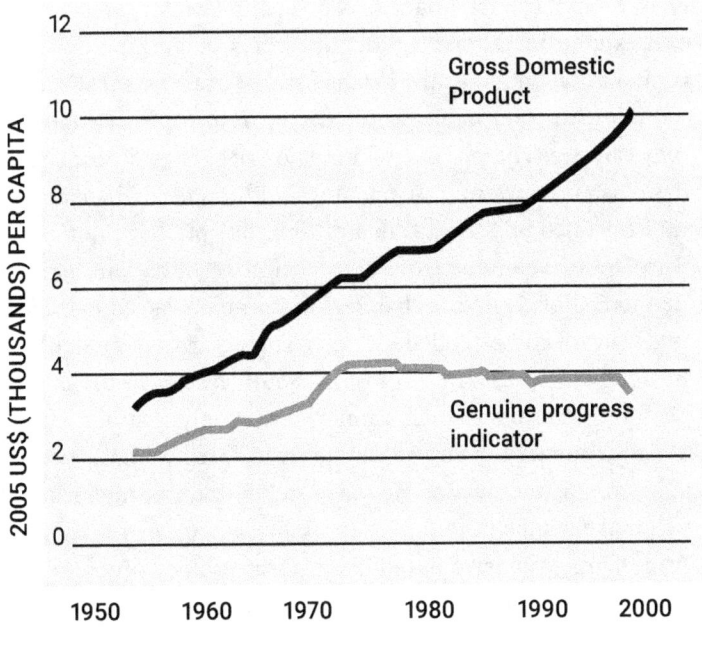

Figure 2.1 Genuine Progress Has Flattened While GDP Soars.
U.S.-based organization Redefining Progress built upon this notion, creating a pathway for Clifford Cobb, Ted Halstead, and Jonathan Rowe to create the Genuine Progress Indicator (GPI), which consists of 26 indicators. *Credit: Costanza, R., Kubiszewski, I., Giovannini, E. et al. "Development: Time to Leave GDP Behind." Nature 505, 283–285 (2014). https://doi.org/10.1038/505283a.*

- Laissez-faire markets (alone) cannot be counted on to find optimal solutions to allocate scarce resources in a timely and effective manner. One of the key assumptions underlying today's dominant economic framework is the idea that the "price mechanism" can always be counted on to drive innovation and the development of new alternatives in an optimally timely and effective manner. Such partial truths are often more dangerous than obvious falsehoods. In this view, when resources or goods become scarce, prices will rise, stimulating innovation and leading to the rapid and effective development of alternative resources or goods. While this mechanism works reasonably well within short time horizons and among easily substitutable goods, that does not mean the price mechanism and markets can solve all of our allocation needs. Understood holistically, we see that some inputs are not substitutes but complements, such as, most critically, natural capital, financial capital, and human capital. As we will explore in chapter 3, key thresholds of multiple forms of capital must be in healthy balance. Money cannot substitute for air to breathe or a viable planet to sustain life. Furthermore, not only can powerful players manipulate prices to effect local agendas (as is currently happening with central bankers on interest rates or Saudi Arabia on oil), but price cannot always drive the development of some critical resources in a timely manner. Global climate change, for example, has led to increasingly severe and extended droughts such that some major cities in both the American South and Southwest have periodically been reduced to less than a ninety-day supply of water. Having already extended their water systems to drain water unsustainably from as far away as Colorado, no amount of higher prices will make a substitute for water magically appear in California. And energy-intensive desalination creates other problems, the very nature of the polycrisis. Furthermore, as critical resources become increasingly scarce, the equity issues magnify exponentially. A healthy living system is capable of self-maintaining and self-regulating. It is one thing to be priced out of buying a Monet; it is another thing altogether to be priced out of access to clean water.

Shifting from outdated mechanistic science to a science of holistic thinking will be hard because reductionist thinking serves a useful purpose. It has also been ingrained in human thinking for centuries and often goes unexamined. It will take great courage for leaders to step back, reflect, and reconnect with the essence of our humanity and the real sources of lasting economic vitality. But grounded in holistic thinking, this viable path out of our interconnected crises is now becoming clear.

With this context in mind, let us now shift to what we see as the eight "first principles" of regenerative vitality in the next chapter.

SECOND EDITION REFLECTION

A fresh read of the chapter on holism ten years later reveals a need to expand upon a foundational premise of the regenerative paradigm and Regenerative Economics.

Bear with me as we drop into the weeds and examine very briefly the history and development of economic thought in the West, the economics by which we generally run the world to this day. It is essential and enlightening to understand how we got to this place, the place we now call the polycrisis. The great economist John Maynard Keynes said it very well. "The ideas of economists and political philosophers, both when they are right and when they are wrong, are more powerful than is commonly understood. Indeed, the world is ruled by little else. Practical men, who believe themselves to be quite exempt from any intellectual influences, are usually slaves of some defunct economist."[50] Let us now explore the defunct (Western male) economists dating back to the Enlightenment whom we remain slaves of to this day.

In the beginning there was Adam Smith. Well not quite. The English moral philosopher John Locke made his seminal contributions on the idea of private property, the foundation of capitalism, some eighty years before Smith wrote *The Wealth of Nations* in 1776. But with this comprehensive, first-of-its-kind work on economics, Smith defined the discipline of classical economics and carved for himself the reputation as the father of capitalism. Smith introduced the idea of the invisible hand of the marketplace—

supply and demand meeting each other through the price discovery mechanism, making the case that markets naturally stimulate desired production and find equilibrium in such a way that the selfish interests of individuals miraculously achieve the highest common good for all. In perhaps the most famous passage from any economics text ever written (including this one!), Smith writes, "It is not from the benevolence of the butcher, the brewer, or the baker, that we expect our dinner, but from their regard to their own interest." Enshrined for posterity, at least in the West, self-interest ("greed is good" Gordon Gekko would proclaim in the 1987 film *Wall Street*) is justified by the "law" of the invisible hand of the marketplace.

Some historical context here is essential. Smith and his peers, who included David Ricardo, Thomas Malthus, and John Stuart Mill, among others, used the phrase *classical economics* to reflect a parallel foundational school of economics to that of classical physics developed in a similar place a century earlier by Isaac Newton. It's likely fair to say that the economists had Newton envy and did what economists have done ever since. They made assumptions. They simply assumed that there was a set of parallel laws in economics to the laws Newton had discovered and proved with mathematics in the physical world of matter. This one assumption can be seen as the original error of economics. This one simple but profound error and what followed are to a staggering degree at the heart of our current crisis in economics. It would not be exaggerating to say that all the crises we collectively refer to as the polycrisis are not in fact problems to solve. They are symptoms of this original error in economics, which in turn is a product of the myth of separation, as I have discussed previously.

Economic historians give Smith a pass because he based this assumption on a prior belief system developed in his earlier work, *The Theory of Moral Sentiments*. Smith was a moral philosopher writing on economics, with a deep religious belief in an all-knowing and all-powerful, benevolent God. Surely in the machine logic of a "clockwork universe" that Newton's laws explained, there must have been a "clockmaker" whose rule applied to the domain of social systems and not just physics. Smith's invisible hand metaphor rested on his belief that humans were bestowed by the Creator with an innate "sympathy" (today probably best translated as empathy) for other humans. Of course, humankind is more complex than that as history makes clear.

The original error of Smith and his contemporaries was to assume without any compelling logic, much less ability to test the hypothesis, that there was an analog in economics to Newtonian, classical physics. Unfortunately, that error has gone uncorrected and even unquestioned by most in the field, despite overwhelming evidence proving the falsification of the premise. Even as a non-formally-trained economist beyond an undergraduate degree, and as a non-formally-trained scientist, I find the perseverance of this grave error so shocking it boggles the mind.

Fast-forward to the next generation of economists, whom we call the neoclassical economists. There were many enhancements to the "rough draft" theories of Smith and his peers, most of them a bit wonkish in nature. But there were also two important and overriding shifts that occurred with great relevance to our present moment. First, there was a conscious drift away from philosophical concerns, for example, the hard questions of fairness and equity. In reductionist fashion, the neoclassical economists explicitly left these questions to the discipline of political philosophy. The artificial divide between political science and economics was born. And in a related development, the discipline would see a mathematical formalization replace philosophical reasoning. With the introduction of rigorous mathematical modeling and differential equations, political economy would become the science of economics, "a science as exact as many of the physical sciences," writes the British neoclassical economist William Stanley Jevons. Meanwhile, similar developments were happening in France led by mathematician and economist Léon Walras, seemingly without much collaboration. Here's Walras: "Pure theory of economics is a science which resembles the physic-mathematical science in every respect."

To fully appreciate the profound implications of this shift, we can look to the American Irving Fisher, described by Milton Friedman as "the greatest economist the United States has ever produced." I am not capable of reading Fisher's seminal work, *Mathematical Investigations in the Theory of Value and Prices*. As the title implies, it's mostly math. But as I scanned it online, this one table, shown in figure 2.2, leaped off the pages to grab my attention.

You can see Fisher making the critical assumptions that allow him to use literally the same equations from Newtonian physics (see column labeled "In Mechanics") to his equations in economics (right-hand

THE NEWTONIAN FOUNDATION OF NEOCLASSICAL ECONOMICS		
§ 2.		
In Mechanics.		*In Economics.*
A particle	Corresponds to	An individual.
Space	" "	Commodity.
Force	" "	Marg. ut. or disutility.
Work	" "	Disutility.
Energy	" "	Utility.
Work or Energy = force x space		Disut. or Ut. = marg. ut. x commod
Force is a vector (directed in space)		Marg. ut. is a vector (directed in com.)
Forces are added by vector addition. ("parallelogram of forces.")		Marg. ut. are added by vector addition. (parallelogram of marg. ut.)
Work and Energy are scalars.		Disut. and ut. are scalars.

Figure 2.2 Fisher's Irrational Assumptions. *Credit: Irving Fisher, Mathematical Investigations in the Theory of Value and Prices (Yale University Press, 1892), p. 85.*

column). What was required was just a few simple assumptions that include the premise that a particle corresponds to a (complex human) individual. Let that sink in.

Newton's physics understood particles to be the basic unit of the physical world, separate from all other particles. So Fisher's economics assumed that humans, too, were simply particles, separate from other humans in the pursuit of their own "utility." Greed is good, formalized in the equations by this one simple assumption, hidden in a dense textbook over a century old. Another striking assumption is that "work" in physics would correspond to "disutility" in economics. The implication is that work is something we only do to get money. No purpose. The equations optimize for utility, which means as little work as possible. So much for the dignity of work!

To summarize, neoclassical economics is the theory by which we run the global economy, the water we all swim in. As a result, it is the theory by which we run the world. It has a conservative wing (free markets, deregulation, privatization, globalization) and a liberal wing (social democracies favoring a robust safety net and a heavier hand from government to regulate the marketplace). Both are expressions of neoclassical economics, built on a foundation borrowed from Newtonian physics, as we have seen, by men who, I suggest, had Newton envy. Whether true or not, they ran headlong into making economics every bit as much a "science" as physics by adding mathematical formalization to the theory so that it could be subject to models for the purpose of prediction. They did this despite being told by physicists at the time that it made no scientific sense.

And critically, both denominations (left and right leaning) of what I'll call the Church of Neoclassical Economics share two fundamental beliefs. First, the economic system exists apart from "nature," with so-called raw materials along with labor and capital as inputs to the closed system. And second, economic growth not only is the source of prosperity but is an imperative to keep the system from collapsing. The first belief directly contradicts advances in physics since Newton, most notably quantum physics, and more recently the evidence of entanglement for which the 2022 Nobel Prize in physics was awarded. Biology, psychology, and common sense tell us that individuals are far more complex than utility maximizing particles, what the economics profession refers to as "economic man." But quantum entanglement means Fisher's assumptions that particles are simply disconnected parts of a machine are simply wrong! Everything is connected to everything in a complex web. They are not separate parts of a machine in which humans have no agency and where there is no whole greater than the sum of the parts. And the second belief, that continuous exponential material growth is physically possible on a finite planet, also violates common sense, as well as that pesky entropy law (not theory) from physics, the second law of thermodynamics, as Herman Daly, his teacher chemist Nicholas Georgescu-Roegen before him, and Daly's colleagues in ecological economics have made clear.

This is not a new critique. It was fifty years ago when economist and systems scientist Kenneth Boulding quipped, "Anyone who believes that exponential growth can go on forever in a finite world is either a madman or an economist." Yet, remarkably, undifferentiated economic growth remains the central and essential objective of mainstream economics to this day. And the thing is, economic growth has worked very well for many people for a long time. It is essential for the many people in society whose basic needs are not being met. It works brilliantly at an individual level, but at a systemic level, it only works until it doesn't. It works until we reach the systemic limits to growth, the title of the seminal Club of Rome study by a group of MIT systems scientists also a half century ago, as discussed previously.

Surely economists are not stupid people, far from it. They have recognized some of the errors of the theory and have spent a century patching the neoclassical framework. Most notably, the Great Depression triggered by the stock market crash of 1929 destroyed the belief that economies would tend toward equilibrium with supply and demand in balance. Our friend Irving Fisher jubilantly declared the stock market had reached "a permanently high plateau" just days before the crash. Oops.

In the postwar redesign of the global economic architecture, the core idea of the brilliant neoclassical economist John Maynard Keynes, for whom the Keynesian school of economics is named, would take root. Government spending could and must be marshalled to fill such "demand gaps" when they arise, like the one caused by the stock market crash leading to the Great Depression. This was a vital "patch" to the neoclassical framework, but the Newtonian foundation remained.

Later, the discipline of behavioral economics would arrive to address the clearly silly assumption that human beings were merely utility maximizing machines. Humans had other preferences and values besides greed. Another patch for neoclassical economics. And finally, the discipline of environmental economics was born to address the so-called externalities of the system, costs not fully priced into the market system, such as the cost of pollution born by those living downstream from a polluting factory. In this way, neoclassical economics has reduced climate change risk to an "externality" that can be "fixed" with, for example, a tax on carbon that internalizes the cost. While a carbon tax with the distributional challenges of who bears the burden thoughtfully managed is without question a smart public policy, it is a patch that is by no means a fix. To quote ecological economist (and philosopher) Peter Brown of McGill University, "There is a difference between a cost that can be fixed with money and a wrong that can never be fixed."

But here's the important point. All these patches and more never addressed the system's fatally flawed beliefs: that the economy was separate from the biosphere, and that exponential growth on a finite planet was physically possible. Neoclassical economics is incompatible with accepted modern science! And yet it is still taught in most of the world's leading universities, and it still drives government policy decisions. It even defines the way we think, just as Keynes presciently warned. It is also the theoretical foundation upon which modern finance rests, both theory and practice. What I call the "finance algorithm" has created systemic "lock-in" with the false assumptions of neoclassical economics, driving us off the cliff.

Let me offer an analogy. For a thousand years, most astronomers accepted Ptolemy's geocentric model in which the sun and planets rotated around the Earth, the center of the Universe. Simple observation told us that the Sun rose in the east, and the Sun set in the west, so an Earth-centric assumption made sense. It also suited the powerful elite in the Catholic Church: one pope with a direct line to God, creator of humanity, as depicted by Michelangelo on the ceiling of the Sistine Chapel. The church would mediate God's will for the universe, divine right from wrong, and lead all of God's children. Talk about elite! Take away the Earth-centric worldview and replace it with the notion that we are but one small speck in a vast universe rotating around one star among trillions, and you pull the rug out from under the identity, assumed power, and authority of the church.

But astronomers started to notice some anomalies that didn't make sense. The stars appeared stationary while the planets moved across the sky. Even more confusing, the planets displayed a retrograde motion whereby they appeared to move backward (east to west) before resuming their normal west to east motion. Ptolemy, for whom the Ptolemaic worldview was named, and other astronomers spent their careers developing elaborate mathematical models to explain these "epicycles"—small circular motions while orbiting the Earth. Just as the neoclassical economists would do centuries later, the early astronomers were devising patches for the seeming anomalies and inadequacies of their theories.

But in 1515, a Polish priest named Nicolaus Copernicus saw what all the astronomers were seeing, but in a new way. "We revolve around the Sun like any other planet." Cautious of the church's disapproval, he first published his theory in 1543, shortly before his death. The Italian scientist Giordano Bruno was less cautious. He faced charges of heresy for teaching Copernicus's heliocentric worldview and was burned at the stake.

Nearly a century after Copernicus first proposed his idea—think about that, an entire century later—Galileo Galilei pointed his telescope into the night sky and noticed that moons were orbiting Jupiter, counter to the Earth-centric assumption that everything rotated around the Earth. With this and other observations, Galileo proved Copernicus right. And yet, the elders of the church literally refused to look through Galileo's telescope. Instead, they tried him for heresy under the Roman Inquisition and placed him under house arrest for life.

More than three hundred years after Copernicus's discovery, with the publication of *Philosophiae Naturalis Principia Mathematica* in 1887, Newton's unified laws of motion would finally explain what Aristotle, Ptolemy, and a millennium of scientists busily constructing their patches had missed. "Of all the discoveries and opinions," Goethe would observe, "none may have exerted a greater effect on the human spirit than the doctrine of Copernicus."

By the dawn of the twenty-first century, the Church of Neoclassical Economics is having its own "Copernican moment." While no one is being burned at the stake anymore, economists from Boulding to Daly and many others questioning the neoclassical worldview have been shunned from the mainstream academy. To earn a PhD in economics today, students must dig deeper down a rabbit hole within the neoclassical framework, rather than do what Copernicus did and question the core assumptions of the framework itself.

Defining the extreme disconnection from reality and the dangerous state of the modern Church of Neoclassical Economics, the Swedish Central Bank awarded its 2018 economic prize "in honor of Alfred Nobel" to environmental economist (recall the externalities patch) William Nordhaus for his Dynamic Integrated Climate-Economy ("DICE") model (can't make it up) that concludes we should target 3.5 degrees of warming because anything lower would "cost too much."[51] Nordhaus understands climate science and knows the scientific consensus since 2015 is that we must stay below 1.5 degrees. Seemingly his flawed logic suggests that with more growth and more money we will be able to "fix" whatever problems arise from climate change. Nordhaus makes absurd assumptions in his work, like climate change won't impact manufacturing because it happens indoors, and while it will affect agriculture, it won't impact growth because agriculture is only 5 percent of the economy. The only explanation is that he is trapped in growth dogma, overconfident, and unwilling to look through the metaphoric telescope himself.

With the introduction of Regenerative Economics, I'm seeking to challenge orthodoxy even further. Not only am I observing the scientific truth regarding the Newtonian error in economics, I'm pushing the discipline beyond the paradigm of scientific materialism itself, as I will expand upon later. I've now spent two decades struggling to find the means and words to effectively communicate even with decent and well-meaning powerful elite who have an identity and vested interests in the growth-centered, "economy-as-machine to be optimized" worldview. Sitting over a quiet lunch after his retirement as the successful architect of the historic merger between Chase Manhattan Bank and JPMorgan, former CEO Bill Harrison struggled to process my simple assertion that exponential growth on a finite planet cannot continue. "It's too big, John, I can't go there." It was not greed or ill intent. You won't find a more gentlemanly banker than Bill Harrison, a breed from a different era. Yet his core identity wouldn't allow him to look through the proverbial telescope. With more than a touch of irony, a decade later Harrison would say on an episode of the "How Leaders Lead with David Novak" podcast, "You've got to get people out of their comfort zone. That's how you keep growing."[52]

This is not a critique of Harrison. It's an observation for us all to recognize how difficult paradigm shift really is. We humans seem to have a weakness when it comes to critical self-reflection, with our identity at stake, particularly when that identity is celebrated and reinforced by our culture, reinforcing our ego. And we don't give up our worldviews and religions easily, both literal and metaphorical. But paradigm shift—what Dana Meadows defined as the highest leverage point for system change—is exactly the project we are called to manifest at this time.[53]

Let's now turn back to our story and see just what a regenerative economy is and what are its guiding first principles.

> Your paradigm is so intrinsic to your mental process that you are hardly aware of its existence, until you try to communicate with someone with a different paradigm.
>
> —DANA MEADOWS

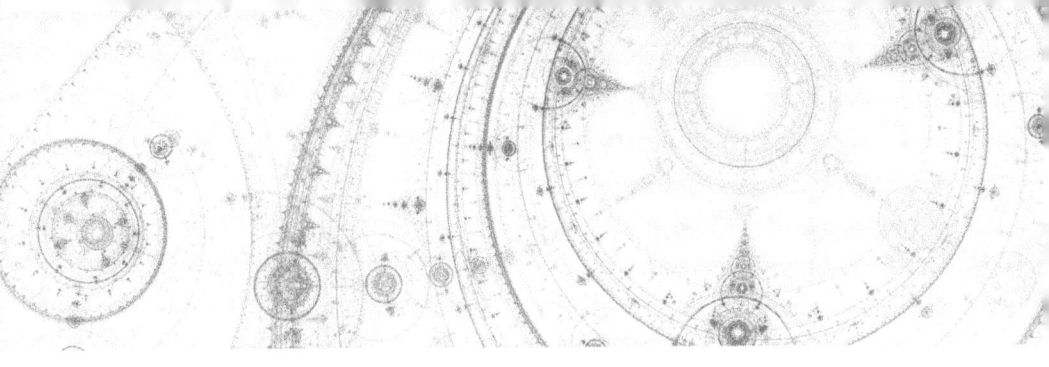

CHAPTER THREE

EIGHT PRINCIPLES OF REGENERATIVE VITALITY

Science tells us that today's dominant form of capitalism uses outdated reductionist thinking that is fundamentally at odds with both the finite boundaries of the biosphere and the laws of systemic health in an interconnected world.[54] What I am suggesting is that we are running the world on a bankrupt theoretical construct, so why are we surprised that it feels so broken?

Let me say clearly again up front, Regenerative Economics is NOT about capitalism versus socialism. From a regenerative perspective, neither the current form of capitalism nor the current form of socialism is a sustainable system. Regenerative Economics is also not merely a mid-ground position. Instead, it demands that we begin at the beginning: with a modern scientific understanding of how all life actually works, which, by the way, is an understanding we did not have in the age of Adam Smith *or* Karl Marx! We will find alignment with certain ideas from both the left and the right but not based on ideology. Rather, we follow the science. Holistic science, that is, a science that embraces and then extends the purely materialist paradigm. In alignment with more left-leaning political thought, Regenerative Economics will shed new light on the importance of fairness, and the unsustainable disease of high and growing inequality. But equally, and in alignment with more right-leaning political thought, it will embrace the dynamism of a truly free enterprise system that taps into the unique essence of human creativity and drive while demanding the resiliency of place and community for systemic health.

Regenerative Economics is not about ending capitalism but about participating in its co-evolution, complexifying it in the evolutionary sense, to produce the next stage beyond capitalism, understood in part as "multicapitalism," recognizing the multiple forms of vital capital, as we shall see. With our new understanding from science spurring this next evolution, the moral, inclusive, and broadly shared vitality and prosperity that its moral philosopher founders envisioned can finally become a reality, grounded in healthy economic networks. The phrase *the network is the system* now defines the change that is transforming the world of technology. It must also be the phrase that defines the transformation of our entire conceptual framework for human economic systems. This is not trivial.

WHAT IS A REGENERATIVE ECONOMY?

Regenerative Economics is the application of nature's process and patterns of systemic health, self-organization, self-renewal, and regenerative vitality to the design of socioeconomic systems.

It is a theory of political economy that transcends the contemporary debate between the neoliberal economics preferred by conservatives on the political right and the Keynesian (or socialist leaning) economics generally preferred by liberals on the political left. In fact, the healthy debate about the role and limitations of state intervention in the economy must continue within a regenerative economic system. However, we will find that the objectives of state intervention (whether incentives, regulation, or direct engagement) will be different from those currently advocated by both the Left and the Right. It will be first and foremost about creating the conditions necessary for a healthy and regenerative system, including removing critical obstacles. We will discuss policy implications at the end of this book.

A regenerative economy, in all its diverse manifestations due to cultural context, scope, and scale, is most fundamentally defined by the following assumption:

> Economic vigor is a product of human and societal vitality, rooted in ecological health and the inclusive development of human capabilities and potential.

Note how different this is from conventional economic thinking, which presumes that economic vigor is a function of the rate of GDP growth. Our assumption leads to the following characteristics of any regenerative economy:

- Acts in ways that support the long-term health of the whole society—a characteristic that underlies "fitness" in an interdependent world;
- Sees economic and financial health as inseparable from human, societal, and environmental health;
- Values richness and diversity, integrity, and fairness;
- Is cooperative at its core yet seeks excellence through constructive competition;
- Responds to the full gamut of human needs, continuously adapting to changing circumstances and evolving to higher and more effective levels of organization.

The critical difference between Regenerative Economics, on the one hand, and both neoliberal and Keynesian varieties of neoclassical economics, on the other, lies in the stated goal of the system. Both neoliberal and Keynesian economics use GDP—a measure of the value of goods and services produced nationally—as their primary measure of economic health. Both seek robust and stable GDP growth as source of prosperity and thus the primary objective of economic policy. A range of new economy efforts now call for alternatives to GDP that measure outcomes of progress and prosperity, most notably the Sarkozy Commission and its "Report by the Commission on the Measurement of Economic Performance and Social Progress," by Joseph Stiglitz, Amartya Sen, and Jean-Paul Fitoussi (2009).[55]

While Regenerative Economics subscribes to these alternative goals to GDP, we hold all goals lightly, since life is an emergent process. We recognize that even our most well-considered goals are likely to leave out possibilities for flourishing we don't yet know about. By contrast, Regenerative Economics seeks first to create the conditions for the development of a mosaic of healthy human networks embedded in healthy societies and the biosphere as the goal. A number of researchers are now working on effective ways to measure healthy development of human economic networks to replace GDP. Some of these efforts are described at the end of chapter 3.

Both neoliberal and Keynesian approaches assume prosperity arises out of healthy GDP *growth* yet fail to acknowledge any biophysical limits to exponential growth. Regenerative economists, on the other hand, assume prosperity arises out of the relationships and patterns of healthy human networks, within the biophysical constraints of the planet and under its physical laws (not theories). The physical constraints are what spur creativity and healthy innovation if we learn to use them in this way. Neoliberals and Keynesians argue over how best to generate GDP growth. Regenerative economists outline a fundamentally different path to prosperity, that is, how best to create the conditions that support the development of healthy human networks.

In essence, regenerative economies build lasting human, societal, and economic vitality by developing the richness, variety, responsiveness, and integrity of inclusive human networks at every level of global civilization. The task at hand for business, finance, and policymakers is to shift into alignment with the regenerative principles described below that give rise to such healthy human networks.

Regenerative design is not new in the realm of agriculture. Integrated organic farms and biodynamic farming date back to Rudolf Steiner. The holistic management of large grassland landscapes using animals as a tool to mimic how life works, an approach to management developed by Allan Savory, has been applied beyond the context of ranchlands. More recently, regenerative design has emerged in the field of architecture, led by pioneers such as Bill Reed in the Regenesis Group and by Jason McLennan, creator of the Living Building Challenge. Both Savory and McLennan are winners of the prestigious Buckminster Fuller Prize.

Regenerative thinking pioneer Carol Sanford has extended the regenerative design principles to the level of the firm in *The Responsible Business* and applied them to enterprise leaders in *The Responsible Entrepreneur.*[56] Under the leadership of Savory disciple Tre Cates, nRhythm has developed further the logic of living systems as applied to organizations of all forms. What is new here is extending the concept of regenerative design beyond individual businesses to the entire global economic system while offering a new lens to consider the profound shifts still needed in our bloated, unstable, and misguided financial system. Regenerative Economics is a new way of seeing what we all see, grounded in first principles not ideology. It's an integration of existing transdisciplinary ideas, adapted to the new context of the twenty-first-century global economy.

Regeneration is the process of life. Natural systems thrive because they are regenerative.

Our body regenerates all of its cells every seven years on average. Sustainability is the outcome, not the design principle. If the human economy and its institutions, and human civilization itself, are to thrive in the long run, they, too, must operate regeneratively. Figure 3.1 is derived from Reed's iconic diagram depicting regenerative design in the built environment (buildings and people) but adapted here to apply to entire economies.

We can see that a multitude of efforts to move from the degenerative, mechanistic design thinking of the "Enlightenment" on the lower left to natural systems design thinking grounded in modern living systems science on the upper right are all part of the journey to a regenerative system that aligns with how we know healthy energy flow networks behave. The low-hanging fruit of energy and material efficiency, the more challenging closed loop business model redesigns, the getting prices true and right, the transparency of integrated reporting, the concept of a triple bottom line—these are all critical parts of the journey.

Something magical happens when we tap into the unique creative and not-yet-seen regenerative potential that exists "above the line" over to the right. As we move above the line, invoking the power

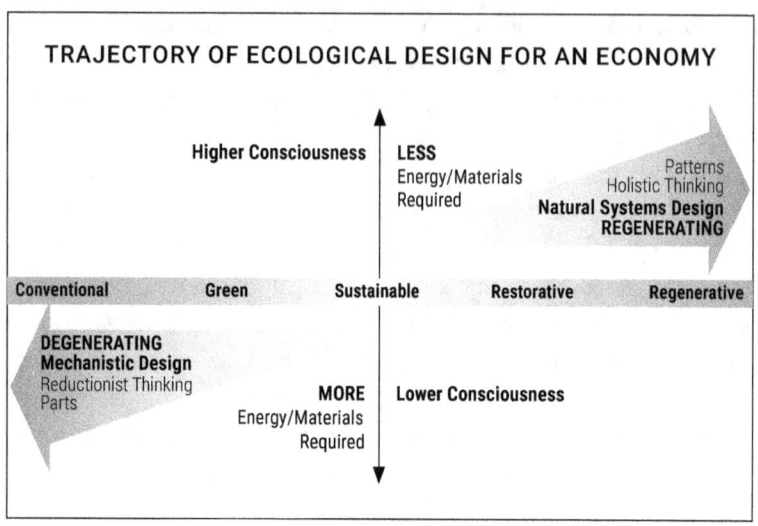

Figure 3.1 From Degenerative to Regenerative Economy. *Credit: Bill Reed and Regenesis Group as adapted by John Fullerton and Capital Institute.*

of holistic thinking that encompasses complexity, not only do we build on all of the efforts below the line, but we suddenly achieve a new understanding of what is possible. For example, only years after the internet was invented did the possibilities of search and social media manifest, unlocking unprecedented "above the line" regenerative potential (and new challenges with extractive and addictive advertising-based business models as well). Understanding the conditions that enable us to unlock this creative regenerative potential, thereby mimicking the abundance found in the natural world, is the key challenge to transforming our economies into alignment with the evolutionary process of life.

We now turn to examine the principles of regenerative vitality, what the principles would imply for a regenerative economy, and then look at some examples of Regenerative Economics emerging in the real world.

HOW DO YOU BUILD REGENERATIVE VITALITY?

EIGHT KEY PRINCIPLES

Close examination of the characteristics of regenerative economies listed on page 41 suggests that they are exactly what we had hoped our free enterprise economic system would be. Since neoclassical economics practiced in numerous varieties has not produced these outcomes, the scientific term we should use for the theory is falsification. Tested. Proved false. That the theory is in conflict with our best scientific understanding of how all life works, we should not be surprised.

I believe that Regenerative Economics represents a more effective realization of the free enterprise economic system fueled by human ingenuity and drive, and made possible by a more acute understanding of how to make free enterprise networks healthy in a complex, interdependent world. Consequently, the second step in building a regenerative economy is to identify the operating principles that lead to and support widespread, long-term, regenerative vitality.

Rather than focus on goals and the metrics needed to monitor progress toward those goals, we will take a "first principles"–based approach. Goals and key performance indicators (KPIs) work well in the reductionist machine paradigm of the clockwork universe. But our focus is on creating conditions for health while holding loosely our desired outcomes. This is the nature of emergence within complexity. This is how we can use our agency to manifest potential. We are working to unlock presently unseen potential. So we simply can't reduce this process to tidy goals. Instead, we will discern, as best we can, what irreducible first principles (to our best understanding) and patterns of systemic health define the regenerative process itself. Our task then becomes to align our economy, its governing institutions, and all the individual networks and organizations that constitute it with these first principles and patterns.

My experiences with regenerative entrepreneurs, practical people realizing the potential of the upper right in figure 3.1 in the real world, as well as my exploration of systems theory, biomimicry, systems ecology, complexity science, and the physics of flow networks, have led me to the following list of the eight "first principles" of regenerative vitality in the context of a macro economic system:

1. Operates in Right Relationship
2. Views Wealth Holistically
3. Innovates, Adapts, Responds
4. Ensures Empowered Participation
5. Honors Community and Place
6. Discovers Edge Effect Abundance
7. Ensures Robust Circulatory Flow
8. Seeks Dynamic Balance

In order to bring clarity to each concept, we will need to drop into reductionist mode (notice!) and describe each one separately and explore its unique implications for the profound economic system transition that awaits us. But, consistent with systems thinking, which demands that we think in relational patterns, for a regenerative economy to be healthy, all eight principles must be present, working together in an integrated whole. So we move into reductionism to explore details, but then move back to holism to understand the system as a whole. Consequently, these design principles are not an à la carte menu from which we can pick and choose, but an overarching pattern of qualities and principles that feed into one another with overlaps. Interactions and creative surprises among them all are to be expected. Please also remember that this is neither the "right principles" nor an exhaustive list. It is context specific, in this case the very high level of the entire economic system. And, just as five artists will make five drawings of the same tree, the regenerative process can be presented in different ways. Life is complex and not reducible to laws alone. Nor is it reducible to mathematics, notwithstanding two centuries of effort by the economics profession.

With these caveats in mind, let us shift into reductionist mode in order to illuminate eight key qualities required for regenerative health in the context of an economic system.

Operates In Right Relationship

As we have seen, both modern science and holistic thinking teach us that we are an integral part of an interconnected web of life in

WHOLES EMBEDDED WITHIN WHOLES

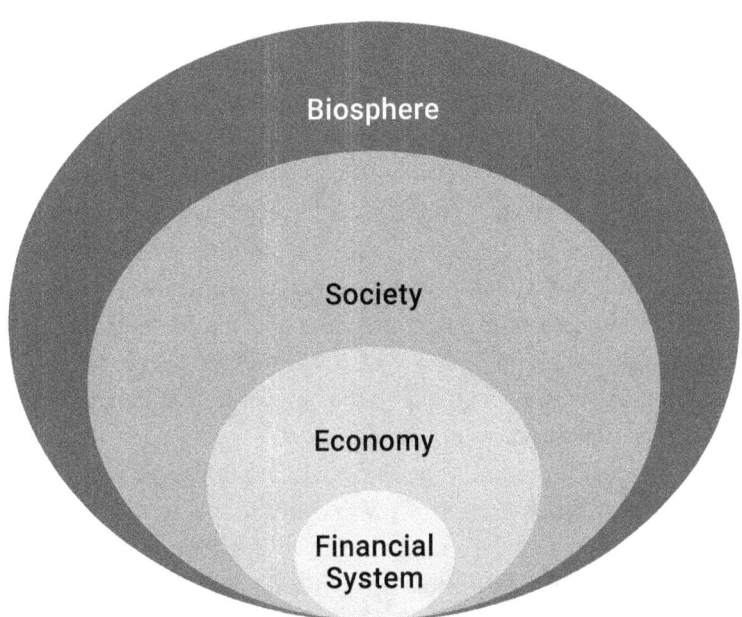

Figure 3.2 Finance within Economy within Society within the Biosphere.
Credit: John Fullerton, Capital Institute.

which there is no real separation between "us" and "it."[57] Theoretical and empirical work by Herman Daly and Robert Costanza, two of the founders of the field of ecological economics,[58] turns the idea that "it is all one system" into a rigorous explanation of why scale and limits matter, and why basic physics confirms that never-ending, exponential material throughput growth on a finite planet is physically impossible. Furthermore, "one system" explains why human economies, properly understood, are so deeply embedded in both societies and the biosphere (as depicted in figure 3.2) that excessive damage to any one part ripples back to harm every other part as well.

Nora Bateson provocatively asks, "Where's the edge of me?" Parts become regenerative wholes only when they combine in symbiotic relationship with one another, creating a unity that is far greater than the sum of its parts. Salmon, for example, play a value-adding role in regenerating life in a river system and associated forests. Even more profoundly, work by biologist Lynn Margulis shows that all complex organisms—from eukaryotic cells to mammals like us—are actually symbiotic collaborations of previously independent smaller organisms.[59] The same kind of symbiotic collaborations of independent entities also describe the interdependent system we call society.

The fundamental definition of fitness in such an interdependent world is to act in ways that serve the long-term health of the whole. In essence, this means that value-adding economic exchanges must be anchored in the context of healthy relationships. Consequently, the first and most fundamental regenerative principle is abundantly clear. Our long-term economic health and even the survival of the human species require that we be in what Peter Brown calls "right relationship" with each other and the broader host systems of which we are part, and upon which we depend.[60]

The most important aspect of "right relationship" is synergetic collaboration. Thus, in contrast with conventional thinking, current research shows that collaboration, not competition, is the defining quality in both business and life.[61] While competition still serves an important winnowing role, collaboration is fundamental because it increases development and reduces risk, thus enhancing resiliency. Margulis, for example, shows that land plants emerged out of an immortal marriage between photosynthetic algae in ponds and lichens on land because the qualities of each enhanced the combination's ability to survive and expand their territory across dry land. In ecosystems, less mature species compete until environmental pressures force them to develop mutually beneficial relationships with other species, which allows them to thrive continuously in more efficient niches. Weeds compete, grow fast, and die. A rainforest is rich, highly evolved, and resilient, and lasts for millennia, providing, in the process, vital services to the whole much larger system (our living planet) of which it is a part.

In other words, as Janine Benyus says, "Life is a team sport."

An understanding of fractal patterns teaches us that all levels within the system must live "in right relationship" as well. Regenerative economies will be built on nested, fractal relationships across many levels, ranging from individual human beings, their families and communities, to their regions, countries, global civilization, and the biosphere as a whole. While each subcomponent can be seen as a "whole," they can never be viewed as separate. Instead, since all levels are interdependent, to whittle away at the health of the small-scale economies (think Walmart suppliers) and ecosystems is to undermine the health of the larger ecosystems as well.

While competition dominates conventional economic thinking, examples of collaborative development abound in the business world already. The open-source movement in software provides a good example, as does social networking tools on the internet. Even large-scale corporations can be seen as an example of complex specialization and supply-chain integration made possible by collaborative efforts. That said, like an adolescent boy reverting to fighting when challenged on the playground, a constant tension and reversion to aggression and competition under duress is to be expected along the evolutionary path. (Recall the Goldman Sachs senior executives aggressively defending their fraudulent subprime mortgage business practices in front of the U.S. Congress.) If the pattern of evolution continues as it has through life, then eventually businesses will evolve mutually beneficial "coopetition" arrangements with each other, the public, employees, and the planet that expand the power, intricacy, resiliency, and vitality of our societal whole.

Let's briefly explore what an economy in "right relationship" might look like. Economies must be understood to consist of many levels of nested "wholes," like a cell within an organ within a body. Each "whole" within a larger whole has unique qualities and contributions. So a local place-based and place-sourced economy is nested within a bioregional economy responding to bioregional physical and cultural needs, which in turn is nested within the larger national and global economies, while a brand is nested within a larger corporation. It's complex. When managing multileveled complex systems, the bias must always be toward systemic health. Decisions are made and implemented with an eye to mutual benefit and health across all levels and systems. If we look at the ideal for educational systems for example, we see that for cultural reasons they are largely decentralized and in the hands of local jurisdictions. So far, so good. However, since effective citizenship is crucial to the entire democratic system, taxes must be gathered across larger-scale jurisdictions and distributed equitably among richer and poorer districts, thus enabling all children to have an equal opportunity to fulfill their potential, and in doing so, contribute to the health of the whole. At least that's the theory.

Decisions are made at the lowest level possible—but not lower—in alignment with the idea of subsidiarity and scale-appropriate decision-making rather than simplistic top down. Thus, in a regenerative economy, the emphasis is on city and regional planning, while national and global agendas focus primarily on issues that cannot be addressed at those lower levels.

In business, "in right relationship" can be seen in the stakeholder theory of management, and even more so in stewardship models of ownership. In the traditional shareholder view, which is still the norm, the stockholders of a company get priority, and the company has a fiduciary responsibility to put their needs first—a responsibility that has largely been interpreted to mean increasing the value of their stock price. Cornell Law School professor Lynn Stout argued persuasively that this interpretation is flawed as a matter of law, and that the "business judgment rule" gives directors of corporations much wider latitude.[62]

In contrast, stakeholder theory, originally developed by R. Edward Freeman,[63] and central to Carol Sanford's depiction in *The Responsible Business*,[64] and of course the entire B Corp movement, redirects business focus by expanding the scope of "who or what really counts." Stakeholder theory describes how management can give due regard to the interests of other stakeholders, including employees, customers, suppliers, communities, financiers, governmental bodies, trade associations, the environment, and even competitors. In a regenerative view, being "in right relationship" with all stakeholders is essential to long-term economic and organizational health. In the future we must co-create, it must be the primary "fiduciary duty" of corporate directors.

"In right relationship" with the Earth means the conventional economic assumptions of the separation of natural resources as inexhaustible inputs and wastes as outputs deposited into the environment without cost and regardless of toxicity are replaced with realization that there are no "externalities" to a healthy, whole system.[65] The only way for the economy to remain viable is to keep a constant eye on maintaining reliable inputs and healthy outputs in the endless flow that circulates throughout and across all levels.

But just as the Earth provides essential life-sustaining functions,[66] so do the functions of a healthy society provide the essentials of maintaining healthy communities, economies, and civilizations. Just as we now know harming the environment is problematic, so too the financial crisis of 2008 provided a harsh reminder that the financial system must be "in right relationship" with the real economy and the larger society in which both are embedded. Furthermore, the relationship works both ways. Harming the real economy through financial malfeasance is deadly to the financial system as well. In an interconnected world, all interests are aligned, whether we realize it or not.

A regenerative economy with these realizations makes profound adjustments, not based on political views or even debates over what human values we must cherish. Maintaining right relationship becomes a systemic requirement for the health of the whole just as obeying the law of gravity is required for the design of an airplane. Such adjustments will include the following:

- Material consumption in the developed world decelerates to make room for developing economies to reach a level of equitable and sustainable material prosperity.
- The new material light economy will be enabled by smart infrastructure and technology investment.
- The global energy system transitions from fossil fuels to 100 percent renewables,[67] an acknowledgment that heat trapped in gasses threatens the health of the whole.
- The agriculture sector transitions to a holistically managed, organic, and in fact regenerative system—that research now shows can be more efficient than industrial agriculture[68]—free of fossil fuel dependency and toxic chemicals.
- Naturally regenerative materials such as wood products are used as primary inputs at a sustainable rate.
- Finite resources are governed by an ethic of thrift; exploiting "Factor Five" resource efficiency potential; and reclaiming, recycling, and remanufacturing as much as possible.[69] Industries from electronics to aerospace that are today dependent upon finite resources are reinvented to be less so.

- The planet's degraded ecosystems are restored bioregion by bioregion to highest functionality. This begins with the natural carbon sinks (natural systems that absorb carbon) we know how to manage: the grasslands, the marshlands, sea grasses and mangroves, and of course the forests.
- The chemical industry is entirely transformed primarily to water-based "green chemistry," or approaches known not to be toxic to health, since we know that neither human nor ecosystem health is possible with destructive toxins in our environment. Everything is connected.
- The primacy of healthy, trusting, "right relationships" over transactions in our system of commerce and particularly in finance is reasserted. For example, we learned in the 2008 financial crisis that the anticipated efficiency gains from extreme securitization in the U.S. mortgage market proved to be not only highly brittle rather than resilient, but highly destructive when the creditor/borrower relationship was not only not "right" but completely severed and often fraudulent, even using the name "liars' loans." It turns out integrity and fair play are not just ethical issues. They are fundamental to systemic health.
- Population growth is controlled, as we recognize that we must slow down and reverse the destruction of all forms of natural capital and the ecosystem function that is essential to the survival of all living beings. The human race must be in right relationship with all life, and we have expropriated far too much of the earth's net primary production for our own good.

Views Wealth Holistically

In keeping with a holistic understanding of true wealth, Regenerative Economics requires that we expand the meaning of "capital" to include multiple forms of capital aligned with our core human values, including the vital patterns of their interdependencies. Regenerative multicapitalism is a more apt description, with multiple capitals "in balance" (see figure 3.3).

Nowhere will the transition to a truly regenerative economy be more challenging than in its value system. True wealth is not merely money in the bank or the accountant's "plant and equipment" line on a balance sheet. It must be defined in terms of the well-being of the whole, achieved through the harmonization of multiple kinds of wealth or capital, and critically, a broadly shared prosperity.

Contemporary economics and finance seek to condense all value into immediate monetary terms (present value) in order to drive decision-making through quantitative analysis, predominantly at the level of the firm or individual. Qualitative factors such as balance, beauty, creative potential, or stress and brittleness—that do not lend themselves to quantification and monetization—fall outside the language of accounting and the scope of mainstream economics and finance. This was done intentionally, to keep accounting simple, perhaps without due consideration to the unintended consequences to our value system (what gets measured gets valued).

Because our decision-making is centered at the level of the firm, our economic decisions also fail to take into account the larger context in which a firm operates.[70] For example, substituting software for people may improve margins and increase the productivity of an individual firm, but it does so without reference to the social costs that ultimately impact the health of society as a whole, including political stability. History is quite clear: Unemployed masses lead to revolution. Those negative impacts are now manifesting in the structural unemployment and underemployment affecting most economies and societies. The current trajectory of our system and our technology choices, such as the increased use of robotics, suggest that this will only get worse in the years ahead.

We also face the twin crises of underemployment and wasteful, harmful, energy/material throughput that continue unchecked thanks to flawed economic thinking. Bottom-line reporting fails to make a distinction between savings made by cutting labor or by cutting energy and material throughput. While common sense says that the economy will do better with more jobs and less pollution, the stock market runs on economic thinking that sees no difference between money saved by workforce reductions and money saved by reducing fossil fuel usage.

At the same time, climate change poses existential risks to all life on Earth, and individual enterprises and people take actions that impact our climate every day—but we have no shared understanding of how to manage these innumerable impacts on the shared commons called the atmosphere. What share of the remaining carbon budget (how much carbon the atmosphere can absorb before tipping the planet into dangerous climate change), for example, should be allocated to General Electric versus General Mills, or Toyota versus Net Jets? Who decides? Such questions quickly bring us to an ethical dilemma where perfect markets, perfectly transparent and integrated corporate reporting, and the most professional standards of carbon emissions management offer little help.

Conceptually these costs are "external" to the firm, but, from a holistic perspective, there are no externalities. In fact, the word *externalities*, coined by Alfred Marshall, Keynes's neoclassical economics teacher at Cambridge—shocker—doesn't make any sense. It is all one system. Externality is an oxymoron, one widely used to this day in economics. Consequently, when a firm makes decisions in its short-term interests, those decisions often have negative long-term impacts on the system of which it is a part, and therefore on its own long-term success and even survival. For example, the same firm that saves money by substituting software for people will eventually face weakened demand for its products and fiscally strapped and deteriorating municipal services where its headquarters are located—all ripple effects of the systemic underemployment it helped create.

It goes further. The Enlightenment concept of the nation-state is a reductionist fiction when looked at through a holistic lens. Governments organized around the narrow self-interest of nation-states also have a mixed record of managing global challenges—from the collapse of global fisheries or the crises in the Middle East to now the challenge of climate change. How do we address the failure of both markets and governments to tackle these threats to the future of people and planet? Readers hoping for easy solutions or silver bullets will be disappointed. No less than a new holistic theory of value and a shift in our collective consciousness will be required. Fortunately, such a shift is underway.[71]

Holism and the physics of flow networks address such problems by suggesting that value and wealth must be defined in terms of the well-being of the whole, achieved through the harmonization of

Eight Principles of Regenerative Vitality 55

multiple kinds of wealth or capital and, critically, a broadly shared prosperity. The key takeaway? The system is only as strong as its weakest link.

Liberating humanity's creative and productive powers—essential to transform our economic system to one that serves the health of the whole—therefore starts by expanding our understanding of value, wealth, and wealth creation to include all forms of capital: intellectual, experiential, social, cultural, living, even spiritual, as well as financial and material.

Concepts like social or human capital, and natural or living capital, are now commonly used in the context of sustainability.[72] The International Integrated Reporting Council (IIRC), chaired by Sir Mervyn King, identifies six forms of capital that business must measure and make transparent to stakeholders.[73] Figure 3.3 shows an expanded and useful list of eight kinds of capital coming out of the permaculture community, itself an expression of the regenerative paradigm. Undoubtedly, you might suggest even further delineations.

Evidence of a growing shift in values toward a more holistic, multiple-capital view of wealth can be seen in the emergence of "stakeholder capitalism,"[74] exemplified by companies such as Patagonia, Dutch bank Triodos, and the rise of the B Corp movement where

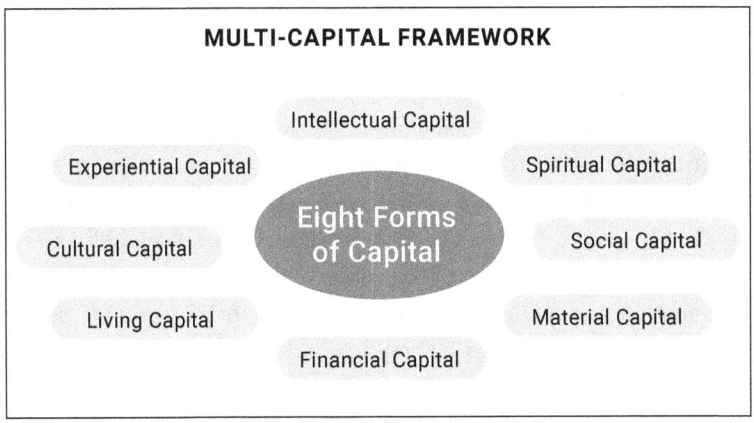

■ **Figure 3.3 Eight Forms of Capital.** *Credit: Ethan Soloviev and Gregory Landau; www.regenterprise.com.*

corporate directors are explicitly empowered by charter to consider all stakeholder interests. Whether that empowerment needs to be explicitly enshrined in new legal code is a matter that some including legal scholar Lynn Stout dispute.[75]

From an integrated perspective, such multiple forms of capital teach us three clear lessons: First, true wealth is not measured in monetary or "financial capital" terms alone. Instead, there are multiple essential parts that make up the "whole" of our true wealth. Unlike the conventional economic assumption that "maximizing the usefulness of stuff" is all people care about, we find that people and economies need a wide variety of services and products—from clean, reliable energy sources to effective collective learning—to remain healthy and strong over the long run.

Second, the relationships of these forms of capital to each other and to the whole are just as critical as the type itself. Despite conventional economics' simplifying assumptions, these relationships are not random, reducible, or freely substitutable for money.

Third, as David Orr points out, the fundamental difference between wealth that can be reduced to money—financial and material capital—and all the other kinds of capital is that "the former are controlled by the laws of accumulation and (all too often) greed, while the other forms of capital—human and natural—are nurtured by affection and foresight."

Where conventional economics concentrates exclusively on scarcity and only two kinds of capital—material and financial—a holistic approach to wealth brings a new focus on abundance. Five of the eight forms of capital—intellectual, experiential, social, cultural, and spiritual—have no limits. Developing them and using them tend to increase the abundance for all. This is our key clue to what can grow on a finite planet! Material and living capital have limits, of course, but with an old-fashioned, conservative ethic of care and thrift, demonstrated as a core value in the natural world, and our innovative potential unleashed, we should be able to maintain these indefinitely into the future while using their abundance surplus to meet our needs. And critically, nature is self-regenerating! If we allow her.

Let's now have a look at what an economy that "views wealth holistically" would look like. In a culture that confuses money with wealth, the financial sector, both the institution and the ideology, is where we must focus our attention. From a living systems perspective, we can view the ideology of finance as a critical obstacle to remove in order to manifest a regenerative economy. That will not be greeted warmly by financiers, but it's not personal. I'm not talking about people, I'm talking about the algorithm and the outcomes it manifests.

At the core, there would be an ethic of sufficiency in contrast to never enough. Once financial and material capital are sufficient to meet basic human needs, creating social capital within community and restoring natural capital in the world are valued above acquiring more financial capital. "Success" is redefined beyond material wealth, power, and fame. Individuals at a deep personal level experience a shift in mindset away from separation and scarcity to one of connectedness and abundance.

Second, cultural pressures drive and reinforce this profound shift. In the business world, the consumer-driven shift to valuing wealth holistically is already beginning to manifest in the food and energy sectors, as well as in the growing role of less resource-intensive industries such as technology, media, and entertainment. *[Note to reader: The previous sentence was written before the rise of AI, a new challenge we must contend with.]* Greater enjoyment of cultural and social experiences replaces the endless individual accumulation of disposable "stuff." More institutions are founded whose purpose is to safeguard both vital natural capital, including the atmosphere and the oceans, and vital social capital, including local or indigenous cultures. This, too, is already happening, as documented by Paul Hawken in Blessed Unrest.[76]

The present mindset of financiers, focused on optimizing financial capital alone, slowly transitions to a new consciousness in service of the regenerative economy as a whole. When it comes at the expense of systemic health, society no longer tolerates the single-minded pursuit of extractive profit regardless of the costs and ever-increasing scale and complexity of the financial sector. In a word, society says no. *[Note to reader: At the writing of this second edition, we now have the speculative and unregulated crypto chaos to rein in, and the challenges mount.]*

The too often corrupt, reckless, and self-serving culture at many of the largest financial institutions—so clearly in conflict with the needs of a healthy real economy—is met by demand for smarter regulation free of corruption and real consequences for bad behavior, including loss of license to operate. This regulation focuses on the largest financial institutions, including breaking them up either by fiat or by punitive risk capital surcharges for the systemic risk they create. At the extreme, governments mustn't shy away from nationalizing bad actors to be detoxified and then released back into the system under new management and proper stakeholder-aligned governance for the health of the whole. Profound policy interventions must occur, including the creation of institutions whose purpose is to counterbalance the excessive power of financial capital.

Evidence of a profound shift in banking taking place can be seen with the growth of the Global Alliance for Banking on Values.[77] Investment banks could be returned to their roots as private partnerships, and the separation of investment banking from commercial banking should be considered. Excessive speculation and leveraged financial engineering that is extractive at its core and destructive to systemic health would be taxed away with "polluter pays taxes" and hard prohibitions. Finance as a share of the economy shrinks materially, and human and technology resources are rechanneled into more productive use by natural market forces.

Innovates, Adapts, Responds

In a rapidly changing world, the best path to "fitness" is to be innovative, adaptive, and responsive to events and conditions by continually learning. Too often our innovation is not adaptive and responsive to the unprecedented context. That needs to change. The transition to regenerative economies, therefore, will depend on our innate, entrepreneurial human capacity to innovate and to create anew across all sectors of society, including but not limited to the business sector. It also depends on our institutions' responsiveness to the needs and well-being of all segments and levels of global civilization and the ecological stresses that we know will accelerate in the years and decades to come.

In a world in which change is both ever-present and accelerating, the qualities of innovation and adaptability are also critical to health. It is this idea that Charles Darwin intended to convey in his often-misconstrued statement: "In the struggle for survival, the fittest win out at the expense of their rivals." What Darwin meant, according to Darwin scholars, is that the most fit is the one that fits best, just as a puzzle piece fits into the larger whole.

While there is little doubt that human innovation and adaptability must play a defining role in the transition to a regenerative economy, we must remember that this applies to each one of us in our own unique way. Not only should every individual be empowered by this realization, it also suggests that overly centralized and hierarchical state bureaucracies and behemoth corporate hierarchies are inherently in conflict with this first principle and must be transformed. Most dynamic and successful businesses understand this already; many government agencies have a lot of catching up to do, recognizing their different purpose. A regenerative organization, regardless of purpose, needs aligned incentive systems to foster conditions conducive to health.

While we must unleash transformational purpose-aligned innovative technologies (and restrain the unchecked development of technologies in the name of "freedom" that are not responsive to the changing context and purpose aligned), we must also seek to rediscover and conserve the centuries-long cumulative wealth of human wisdom dormant in our own civilization as well as that which resides today in indigenous cultures. Once upon a time, long before our current obsession with short-term efficiency, many in our species lived regeneratively, in harmony with nature. We must now remember how.

At the same time, both private and public institutions must also become more responsive to the needs and well-being of all levels and sectors of their society. Free enterprise was supposed to be responsive to human needs, and democracy was supposed to be responsive to citizens—yet this is not how things have turned out. Whether it is coolly calculating the cost-benefits of poisoning local water sources or cutting costs by creating sweatshops in the Global South, global capitalism has become notoriously unresponsive toward the needs and well-being of the larger public, including its customers and employees. Democratic governments dominated by monied interests often become similarly unresponsive to the needs and well-being of the citizens they supposedly serve—particularly when public needs for, say, affordable health care, fair elections, or clean water conflict with the desires of certain powerful donors. When one donor, casino tycoon Sheldon Adelson, can influence the course of America's and Israel's foreign policy on a matter as important as Middle East peace and the nuclear agreement with Iran, we know we have a systemic breakdown, irrespective of one's views on the substance of the matter.[78]

What would an "innovative, adaptive, and responsive" economy look like? First, it would require a fresh perspective to consider what antitrust laws would imply. While monopoly power certainly runs against systemic health, our metrics would need to expand beyond competitive market impacts to include a broad understanding of measures of systemic health, as we will discuss. If we first see and then understand the design principles of a regenerative forest, we could certainly design supportive policies for a regenerative economy. The implications will be far reaching.

Huge command-and-control global business enterprises that pursue efficiency through economies of scale at all costs are transformed or replaced by more innovative, agile networks of interconnected business webs, creating value through enhanced relationship-centric exchange, adapting and responding to the needs of the whole system, not just single-firm shareholder interests in the short run. Easier said than done; just ask my publisher and the entire book industry that has been "Amazoned," or the music industry. Second, our innovation would be driven by what's essential to the health of the whole, not our misguided endless desires for convenience and material wants when they conflict with the health of the whole.

The rigid hierarchal systems that undergird today's centralized, bureaucratic states in which participants feel little agency are replaced by decentralized, innovative government centers at the regional, state, and local levels with decision-making retained as close to the communities they affect as possible, while only those decisions that cannot be managed regionally or locally (the management of certain security threats and climate change, for example) are referred up to more central authorities.

Entrepreneurial and low material throughput creative sectors of the economy flourish and grow, both for-profit and not-for-profit.

Public policy works to ensure they remain aligned with the core purpose of promoting and sustaining human prosperity in an economy of permanence.

Ensures Empowered Participation

Merriam-Webster's Dictionary defines "participation" as "the state of being related to a larger whole." The American College Dictionary defines it as both "taking part in an action" and "sharing in the benefits." Finally, theoretical ecologist Robert Ulanowicz notes that, in an interdependent system, fitness comes from contributing in some way to the health of the whole, or as he puts it, from "the ability to play a constructive role in the web of processes." For example, if the lungs do not take in enough oxygen and the circulatory system is weak, the muscles in the legs won't function well, the person becomes sedentary, and the whole body (and mind and spirit) degenerates.

If we put participation together with empowerment in the context of the human economy, we find that the quality of "empowered participation"[79] means that all parts must be "in relationship" with the larger whole in ways that not only empower them to negotiate to meet their own needs but also enable them to add their own unique contribution toward the health and well-being of the nested, larger wholes in which they are embedded. In other words, everyone matters, and the health of any human economy is systemically dependent upon everyone's unique contribution to the health of the whole.

This quality of empowered participation validates our deep moral yearning for an economic system that enables a life of dignity for all, and a chance to participate in the system in order to prosper and realize one's potential. In other words, *inclusivity is implicit in regeneration*, but not based on moral choice alone. It's implicit simply based on the science. It also explains why, as Martin Luther King Jr. put it, "the arc of the moral universe is long, but it tends towards justice." That arc explains the long push from early Greek democracy and the invention of laws that apply to all men, to America's Bill of Rights, to the civil rights movement of the 1960s, and to the Arab Spring of 2011. Honoring the essence of individuals can be seen in all the great human rights reform movements: civil rights, women's rights, LGTBQ rights, and human rights. Unleashing the unique potentials of the millions of individuals in these disempowered groups would unleash a tidal wave of vitality undreamt of in current economic theories.

For starters, a genuine democracy is fundamental to the principle of empowered participation, a self-evident truth. Removal of money from politics—using publicly funded elections, limits on contributions, and a diverse free press—allows for the election of government officials concerned primarily with the needs and well-being of the whole society, not just the interests of powerful donors, be they corporations or individuals. In the United States, the overturn of *Citizens United* coupled with public election funding is therefore fundamental to the realization of a regenerative economy.

As with all of the principles, empowered participation applies at all scales, from individuals, communities, and regions to nation-states and global-level entities. Achieving empowered participation that is integrated across levels ultimately depends upon a broadly accepted culture that values empowered participation at all levels.

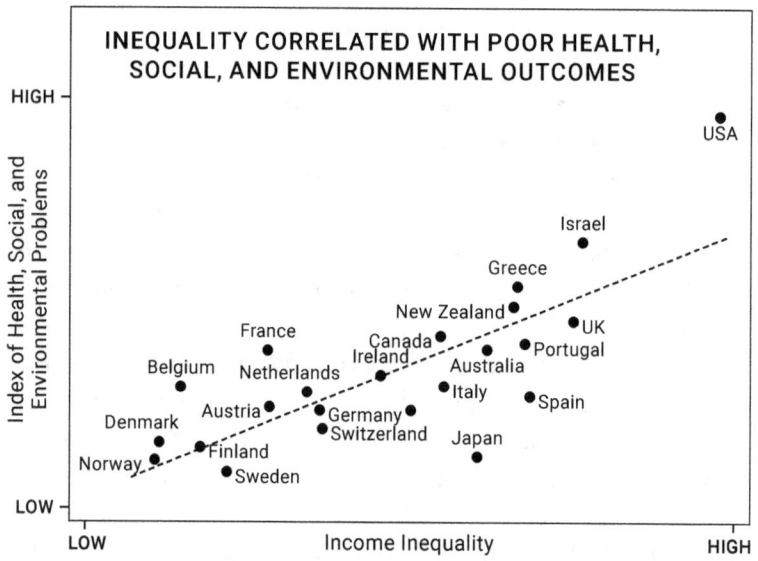

■ **Figure 3.4 Aggregate Index of Health, Social, and Environmental Problems.** *Credit: Pickett, K., Gauhar, A., Wilkinson, R. and Sahni-Nicholas, P. (2024). The Spirit Level at 15. London: The Equality Trust. DOI: https://doi.org/10.15124/yao-de9s-7k93.*

Critically, it also demands enlightened servant leadership and the wise exercise of power with an eye toward the health of the whole.

Research by Kate Pickett and Richard Wilkinson shows that extreme inequality, which snuffs out "empowered participation," harms overall systemic health, not just the health of the disadvantaged.[80] As you can see in figure 3.4, developed countries (inclusive of the well-off within them) with high degrees of inequality, like the United States and the United Kingdom, perform worse on a long list of health and social problems than more equal societies such as Norway, Sweden, and Japan.

Consequently, what is an ethical position to most of us is also a systemic requirement of a healthy economy, not a nice thing to have when we can or choose to afford it. By acknowledging the critical role that empowered participation plays in systemic health, we then recognize universal rights to fundamental needs of quality health care, quality public education, and access to clean water and affordable housing. Again, this is not only for ethical reasons, but because such empowered participation enables individuals to contribute their unique talents, which are essential for the collective benefit of the economic system as a whole, even if we have no idea what those unique contributions will be in advance. Similarly, public investment in public goods—core infrastructure, healthy ecosystems, open access to information, and more broadly the prioritization of a healthy commons in all its forms—must also be enhanced for economies to thrive.

At the same time, this finding redefines the debate on inequality more generally. Regardless of what one thinks about exorbitant compensation and extreme inequality as an ethical matter, the study of interdependent systems tells us that extremes of wealth and power are harmful to systemic health because they undermine the empowered participation of all the other members of a democratic society. For example, powerful corporations and the ultra-wealthy create PACs to influence politics in the U.S. in ways that serve their own self-interest while often subverting the will and well-being of the public at large, as well as the health of the larger social and economic systems of which they, too, are a part. This means that the extreme levels of CEO compensation common in the United States not only waste company resources and raise very real moral questions. They also can be directly linked scientifically to the destruction of systemic economic and social health while risking political upheaval. This obviously harms the powerless. The key insight here is that it also harms the powerful and their families. It's all connected.

Still, while building such broad-based power and wealth-sharing into the design of the system will be challenging in a market system dominated by high levels of concentrated private ownership of capital, a great deal of evidence suggests that new approaches to ownership and participation are already at hand. These range from the best-in-class, widely distributed stock options and profit sharing in many Silicon Valley enterprises and thoughtfully conceived employee stock ownership plans (ESOPs) in large mature companies, to the age-old and popular private partnerships in legal and other professions and the enormous resiliency of worker-owned cooperatives in Spain, Italy, and elsewhere in the world.[81] Goldman Sachs was a much better private partnership, with greed restrained by self-interest, than it is a public corporation—exploiting taxpayer "too big to fail" subsidies for private gain while pursuing many activities that serve no social purpose, and much worse.[82]

Of course, power sharing must be done skillfully, with the goal of seeking a balance that is healthy for the whole in the relevant context. Since labor unions grew out of a system in which individuals were not empowered to negotiate their needs sufficiently, many labor leaders of the past have taken an overly antagonistic stance. While understandable, such actions have sown the seeds of destruction as well, as evidenced in the U.S. auto industry in the 1980s and in public education to this day. A new generation of labor leaders in the United States with a more constructive eye to the health of the whole is pointing the way for a more constructive labor movement, one aligned with the principles of regenerative vitality.

Let's have look as what empowered participation looks like in practice, and let's be blunt. America's self-serving elites—from Big Business to Washington, from Wall Street to Silicon Valley, from entrenched special interests in all their forms to corporate boardrooms, big labor, and increasingly the media—institutions far and wide have lost legitimacy in the public eye. An integrated stream of empowerment that runs from bottom to top means the jig is up for self-important elites who conflate the manipulation of the system for their own personal power and fortunes with meritocratic success.

Empowered participation requires that human beings are treated not merely as substitutable units of labor—mere "particles" in the algorithms of economics—but are valued for the unique contributions that their creative essence and entrepreneurial energies can and must make to the enterprise and to the society at large. After all, it's a human economy we care about! Continuous investment in human capital to ignite this creative human potential and catalyze collaborative, lifelong learning in our rapidly changing society is essential for systemic health and commonsense priority.

The institution of education in the West must reinvent itself to break free of the limitations of a reductionist worldview that we now know does not reflect reality. Instead, a plurality of education systems and designs, drawing on our latest scientific understanding of how life works, as well as our ancient ways of knowing, develop empowered and critically thinking individuals. Success will ensure that everyone is invited to bring forth their unique potential in a synergistic weave with other members of society rather than be treated as a cog in an industrial machine.

The nature of ownership of the firm and critical economic infrastructure evolves to enable economic empowerment and less concentration of wealth and power. Expanded experimentation with direct pension fund business ownership in negotiated partnerships,[83] cooperative forms of ownership, purpose trusts, private partnerships, and broadly distributed equity ownership of business enterprise is the norm.

Corporate governance evolves to embrace the empowered participation of all stakeholders. The German requirement for labor representation on boards of directors is a successful demonstration of this principle already in action. Similarly, we are beginning to see the rights of nature reflected in corporate governance. Ultimately governance must facilitate wiser decision-making that addresses the health of the whole as the single unity that it is.

Ecological challenges are addressed not only through large-scale investment and rollout of emergent technologies but through holistic solutions that enable broad, active participation and consensus building in the evolution of the human project. The economic architecture economy not only ensures secure access for all to food, clean water, shelter, clean energy, and education, the essentials that provide a life of dignity. It also provides opportunities for all individuals to manifest their potential and, in the process, co-create the economy and society through their collaborative participation.

Honors Community and Place

"There are no unsacred places," Wendell Berry implores. "There are only sacred places and desecrated places." Hard to say it better than that. In the context of a human economy, we must begin by understanding the truth that human culture is an expression of the place where it manifests. Different in the arctic than in a rainforest. So, too, for place-sourced local and bioregional economies, the cellular scale foundation of the global economy. The growing interest in bioregionalism should be seen as the regenerative economy emergent in response to the pressures caused by our unhealthy system. But of course, this is but one of eight principles, not a silver bullet. Living systems demonstrate all at the same time.

No two places or things in our world are ever the same—even identical twins have differences. This diversity creates the richness that is essential to system vitality. It fills niches, provides choices, adds opportunities, discovers new ways, and increases excellence through constructive competition. Furthermore, just as each ecosystem comes to embody unique adaptations to a particular place, so each human community embodies a mosaic of traditions, beliefs, and potentialities, each uniquely shaped by long-term pressures of geography, history, culture, environment, and changing human needs.

Honoring the uniqueness of people and place, a regenerative economy builds resilient individuals, communities, and entire bioregions by developing their distinctive potentialities informed by the essence of their individual story and being. Modern capitalism's rush to a monoculture of chain stores driven by "efficient, scalable" business models has desecrated place in ways that have increasingly well-understood social consequences.[84] While we discount these issues as the price for progress, it does not need to be this way. In fact, the tide is already shifting back into alignment with the principle that "honoring community and place" is integral to system health.

Honoring communities of place can be seen in the relocalization movement that began with local food and community-supported agriculture—now also extending to a global, connected mosaic of place-centered economies. The growing efforts to "relocalize" are also reflected in the "slow movement" and its various branches that advocate for a cultural shift toward slowing down life's pace and reconnecting with place—Slow Food, Slow Money. It's reflected in the surging interest in the Business Alliance for Local Living Economies (BALLE),[85] farmers markets and farm-to-table restaurants, the Transition Town movement,[86] and local community capital initiatives led by pioneers like Michael Shuman, seeking to redirect community savings back into community investment,[87] as well as the plethora of local and complementary currency initiatives.

The burgeoning craft brewery movement, for example, and other local initiatives demonstrate our desire to reconnect our businesses—and our consumer and investing dollars—with community and place. Although they are no substitute for direct interpersonal connection in the context of a culture rooted in distinct geographic place, healthy digital networks and virtual communities of practice on the web also support many critical functions of physically rooted places.

Unfortunately, instead of a free enterprise system that works to develop human potential, today's global corporate capitalism too often seeks to maintain its exploitative advantage by blocking the rights and stifling the potentialities and well-being of citizens, employees, and often even its customers worldwide. Corporations that do not honor the unique richness of place-based communities and human potential run roughshod over anything that stands in the way of profit. The drive for scale demands commodification, from Starbucks and McDonalds to Amazon and Walmart. Our places and unique cultures become "desecrated." We lose some of our humanity in the process, creating conditions for degeneration rather than regeneration.

Similarly, instead of a deeply felt connection to place, we now have "placeless" global corporations that move their headquarters and factories around the globe in response to tax, labor, and environmental standards, all in the name of optimizing "shareholder value" as still taught in finance by most of our leading business schools. The consequences of corporations that disregard people and place are often catastrophic to the communities in which such placeless corporations operate. To comprehend the horrors of business enterprise disconnected from place, one need only consider the numerous industrial tragedies in far-flung locations, ranging from factory collapses in Bangladesh, and stressed workers jumping out of buildings in China, to rivers fouled with oil in Latin America.

Global expansion is often driven by an empire-building mentality that tends to exacerbate disconnection from place by justifying exploitation of subject regions. Such conveniently rationalized callousness explains the strong backlash seen in the 1999 Seattle World Trade Organization protests against globalization and so-called free trade agreements, as well as Joseph Stiglitz's recent article, "On the Wrong Side of Globalization."[88]

Indeed, the challenges of managing a healthy, global business network while disregarding people and place have tripped up many who have tried. Just ask Walmart about Mexico or India, or Apple, Google, or JPMorgan about China. Many are forced into a retreat to their core home locale after embarrassing and expensive blunders, but some will succeed. If global civilization is to prosper, the responsibility of the successful global corporate leaders to the health of the whole will be critical.

When a business successfully extends beyond its place of origin, more often than not it continues to be what Regenesis Group calls "place-sourced." It is defined by—and retains its connection to—the unique qualities and culture of its home place. For example, a Dutch multinational will tend to remain distinct and true to its "essence" in a way that will be quite distinct from that of a Brazilian company, creating healthy diversity in the process. But only if it honors community and place and finds a niche within which to "fit best."

In flow network terms, expanding from local to regional and ultimately to global contexts will require great attention to and advances in structural intricacy to support higher levels of connection. Matrix management seeking to harmonize global product strategies with regional geographic strategies are evidence of this higher level of structural intricacy. I can share from lived experience; this is hard to get right. We are still growing into our globalization and learning its nuances and limitations. The imperative must be for global business to honor place, just as an aerospace engineer had better respect the law of gravity. This demands collaboration with place-based organizations as a precondition to global success even at the expense of short-term efficiency.

Aligning today's globalization with the notion that regenerative systems must honor the richness and diversity of place poses a profound challenge. Today's local versus global, either-or thinking will not lead to effective solutions because systemic health requires integration across scales. Instead, if global enterprises want to be successful over the long run, they will need to develop more intricate connective tissue to unify their increased complexity, building resiliency in the process. But such resiliency comes at a cost of efficiency, as we will see below. As global enterprises learn how to increase collaboration and to honor place, they must also be more intentional about the very real but circumscribed benefits of their global reach. Globalization is not, as current thinking would lead one to believe, inevitable for all; a healthy human economy can and must be built on the foundation of healthy local, regional, and multi-nodal economies that honor their people and places.

Let's see where we need to go to truly align with this principle. First, public policy must encourage and fortify a diversity of unique, collaborative, place-based economies at multiple scales from community, to city, to bioregional. Each is a core node in a global interconnected economy that engages freely and equitably in trade from a position of place-based resilience and strength, not desperation. This represents a new development paradigm, in stark contrast with the debt-based export paradigm of the World Bank and IMF, inspired by and staffed with neoclassical economists. It will require a new layer of financial intermediaries dedicated to flowing financial and non-financial resources to support such a bottoms-up development paradigm that today's private sector doesn't naturally address. Samantha Power and Tyler Wakefield's Bioregional Financing Facility project is just such a new layer of financial intermediary that is exactly the kind of responsive innovation we need.[89]

Anchor institutions rooted in the community, such as hospitals and universities and even sports teams when committed to place such as the Green Bay Packers, work with local government and other community-based institutions to provide an economic foundation for place-focused economic initiatives aimed at improving the resilience, prosperity, and sustainability of their communities.

Cooperative ownership models of place-centric economic networks thrive, building on the example of the Mondragón cooperatives in the Basque region of Spain, with €11 billion of turnover across eighty-one cooperatives and one hundred subsidiaries employing sixty-eight thousand people, all owners empowered to participate in the strategy and key decisions of their businesses,[90] and the even larger network of employee-owned enterprises in the Emilia-Romagna region of northern Italy. In the U.S., the Evergreen Cooperatives[91] and the Oberlin Project[92] in Cleveland, Ohio, are promising new experiments being replicated in many regions.

Monoculture chain stores that maximize "efficiency" are replaced by clusters of local and regional unique and more complex businesses that arise out of and honor the uniqueness of culture and place, beginning with restaurant businesses and more generally growing out of local business support networks like the Business Alliance for Local Living Economies and the amazing work of Rising Tide Capital led by Alfa Demmellash.

Prosperous global corporations remain place-sourced in their culture and become genuinely connected to more distant communities as supportive partners, not extractive predators. More global corporations follow the business strategies of enlightened companies like DNV GL, the global-shipping-certification leader that has opened over thirty offices in China in order to operate close to its customers and to understand the local community context of its business. While DNV GL has offices that connect it to "place" all over the world, at its core it remains a Norwegian company with a Norwegian business culture ("place-sourced") no matter where in the world it is operating. Where some global banks, for instance, seek to win business by systematically hiring their clients' children, or apply even more blatant forms of corruption with local officials, DNV GL constantly talks internally about ethics and insists on doing business the way it's done in Norway, even if it means slower expansion in China or elsewhere. The company has been around for 150 years.[93]

Discovers Edge Effect Abundance

Brain research and sociology both indicate that the cross-fertilization that comes from stepping outside one's usual silos leads to tremendous bursts of creativity, synergy, and satisfaction. "Edges are about increased potential of relationship and exchange," says Bill Reed. "They are the bridge and arbiter of relationships—the more edges we have, the richer the potential to improve the resilience of life." Consequently, a regenerative economy works hard to find ways to cultivate common cause synergy and cross-fertilization at the "edges." Notice how nicely the principles work together and complement each other, in this case, edges with right relationship.

Honoring the uniqueness of people and place is essential because diversity is critical. Yet, because collaboration is also essential, all those unique people and places must find ways to work synergistically. Unfortunately, genuine collaboration is often rare today because our society is deeply fractured into competing interest groups and siloed specialists whose livelihoods often depend upon staying in sync with dominant beliefs. Step out of line in corporate-owned media, funder-conscious academia, or profit-maximizing medicine, for instance, and you will find yourself on the street. The myth of separation at the heart of so much divisiveness, whether it's racial, religious, or class-based, not only causes tremendous social strife but violates the first principles of regenerative vitality. Of course the health of our societies suffers.

How do we change this? Ecologists suggest that creative synergy emerges best at the "edges" of systems, where the bonds holding the dominant pattern in place are weakest, and the opportunities for diversity and novelty are the greatest. With this diversity comes life's abundance, but also risk. For example, the edges where rivers meet the ocean breed rich salt-marsh estuaries teeming with a diversity of life. On land, prior to the industrialization of agriculture, farmers who understood the fertility that occurs at the edges planted hedgerows to create artificial "edges" where pollinators would dwell and where the soil would be buffered from the wind.

In human networks, creativity and abundance often emerge in cosmopolitan cities like New York York, London, or Mumbai, where diverse ideas intersect and opportunities to pursue novelty outside mainstream pressures are more open. Similarly, the regenerative projects we have studied all exhibit deepening relationships and hard work around the "edges" between different sectors of the economy—private, public, NGO, and philanthropic—and between different socioeconomic groups that do not always coexist comfortably or have opportunities to connect with one another around a common purpose.

Finding common cause is also a way to nurture unlikely collaborations. Nowadays, for instance, social conservatives and liberals are increasingly finding common cause over caring for the environment. Joel Hunter, the leader of a conservative Christian Evangelical church and a member of the board of directors of the regenerative First Green Bank, expresses the connection this way:

> I didn't agree to being on the Board of First Green Bank because of my banking expertise, I did it because I have been a long-time advocate nationally and internationally for what Christians call "creation care." For a Christian, the scripture is really clear on this. It was the first order in the Garden of Eden, Genesis 2:15: "And the Lord God took the man, and put him into the Garden of Eden to cultivate it and to keep it." That order was never rescinded, it never expired. That wonderful gift we were given should continue to be a resource for everyone, especially the poor. So advocacy for the sustainability of this planet is really advocacy for the poor and the vulnerable. Our goal is to add to the earth's capability of production and cultivation. That coincides with the regenerative goal you are talking about.
>
> (Excerpted from Capital Institute's soon-to-be-released "Year in the Life of a Regenerative Bank" *Field Guide* project.)

Yet, nowadays, the environment is not the only source of common cause. The Chicago-based group Manufacturing Renaissance, also a *Field Guide* subject, is forging common-cause collaboration among government, the private sector, organized labor, educators, and civil society in hopes of countering the relentless stream of plant closings and off-shored jobs by creating programs to support their regional advanced manufacturing sectors.

The benefits of interactions taking place at intersections and around common cause are often both profound and subtle. Regardless of the degree of success of a particular project, we have consistently found that working collaboratively across edges—with ongoing learning and development sourced from the diversity that exists there—is transformative for both the communities where the exchanges are happening and for the individuals involved. This vast, untapped creativity to be found "working the edges" of unique places, rooted in deeply "empowered participation," has tremendous potential for individual and group regeneration, giving rise to numerous personal "aha" moments and subtle shifts, some very small and some large and profound.

Consider what an economy that cultivates "edge effect abundance" would imply. First, place-based initiatives built around locally rooted anchor institutions work to create new abundance at the intersections of various stakeholder groups ranging from local businesses and unemployed youth to state and local governments, community groups, and faith-based organizations.

Second, large companies with a wide range of core competencies—operational, technological, marketing, financing, and more—become "networked platform companies" that create abundance (including value for themselves) by providing services that minimize costs and facilitate interactions between intersecting groups. Platform companies are now commonplace within the technology sector. However, too often they operate purely to extract the network benefits purely for themselves, rather than for the health of the whole. You only need to look at what Spotify has done to extract value from millions of creative artists to see how *not* to do this. Such platform companies host vibrant economic exchanges and could find numerous new ways to leverage their assets in mutually beneficial innovation and infrastructure on the edges between private-sector industries, between the public and private sectors, and between those and NGOs.

As a positive example of what's possible for large asset-rich companies, consider Peter Bakker's leadership at TNT, the €6 billion Dutch postal company, prior to him becoming president of the World Business Council for Sustainable Development.[94] Bakker used his experience in Africa to form a partnership between TNT and the World Food Program. TNT leveraged its logistics assets to great effect in the challenge of emergency food relief. The impact on TNT employees was transformative, giving new purpose to many, improving employee retention, and saving TNT money in the process. Previously unseen potential was released by working the edge between daily postal service in Holland and famine relief in Africa.

Government entities would work proactively across the edges, leveraging the strengths of the private sector, for example, in areas of technology research that gave rise to the internet and to many other innovations. Government entities also work collaboratively with the NGO sector where social entrepreneurs with close community relationships are finding innovative solutions to seemingly intractable social challenges that have stymied the public sector.

Instead of working to weaken policies designed to protect social and ecological systems, competitive businesses use their power to catalyze collaboration within industry sectors and with the public sector to advance policies and practices that sustain the social systems and ecosystems in which they all operate. This is done out of informed self-interest, not merely for the public relations benefits Healthy "coopetition" displaces extractive competition.

Environmentalists and social justice advocates work together rather than at odds on strategies that restore both ecological and social health, both essential to true human prosperity and interdependence.

Ensures Robust Circulatory Flow

Just as human health depends on the robust circulation of oxygen, nutrients, and so forth, so too economic health depends on robust circulatory flows of money, information, material and energy resources, and goods and services to support exchange, to flush toxins, and to nourish every participant at every level of our human networks. The circulation of money and information is particularly critical to individuals, businesses, and economies in reaching their regenerative potential.

The central role that circulation plays in new economy thinking can be seen in work ranging from Bill McDonough's *Cradle to Cra-*

dle,[95] to Hawken, Lovins, and Lovins's *Natural Capitalism*.[96] Following the living systems model, which uses the waste of one process as the fuel for another, these circulation-centered business models seek to transform businesses from sellers of products or assets to providers-of-services, turning the waste of one process into the resources for another (a closed loop circle). Waste equals food.

Drawing on the economic work of Kenneth Boulding,[97] and that of Walter Stahel and Geneviève Reday on closed loop systems,[98] those seeking to build a "circular economy" are generating interest by showing how shifting from a linear "take-make-waste" system of material flow to a circular "reclaim, recycle, remanufacture, regenerate" design can help boost business vitality, community health, and profits all at the same time. A recent report by the Ellen MacArthur Foundation produced by McKinsey & Company makes the business case that transitioning to a circular economy translates into a trillion-dollar business opportunity in terms of cost savings that can drop to the bottom line.[99] The foundation is now helping leading companies from Ikea to Cisco see if they can seize this opportunity. Time will tell. But if whatever financial savings materialize are merely reinvested in more growth, nothing much will be accomplished, a stark reminder that in the regenerative paradigm, all first principles must be honored. They don't work in isolation.

The role that robust circulation and exchange play in enabling regenerative vitality is also obvious in the growth of today's information economy. Ignoring for the moment its invasive, exploitative, and destructive ad-based business model, one need only consider the incredible economic potential that Google's search-engine sitting atop a highly connected internet unleashed for connecting ideas and people and empowering intelligent decision-making while stimulating economies. Intriguingly, from a systems view, this vastly expanded potential for information exchange and social networking is but the latest expression of a much older, extremely important pattern of development in all regenerative flow networks. It's hard to think of a technological advance that is inherently more regenerative than the internet. It's up to us how we use the tool.

The robust circulation of money, the economy's bloodstream, is particularly critical to its regenerative health. "The rate of circulation of money at local and regional levels may be the most critical measure of economic health," notes Capital Institute science adviser Dr. Sally Goerner. Like a body with poor circulation to its limbs, an economy cannot be healthy if money from profits and savings are systematically sucked from the periphery into the center, or trapped upstream behind a dam. Unfortunately, too often this is precisely what neoliberalism's hyperefficient, globalized, financialized, and centralized version of capitalism does. Its relentless pursuit of "economies of scale" constantly drains money, people, and resources from local communities and the real economy in the periphery while shifting the burden of the real costs it creates to other parts of the system. Walmart workers on publicly funded food stamps are but one familiar example. Recent work by the Belgian financier Bernard Lietaer suggests that a proper restructuring of our banking system to increase cross-scale circulation of credit would go a long way toward creating both a more sustainable financial system and widespread, long-term prosperity.[100]

In this way, the constant concentration of money and thus power within the global banking system and within large retail chains like Walmart and Amazon, who use their power to extract positive net working capital from their weaker suppliers, serves to reduce the effective circulation of money to the middle and lower levels of the economy. Community banks, community cooperatives, loan funds like the one managed by RSF Social Finance,[101] complementary currencies, and buy local movements are all expressions of an intuitive drive to increase the circulation of money and credit at the local and regional levels by reasserting relationship (principle one: "in right relationship") at the heart of transactions.

One particularly critical form of circulation—reinvestment in the system itself—is often overlooked in economic discussions. As we have seen, the single most fundamental factor of systemic health comes from being "self-feeding," that is, from continually channeling money and resources back into building and maintaining systems and processes the organization needs to survive. This thought applies to individuals, businesses, communities, and economies at all levels, both in the real world and in the digital world.

This, of course, is not controversial. Any wise businessperson understands the importance of investing in R&D, as well as the professional development of a firm's people. Unfortunately, in their rush to maximize short-term profits, Wall Street in general—and "financial engineers" specializing in leveraged buyouts in particular—often sacrifice this vital component of long-term health by cutting R&D and eliminating professional development to boost short-term profits in order to maximize the value of an "exit" for themselves and a small group of private investors. All too often, after the financial extractors have taken their money and are gone, the consequences for the business are disastrous. Norwegian DNV GL, on the other hand, reinvests a remarkable 5 percent of sales in long-term research not directly connected to specific product development. Again, this is the same DNV GL that has been in business for 150 years.

An economy that promotes "robust circulatory flow" analogous to the miraculous and highly efficient metabolism of a healthy living organism is beyond anything we see today in the circular economy movement. It would demand an unprecedented redesign of business models. Most critically, it demands reimagining entire business ecosystems since no individual company can do this on its own. The goal is to ensure enterprises cease from selling products that create waste (cars, heating oil emissions) and transform to companies that provide services in closed loop models (transportation, warmth).[102] The linear flow, extractive industrial economy will need to be profoundly remade in the coming decades, creating ecological and financial efficiencies that do not merely trigger a "rebound" in demand and thus more growth that cancels the benefits. We need efficiency harnessed for systemic wealth holistically understood as we have seen, not ever-increasing financial wealth alone.

As the retreat from "peak globalization" accelerates,[103] the most centralized global businesses increasingly decentralize as they strive to reduce material and energy throughput, while more place-based and bioregion-centered business ecosystems rooted in culture and committed to local and regional sourcing have gained competitive advantage and even begin to trade with one another.

We will need to see the financial services industry first restore trust, no easy feat. Then the robust circulation of credit is job one for finance, as credit is the life blood of economic metabolism. Financial wealth will need to be less concentrated in the speculative centers of Wall Street and London and become more broadly distributed directly into productive enterprises in the real economy across local, bioregional, and global scales. Economies exhibit a more diverse and more decentralized array of financial services firms, and even currency systems, improving money circulation in the process. Success will demand sharply curtailing the extractive, speculative excesses that increasingly define finance.

Enterprises that accelerate the exchange of high-quality vital and sought-after information, and those that turn information into useful knowledge, will thrive—but only if their services and business models are aligned with all principles of a regenerative vitality. The next generation of Googles, Facebooks, and Amazons will circulate personal data only in the context of a "right relationship" between the individual owners of that data and those who want to purchase access to it. Perhaps extractive data practices feeding the digital advertising machine are diminished by eighty percent in the process. You read that right. In fact, we should ask why we subsidize advertising at all with a tax deduction if we need to discourage excess consumption in the developed economies.

We will see enterprises in the private, public, and NGO sectors make dramatic increases in investments in their employees' continuous learning and development and in long-term research as top priorities, not luxuries when times are good. A living economy is a learning economy, developing, circulating information and knowledge not to be extracted for profit, but to best participate in and contribute to the essential evolutionary process of life.

We will see new metrics for economic vitality developed to monitor the healthy circulation of materials, information, and all forms of money. These new systems of measurement help redefine economic goals for policymakers, replacing misleading monetary aggregates such as GDP and complementing sensible outcomes metrics aligned with long-run societal well-being.

Seeks Dynamic Balance

Where a host of Eastern practices from yoga to Buddhism taught us to value balance, the hard science of holism now confirms for us that balance is more than just a nice way to be; it is essential to systemic health of an economy, just like for our body. Like a unicycle rider, regenerative systems are always engaged in a delicate and dynamic dance. Achieving balance requires that they harmonize multiple variables instead of optimizing single ones.

Conventional economics and finance are designed to optimize "efficient returns to financial capital" as the objective. Because it is reductionist, this practice makes sense only when one is focused on parts (in this case, financial capital), but it fails when one considers the health of the whole that is by definition only as strong as the weakest link. Just as an athlete who works out hard in the gym but eats an unhealthy diet will eventually fail, so must return on invested capital, while important, be kept in balance with the multiple kinds of capital that all play a role in the long-term systemic health of the firm, society, and the planet.

Not only must multiple forms of capital be in balance (our "holistic wealth" principle above), but multiple critical variables must be

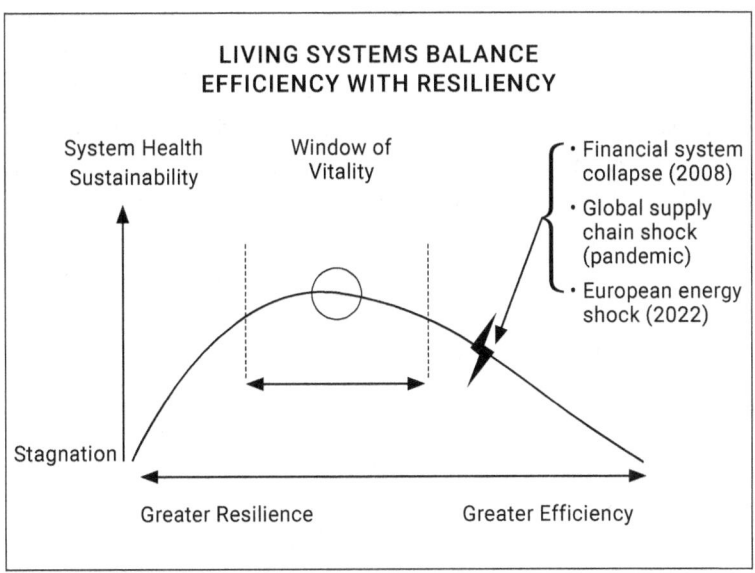

Figure 3.5 **Window of Vitality.** Credit: Robert E. Ulanowicz, "The Dual Nature of Ecosystem Dynamics" Elsevier, May 2009. https://people.clas.ufl.edu/ulan/files/Dual.pdf.

as well. Theoretical ecologist Robert Ulanowicz and his colleagues used the balance of small, medium, and large organisms found in nature to identify the optimal balance of system resilience and system efficiency. In the process, Ulanowicz showed empirically why an emphasis on increasing scale and efficiency is useful up to a point, beyond which it is destructive to the system as a whole. Ulanowicz's work even provides a way of measuring this balance point within a dynamic "window of vitality."

One final but critical point about this window of vitality. The optimal balance point moves depending on the surrounding context. Just like a sailor changes the sails depending on wind conditions, as environmental chaos accelerates with increasing climate change impacts and associated chaos in the years and decades to come, the center of this "window of vitality" will move more toward resiliency. Yet our economic system has been wired for efficiency by the errors of neoclassical economics.

While such balances that define healthy systems in the natural world are often easy to observe, today's dominant economic belief system's obsession with efficiency does not give up easily. In finance, for example, the collapse of 2008 was the direct result of decades of globalization and deregulation combined with the innovations of derivatives and securitization, all done in the name of efficiency, but with the unintended consequence of destroying system resilience, leaving dangerous fragility. Indeed, since the global economy lacked sufficient resilience,[104] it would have collapsed were it not for unprecedented interventions by central banks to shore up the seemingly "efficient" but deeply reckless and fragile financial system. Nevertheless, we now face even bigger "too big to fail banks" in the pursuit of extreme-scale efficiency, supported by the artificial resilience of unprecedented central bank support around the world and a massive investment of public effort to control these behemoths through regulation—a losing proposition in my judgment. Meanwhile, their leaders claim that "scale has always defined the winner in banking,"[105] as if banking, the systemically vital circulatory system of the global economy, could be reduced to a boxing match. Nor does their claim happen to be true, as demonstrated by research on values-based banking showing that medium and small-sized sustainable banks outperform the mega banks on a sustained basis.[106] There is one caveat. Such values-based banks are not paying their bankers multimillion-dollar bonuses. Doing so demands systemic extraction.

Again, the bard finds the words better than me. "We identify arrogant ignorance by the willingness to work on too big a scale and thus put too much at risk," Wendell Berry reminds the bankers, "because the arrogantly ignorant are often blinded by money invested; they cannot afford to see bad consequences."

Our banking system needs a balance of small, medium, and large, with an awareness that "too big" is particularly dangerous, and an understanding that the biggest in particular must act in a way that supports the health of the whole. Is that behavior possible as a publicly traded private company? Unclear to me, to say the least. The same applies to all other critical circulatory systems of the economy including energy, fresh water and wastewater, and telecommunications, all of which have evolved toward ever greater centralization and scale driven by a flawed ideology that promotes economic efficiency at the expense of system resiliency. As a result, all economic sectors will need to shift to more decentralized models to restore the critical balance that defines healthy systems.

In sectors of the economy where there are natural benefits to society to have common platforms, such as in technology infrastructure (from social networks to the global communications network, to stock exchanges and money systems), regulatory regimes need to evolve with fresh understanding of systems dynamics. Anticompetitive threats must be managed. But so too must we take necessary steps to ensure that system resiliency is maintained, even when it comes at the expense of some (misguided) system efficiency. Look to the oak tree in a forest as the model. It is not a parasite.

Modern capitalism's relentless drive for global efficiencies and economies of scale, combined with deficient shareholder-governance, and the short-term bias of capital markets and finance in general, has many rightly concerned about the excessive power and influence of today's largest global enterprises. We yearn for more human-scale enterprises, and we heartily endorse E. F. Schumacher's maxim that "small is beautiful." Yet few remember that Schumacher also once said that, if everyone were for small, he would be for big! The study of fractals affirms Schumacher's intuitive affinity for both small and big by showing empirically that both are important. It's the balance and integration of the two that is essential.

Of course, dynamic balance applies more broadly as well. Let's consider just a few key issues for our consideration in the context of regenerative systems, beginning with the elephant in the room, wealth and power. The Great Depression, as well as the collapse of every great civilization over the last five thousand years, proves that extreme inequality and excessive concentration of power leading to oligarchy inevitably causes the system to collapse—with disastrous consequences for all.

If our aim is to avoid economic and social collapse, then just as a series of mini-quakes restores balance by releasing pressure building toward a catastrophic earthquake, so must we find ways to periodically release pressures building from today's extreme inequalities, before our next "big one" occurs. Progressive income taxation and, most crucially in my view, an inheritance tax of 100% above some threshold per beneficiary—for society to decide, but I'll put $25 million up for discussion—would serve this purpose. Of course, one can make the case for far less, but I'm trying to make it easier to accept. Similarly, the ancient Judeo-Christian tradition of debt jubilees served the purpose of resetting an equitable balance within society. But importantly, this is a scientific recommendation, based on our best understanding of how living organisms thrive. It's not simply an ideological preference open to debate.

A second issue concerns competitive individualism and collaborative community. The need for dynamic balance can also be seen in modern society's long-running battle between the rights of the individual and those of the community, as well as the opposing pressures to compete and to collaborate. A holistic approach teaches us that both competitive individualism and collaborative groups play important roles in systemic health. Competitive individuals advance learning by pushing envelopes, increasing quality, and challenging others to do the same. Yet even the most gifted and powerful individuals cannot compete with the power of collaborative groups, as smartly described by E. O. Wilson and David Sloan Wilson: "Selfish beats altruism within groups. Altruistic groups beat selfish groups. The rest is commentary."[107]

Furthermore, history shows that unchecked competitive power leads to monopoly and even oligarchy. The unrestrained extension of competition taken to its logical extreme is war. A society that intends to continue must balance power with restraint, yet restraint is not a quality found in the philosophy of "never enough" that drives modern capitalism.

Consequently, individual and community needs are not only inseparable, but their unique contributions are mutually beneficial. The challenge lies in finding ways to balance that delicate dance, the flexibility (freedom) upon which individualism thrives with the constraints (rules/procedures/regulations) required for community and collaboration.

A third issue concerns flexibility and constraint. The need to balance flexibility and constraint suggests that, while intelligent regulation is necessary for achieving systemic health, we will not be able to regulate our way to healthy financial or economic systems. Instead, regenerative systems are arranged to self-regulate by design rather than depend on ever greater externally imposed regulation (as demonstrated by our overall response to the recent financial crisis) with its inevitable unintended consequences to systemic health.

For example, the logical new liquidity constraints imposed on global banks to reduce the funding mismatches that led to the collapse of Lehman Brothers are having the unintended consequence of discouraging banks from using their balance sheets to finance long-term and illiquid renewable energy infrastructure projects when the health of the entire system depends upon it. On the other hand, the excess capital requirement for the largest, "systemically important" (meaning "too big to fail") banks such as JPMorgan is an example of a well-designed "self-regulating" incentive. Goldman Sachs's equity analysts and others have called for JPMorgan to break itself up, in part as a response to these new capital requirements. (In my opinion, those requirements should be much tougher, accelerating the systemically desirable shift.) From a systems science perspective, this is a policy-imposed self-regulating feedback loop, much more effective than a fresh army of regulators looking over JPMorgan traders' shoulders with a fresh set of rules to monitor.

In living systems, self-regulation comes from a complex and hard-won balance of positive and negative feedback systems evolved over long periods of time. In human networks, creating naturally self-regulating economies will require similarly hard-won cultural shifts along with legal and moral constraints that allow the messiness of learning to continue.

These nuances demonstrate the fact that systemic health is not a product of any single extreme, be it global versus local, big versus small, resilience versus efficiency, or any other quality. System health is complex, a product of intelligent design and structure. Dynamic balance plays a key role.

Again, let's imagine what an economy "seeking dynamic balance" will look like once it arrives. First, it will reject extremes and simple solutions. Instead, it will manage the endless, delicate dance of striving for balance in interdependent systems. Dancing with complexity is a core function of regenerative enterprises and economic networks, replacing the mechanistic approach of management by objective that we experience today in most organizations.

Instead of setting rules using traditional reductionist assumptions, policymakers and regulators will use a principles-based systemic architecture and associated objectives to design policies that encourage systemic balance. For example, governments seeking systemic health regularly intervene to reduce concentrations of economic and political power in the world's largest corporations, recognizing, as Milton Friedman's mentor H. C. Simons did, that capitalism naturally tends toward "economies of scale" and bigness in the name of efficiency, resulting in extremes in the distributions of wealth and political power. Teddy Roosevelt's passion for trust-busting suggests that he was an early intuitive systems thinker.

Policies will be crafted to foster a balanced and sustainable financial sector—with small community banks that take risks by creating and circulating credit locally, efficient regional banks, and global banks that are constrained in their scale and power to ensure that they serve the public good and not merely their own short-term self-interest. Entire new categories of financial and other resource intermediaries will be created to serve the needs of the commons, and ecological health across all scales from the hyper-local watersheds to the global atmosphere, the foundation of a regenerative economy.

Policymakers will restore a healthy market-system balance between systemic efficiency and systemic resilience by rebuilding resilience that has been destroyed and restraining the excessive power of economies of scale where necessary. Examples of financial policy initiatives that are aligned with the latter goal include excess capital buffers for "too big to fail" banks as discussed above, a financial transaction tax to create a feedback loop that discourages excessive speculation, and positive incentives that encourage long-term investment in the things we need, beginning with investments that will drive the transition of our energy system away from fossil fuels, and our destructive industrial agriculture system toward regeneration. We will see experiments with modification of central bank mandates to support such efforts, particularly the dominant central banks of the global economic order.

Given our historical bias toward efficiencies of scale, the pendulum swings back toward more diverse and distributed solutions, particularly with respect to critical infrastructures, energy, food, and water, following the model of distributed computing networks.

RETHINKING CAPITALISM

> Capitalism does millions of things better than the alternatives. ...However, it is totally ill-equipped to deal with a small handful of issues. Unfortunately, they are the issues that are absolutely central to our long-term well-being and even survival.
>
> —JEREMY GRANTHAM

Like all vibrant, long-lived systems, a regenerative economy must be designed to work as an integrated whole. It must not only value all of its parts, but it must also nourish, develop, and empower them. It must maintain balance, circulation, innovation, and learning because these, too, are essential to holistic health. It honors community and place and cultivates common cause synergy at the "edges," because only in bringing forth and connecting the unique colors of each element in synergy can full vibrancy be achieved.

Since systemic health occurs only when all parts are working "in right relationship" with one another, our ability to achieve a regenerative economy with lasting economic and social vitality will depend upon our ability to nourish and develop multiple kinds of capital, at all levels of today's global civilization, while learning to effectively balance and integrate the key principles of regenerative health.

We believe that developing a regenerative economy around these principles and investing in the creation of holistic wealth represent the next stage in the evolution of capitalism. However, to understand the change in store, let us first examine what *capitalism* means.

The conventional definition of capitalism is an economic and political system in which private property over public control is the norm, and the country's industry, finance, and trade are controlled primarily by private owners for profit, rather than by the state. Capitalism is also characterized as a competitive market economy using the price mechanism to clear markets, where the goal is to maximize profits and accumulate wealth. While such a system may at one time have been a glimmer in Ayn Rand's eye, it does not exist in what we call the modern capitalist economy today.[108] Instead, we have a highly complex, interconnected system, dominated by multinational corporations operating under the flawed and dangerous ideology of shareholder primacy that bears little resemblance to a theoretically pure "capitalist" system.[109] While the genuinely private control of small-scale means of production that Adam Smith originally imagined is still present, today's economies are dominated by enormous private enterprise, often driven by competitive short-term dynamics, and "owned" by mostly passive, short-term shareholders who exhibit only very limited control. Such massive global enterprises are a different beast altogether from what Adam Smith could imagine, just as a lake is different from a puddle.

Too often, large multinational corporations, trapped in the reductionist, finance-driven ideology of modern capitalism, demonstrate predatory behavior devoid of any understanding of the critical regenerative role they must play as part of a larger system. At the same time, they must compete fiercely to "win" in accordance with the norms of the system. Control is largely surrendered to powerful CEOs and their boards, and to their short-term shareholder value-maximization-above-all-else-at-any-cost paradigm grounded in a broken definition of "fiduciary duty." At the same time, real asset owners like pension funds and endowments too often cede their long-term stewardship duties to short-term speculators, paying little heed to their ownership responsibilities.

In short, there is no pure "capitalism" any more than there is pure, centrally planned "communism" or "socialism." The term *capitalism*, used more liberally and democratically, is still useful in referring to a market economy in which the private sector is the primary, but not the exclusive, owner of the means of production.[110] It is augmented by large and powerful state actors, and a diversity of alternative forms of enterprise, including cooperatives and nonprofit social enterprises. Typically, the most dynamism and employment growth exist in small and medium-sized enterprises even though they don't attract the attention of the giants. This more generalized vision of capitalism is subject to varying degrees of governance by the democratic process and managed for the common good.

If this more democratic vision of capitalism is to succeed, it must embrace a holistic worldview and learn to mirror the lessons of regenerative systems. The implications of a world where wealth is viewed holistically, empowered participation makes innovation common and adaptation easy, circulation is robust, community and place are honored and edge effect abundance at their intersections is facilitated, and polarities dance in dynamic balance and in right relationship with everything else are far-reaching and profound. Yet, in some ways, this vision also brings us back to our original free enterprise roots while clarifying where current capitalism went wrong.

This is not just theory, although a broadly shared conceptual framework such as the one we offer here is an essential start. Meanwhile, triggered in part by the financial crisis, but with roots going back much further, a growing new economy or "future of capitalism" movement is emerging. Some are calling it The Great Transition. It is gaining momentum and already reinventing capitalism along regenerative lines, still below the radar of the mainstream press. The next chapter seeks to shine a light on just a few dimensions of this emerging movement.

SECOND EDITION REFLECTION

The eight principles of regenerative vitality have aged quite well. On several occasions, I have sat with colleagues to consider what changes would be helpful. While the list is not perfect, again and again I have concluded that any changes I could make would not result in any meaningful benefits in terms of either accuracy of my evolving understanding or effective communication. These discussions have shed more light on the challenges of reductionism itself—reducing the complexity of the process of life to as few "first principles" as possible—irreducible without sacrificing critical meaning. Second, they reinforce the primary challenge, which is the communication of an ecological concept to a mechanistic-thinking world. The discussions have not revealed any genuinely new insights demanding a revision of the principles themselves.

Let me offer two examples. Recently, regenerative thought leader Carol Sanford came out with her own set of regenerative principles. Naturally, there was tremendous overlap, and Carol's perspective is both valid and important. Nonetheless, two fundamental differences emerged. First, she considers both "holism" and "potential" as principles of regeneration, while she excludes several in my formulation. I know from our conversations that she does not think these are wrong. She just saw what rises to first principle status differently than me.

While I certainly understand where she is coming from, I don't consider either of these as examples of design principles. Instead, I agree with Smuts, who coined the term *holism* and sees it as "the universal principle that explains matter, life, and spirit." As such, holism is both structure and process at the same time, and it sits above regeneration in the layers of reality of my thinking, just as biology sits "above" physics. By this I mean that biology must honor the foundational laws of physics, but the opposite is not the case. To consider holism as merely one of several principles of regeneration reduces its primacy in importance in my way of thinking. But at the same time, regeneration does indeed require holistic understanding. The bigger point is that the paradigm shift we must grasp is a shift out of reductionism and into an enlightened and more reality-based holism, inclusive of the reductionist method, used where appropriate. Allan Savory likes to say that reductionism works well for the complicated things we make (from microchips to rocket ships), whereas holism is required to understand and dance with the complexity of the things we manage (like our health, our organizations, and our economies).[111]

Regarding potential, again we both agree that regenerative potential is fundamental. For me, it's more of an outcome than a principle. Unlocking unseen potential is the outcome of the regenerative process, and the reason it's rational to remain hopeful, in spite of having considered all the facts. You can see the nuance involved in describing what constitutes "first principles." As Stuart Kauffman says, life is not reducible to neat laws and equations. But it does have strong tendencies to follow patterns, and it does seem to demonstrate first principles.

I did make two subtle yet important modifications to my eight principles, both in response to thoughtful student observations in my course. First, we modified "Seeks Balance" to "Seeks Dynamic Balance." The idea has always been balance as a unicycle rider experiences it, not as seen with a static scale. The concept is an endless dynamic process of seeking and responding to ever-changing conditions. Which is also why a goal in one context may no longer be the appropriate goal the moment the context shifts. This is the nature of holistic thinking within complexity in contrast to reductionist thinking to engineer static, controllable machines.

Second, in one class there was a question about the concept of innovation as we now experience it, particularly coming out of Silicon Valley. This was a perceptive question. As a result, when I talk about this principle, I always stress that we need innovation that is adaptive and responsive. In other words, living systems are indeed innovative, but they innovate for the purpose of keeping the system adapted to the changing context and responsive to those changes. Subtle tweak in language, profound change in meaning of the principle.

Finally, I am indebted to my colleague and visual thinker Kate Raworth, creator of the Doughnut Economics framework to help us visualize and integrate the ecological and social constraints introduced by the discipline of ecological economics.[112] Kate suggested that I create a visual for the eight principles of regenerative vitality, a picture to communicate far better than words alone. I listened and we created a mandala of sorts, depicted in figure 3.6. It is now in its third iteration after our course community member Robert Althuis pointed out the significance of the number eight in Chinese philosophy. Eight symbolizes prosperity and wealth,

ALIGNMENT WITH LIFE'S PRINCIPLES UNLOCKS REGENERATIVE POTENTIAL

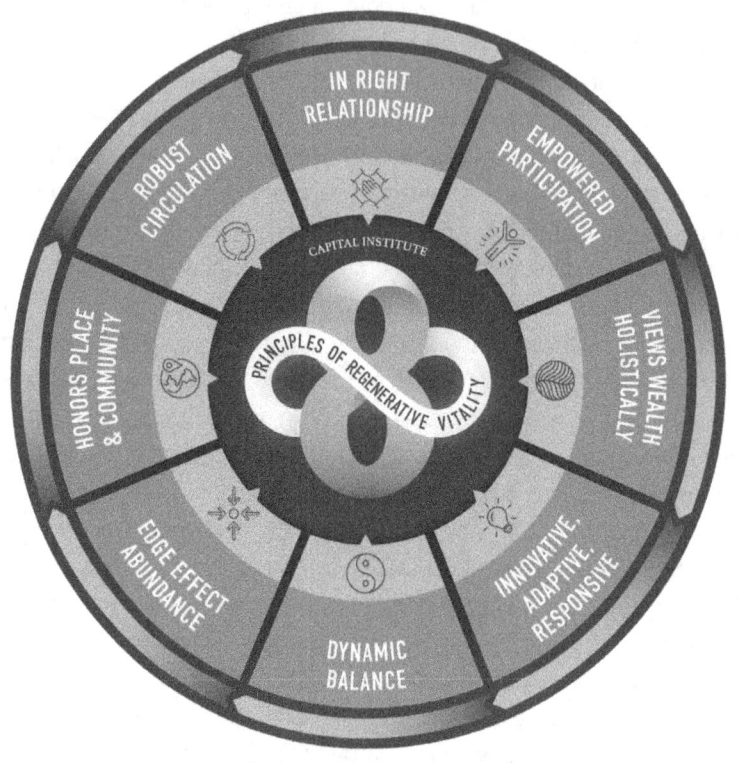

Figure 3.6 **Eight Principles of Regenerative Vitality.** *Credit: John Fullerton, Capital Institute.*

but is also associated with balance, harmony, and the infinite, which we now highlight at the center of the latest version of the mandala. Turns out the number eight is the infinity symbol turned on its side as well! A beautiful synchronicity hidden in plain sight. The connecting arrows around the outside are meant to communicate connection and dynamism. The notches into the single center suggest connection to an overall unity, a single whole greater than the sum of the parts. I hope a picture can tell a thousand words!

In summary, the idea of a Regenerative Economics rests on three premises:

First: The economy is a living system, albeit an unhealthy one.

Second: There are patterns and principles that describe all living systems. This is now accepted science not opinion.

Third: If the human economy is to be a healthy system, not only to sustain itself over long periods of time, but to manifest human thriving within a healthy biosphere, then it, too, will need to follow these same patterns and principles. Or someone will need to make the case that the human economy is the only known exception to the rule of what constitutes the qualities of healthy living systems.

By aligning the design and functioning of our economy with our eight principles of regenerative vitality serving as a first approximate guide—not some notion of whole truth—we will create the conditions for health in our economic system and thus participate constructively in the evolutionary process we call life. As bioogist Janine Benyus has observed, "Life creates conditions conducive to life."

The universal dwells in the concrete particular. Neither is real nor truly apart from the other.

—*Jan Smuts*

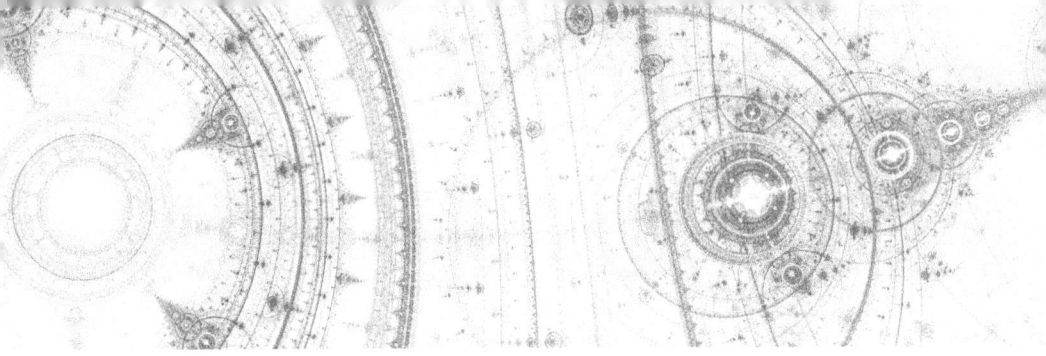

CHAPTER FOUR

REGENERATIVE ECONOMICS EMERGING IN THE REAL WORLD

The good news is that the entrepreneurial creative spirit at the heart of our free enterprise system, the vital baby we must not throw out with the bathwater, is inherently regenerative. Every day, new manifestations of this regenerative heart are emerging all around us. This regenerative energy is the driving force behind a great deal of new value creation and some of the most successful innovations we've ever seen. But without a regenerative lens to see in a new way, often this concrete emergence of regenerative economies remains hidden in plain sight.

The internet is perhaps the most profound regenerative innovation of all time, enabling mass connection, and the circulation of information, and even emotion on a scale and with an ease previously unimaginable. That's what potential is, previously unimaginable. If we examine what it was that created the conditions for the internet to emerge, we will find our eight principles. I invite you to give it a try. You may not find all eight, but you'll see several for sure.

Like any tool or technology, we must learn to use it wisely, again in alignment with how life works. So, while social media and all platform businesses hold great potential, the unnecessary extractive business models attached to them have caused great harm. It's the business models that are out of alignment, not the internet or even the concept of social media. As a result, few look at the internet and recognize the vital energy flow network of a regenerative economy today. We see it as a technology being monopolized by a handful of companies whose extractive methods are highly degenerative to human and systemic health. But the internet most certainly is and can be regenerative if we learn to manage it wisely.

The regenerative qualities emerging in these real-world examples serve as beacons of hope and inspiration, and indicators that economic transformation without catastrophic collapse is not only possible but well underway. If only we had eyes to see the metamorphosis taking place under the radar.

REGENERATIVE MOVEMENTS IN ACTION

I don't consider regeneration to be a movement. But a multitude of movements are underway that most certainly exemplify the regenerative process working its way into our economy. Often viewed as disconnected "feel good" activities outside the mainstream capitalist system, we see these activities as interconnected and in alignment with the regenerative economy framework, that is, in alignment with the natural order of all things in the universe. Collectively these forces provide living proof that regenerative economies are emergent, and it is the mainstream capitalist system that is under existential threat if it does not adapt.

[Note to reader: I have elected to again profile the examples below from the first edition to highlight some of the true pioneers, even if they didn't identify with the regenerative paradigm. That's the thing about regeneration—it reflects our natural, intuitive response to the challenges we collectively face. Today an entire book could be written with fresh initiatives, such as many included in Our Biggest Deal: Pathways to Planetary Prosperity, *by Aaron William Perry (2025).]*

Social Entrepreneurship and Purpose-Driven, For-Benefit Enterprises. The burgeoning field of social entrepreneurship is the regenerative economy, even if the practitioners aren't aware of the term. As social entrepreneur observer David Bornstein writes, "Social entrepreneurs identify resources where other people only see problems. They view villagers as the solution, not the passive beneficiary.[113] In other words, they see potential hidden in plain sight. Social entrepreneurship is now a strong area of interest in leading business schools and exploding around with world through organizations like Ashoka. For-benefit enterprises can be either for-profit businesses with an explicit social and/or environmental objective or nonprofit enterprises with sustainable business models.[114] A particularly interesting development involves "B Corps" (in contrast to conventional C Corps) that demonstrate "business as a force for good." B Corps sign up for a set of best practices including a corporate charter declaring that directors "shall give due consideration" to all stakeholders, not just shareholders. It is a direct response to the shareholder primacy presumption that corporate directors invoke as their fiduciary duty to uphold, leading to many corporate decisions with adverse societal consequences. So far twenty-seven states have passed B Corp legislation in the U.S., and there are over one thousand registered B Corps around the world, including many young entrepreneurial ventures as well as iconic names like Patagonia and Ben & Jerry's. In April 2015 Etsy became the first publicly traded B Corp.

[Note: As of this second edition writing, there are now nearly ten thousand B Corps in the world, just the kind of growth story we need.]

Microenterprises and Microfinance. Despite their extremely small size, "micro" enterprises are the cellular fabric of economies and add massive value to economies by providing over half the employment in most economies and much of the new job growth opportunities, and by strengthening the purchasing power of a large percentage of the global population while also lowering costs and adding business convenience. Yet despite their importance, such enterprises often have little or no access to commercial banking or finance. Using the principle that "credit is a human right," Nobel laureate Muhammad Yunus and his Grameen Bank of Bangladesh helped rectify this situation by pioneering the concept of microfinance organizations, which focus on making small loans to micro-businesses and poor people, particularly women, to help them achieve self-sufficiency. Grameen's extremely effective strategy of organizing groups of borrowers and teaching them both business and technical skills caused it to grow from fewer than 15,000 borrowers in 1980 to 9.4 million today—97 percent of whom are women. Loan repayment rates are similarly impressive, often nearing

100 percent. Microfinance is now a relatively mature global industry, although it does have blemishes to its reputation when business models shifted to become profit driven rather than guided by the principles of "right relationship" and "holistic wealth."

Relocalization, Slow Food, Slow Money. Relocalization organizations strive to build more resilient societies by relocalizing the provisioning of food, clothing, shelter, and energy, as well as currency, governance, and culture. Their immediate goals are to strengthen local economies, increase community food and energy security, and dramatically improve social equity and environmental conditions. While working primarily within their communities, these groups also share knowledge, experience, and educational resources within communities of practice such as the Business Alliance for Local Living Economies.[115] Slow Food, a variation on relocalization, works to promote local foods and preserve centuries-old cultural traditions of food preparation and production while opposing fast food, industrial food production, and globalization. Slow Food's motto is "good, clean, and fair." Started in 1986 to prevent McDonald's from setting up a franchise at the bottom of the Spanish Steps in Rome, the Slow Food movement has expanded to over one hundred thousand members in 150 countries. Slow Money, inspired by the Slow Food movement, catalyzes investment to local food enterprises and organic farms, connecting investors to the places where they live and "bringing money back down to earth," as founder Woody Tasch poetically says. Since its founding in 2010, $40 million has been invested in over four hundred small food enterprises.

[Note to reader: Now $100 million in a thousand projects.]

Impact Investing. Impact investing, a not so new label on an old idea, is now a recognized phenomenon, with increasing numbers of individuals, families, and progressive institutions seeking to better align their investment capital with their values in primarily early-stage companies and projects that harmonize financial, social, and ecological returns. Not only does impact investing help address social and/or environmental problems while turning a profit, according to the Rockefeller Foundation, it could eventually provide a way to "unlock substantial for-profit investment capital to complement philanthropy in addressing pressing social challenges." Indeed, a growing number of philanthropic foundations are increasingly using their corpus for mission-aligned, "program-related investments," and some, like the F.B. Heron Foundation, have declared the intent to have all of their investment portfolios invested for impact. Of course, Community Development Financial Institutions have been "impact investing" in the U.S. for decades, while the world's numerous development banks have been investing for positive "impact" on a global scale built into their charters. The lack of alignment of mainstream finance with the eight principles of regenerative economies is certainly one of the key obstacles to the transformation of our economies.

[Note to reader: Today the Global Impact Investment Network (GIIN) estimates the total impact space exceeds $1.5 trillion of invested capital. At the same time, impact practitioners such as TWIST (Together We Invest for Systems Transformation) and the TransCap Initiative (Systemic Investing for Sustainability) have moved closer to a regenerative approach with their shift to systemic impact investing (or "systems change investing"), recognizing that the transformation we desire cannot happen one company at a time, no matter how ambitious. This is welcome progress.]

Global Alliance for Banking on Values (GABV). GABV is a growing independent network of global banks committed to values-based banking in service of sustainable development. Peter Blom, (former) CEO of the perennial "Sustainable Bank of the Year," Triodos Bank in the Netherlands, is the founding chair of GABV, which seeks to collaborate among its members rather than compete. Less well-known than impact investment, but equally vital given the importance of a healthy banking system in service of the transition to regenerative economies, GABV is now made up of twenty-five licensed financial institutions with combined assets of $100 billion that together touch the lives of more than twenty million people in thirty countries.[116]

Integrative Design Collaborative. A network of green building consulting, living system design, and education organizations, working to lift building and community planning into full integration and co-evolution with living systems. The work of architect Bill Reed, a principal of this group, centers on creating the framework for and managing an integrative, whole-systems design process in order to improve the overall quality of the physical, social, and spiritual life of our living places and therefore the planet.[117] In Reed's view, truly regenerative building designs should create "net energy," including but not limited to electricity that can be put back into the electric grid; embody a circular approach by using natural systems to treat wastewater in ways that enhance groundwater and soils and mitigates downstream flooding by slowing run-off; and regenerate depleted soils on community farms to support healthy food systems, build biodiversity and organic matter, and sequester carbon in the process. Finally and most critically, they should build community around shared values while educating members of the community about the regenerative principles that must be deployed in all walks of life, including creating "value-adding" relationships (social capital) extending far beyond both the buildings themselves and the immediate communities in which they are built.

NGOs (Non-Governmental Organizations) and Other Forms of Social Enterprise. Paul Hawken, author of regenerative business touchstone *The Ecology of Commerce* (1993), calls the burgeoning NGO sector "the largest movement in the world that no one saw coming."[118] Usually set up by ordinary citizens and either run by volunteers or funded by foundations, private persons, or governments, NGOs devote themselves to critical issues that require long-term attention and where neither market nor government solutions are viable on their own—such as climate change, malaria prevention, or even rethinking global capitalism! Well-run NGOs often enjoy a high degree of public trust because they work to address the broad concerns of society. According to Wikipedia, there are at least ten million NGOs in the world in 2025, with India and the U.S. accounting for the largest share. If NGOs were an economy, it would be the fifth largest in the world, employing millions of people. Yet it is highly distributed (healthy, not efficient, as capitalism would suggest). As a result, it is difficult to even see.

CREATIVE REGENERATIVE PROJECTS AND ENTERPRISES OF THE *FIELD GUIDE*

[Note to reader: These examples, too, are now over a decade out of date, yet a review today will reveal how we have been observing the emergence of the regenerative economy for quite some time. While new in the awareness of many, it's not a new phenomenon. Recall that Einstein pointed out that it is the theory that determines what we are able to see. The emergence of a regenerative economy has been underway for decades now, often right under our noses. Let's have a look back.]

In addition to the broad regenerative, process-aligned movements described above, a vast number of unique and creative regenerative learning projects, enterprises, and experiments are also taking place. In order to illuminate how Regenerative Economics works in practice, Capital Institute's *Field Guide to a Regenerative Economy* has been exploring how the regenerative principles emerge organically.[119] They typically arise at the small-scale, rooted in place outside the mainstream, where pressures to conform to the current paradigm are not as intense, and where hunger for innovation is strongest, often out of necessity. Yet we increasingly find organizations earnestly aspiring to be regenerative, even if it is still unclear what that might look like, operating inside the mainstream and at the global level as well. Norway's DNV GL, the multibillion-dollar, global safety-certification company that recently celebrated its 150th anniversary, is a prime example of the latter.[120]

Since we began *The Field Guide to a Regenerative Economy* project in 2010, we have had the privilege of sharing the stories of over twenty-five projects and enterprises that are exemplary of the emergence of regenerative principles in the real world. It's important to see these stories as emerging manifestations of this entirely new paradigm. There is no pure model of a regenerative company, and all enterprises must for now operate within the very degenerative global economy. But it's impressive to see the clear trend of movement in a regenerative direction, all of these entities learning as they go. The discussion below is merely the tip of the iceberg.

REGENERATING CITIES AND THE BUILT ENVIRONMENT

Manufacturing Renaissance (Chicago, Illinois) is forging unlikely partnerships among government, organized labor, educators, the private sector, and civil society by creating programs to support the regional advanced manufacturing sectors. One of its immediate projects has been to develop the next generation of advanced manufacturing leaders by educating a generation of inner-city high school students at Chicago's Austin Polytechnical High School.

The Evergreen Cooperatives (Cleveland, Ohio), a partnership of the Cleveland Foundation, the Democracy Collaborative, the city of Cleveland, and several "anchor institutions" including local hospitals, is creating a grassroots solution to the crisis of poverty in inner cities by developing a network of locally anchored, worker-owned businesses to generate locally anchored jobs and greater local empowerment and wealth-building. Evergreen Cooperatives now includes Evergreen Energy Solutions, Evergreen Cooperative Laundry, and Green City Growers Cooperative.

Detroit Kitchen Connect (Detroit, Michigan), another example of the "edge effect" in action, is a kitchen incubator that is finding creative and intentional ways to use underutilized resources to forge closer social relationships, bringing people together who might not otherwise connect, through the shared love of food. The leaders describe their strategy as the power of the "uncomfortable." They also grapple every day with two sometimes competing realities: the need right now for food and well-being in an inner city, and the long-term need to shift to a different food system entirely to sustain the health and wellness of the planet.

REGENERATING THE LAND AND FOOD SYSTEMS

Grasslands, LLC (Bozeman, Montana), a "custom grazing" business inspired by and linked to the decades of developmental work of Allan Savory, is now operating ranches in South Dakota, Montana, Hawaii, Florida, and New Zealand. It uses holistic management practices to regenerate overgrazed land using herds of animals, managed as nature always has, in symbiotic "right relationship" with the grasslands. The result is reversing desertification by increasing ground cover, increasing biodiversity, water retention, soil quality, and carbon sequestering ability. In essence, this practice harnesses the power of the photosynthetic process and converts it into ecological, human, and financial capital. Given that nearly one-third of the Earth's land mass is dry brittle grasslands (think Mongolia, Argentina, South Dakota), if these projects can successfully inspire imitation aided by the global training efforts of the Savory Institute and others in order to reclaim land that has been degraded by conventional livestock management and human population expansion, the implications will be game changing for the planet. Unfortunately, a reductionist approach to climate change sees cows as a problem. The problem is not the cows, it's how they are managed in the industrial feedlot system to maximize profits. Huge regenerative potential lies unseen, as Savory and colleagues have demonstrated around the world. Full disclosure, I am a co-founder of Grasslands, LLC and a board member of the Savory Institute.[121]

Grupo Ecologico (Sierra Gordo, Mexico), founded by Martha "Pati" Ruiz Corzo and her husband, Roberto, is a not-for-profit collaborative that not only catalyzed the creation of the only locally governed biosphere reserve in Mexico but also has helped put in place a variety of innovative funding mechanisms empowering a network of highly resourceful, impoverished small farmers and ranchers to assume the roles of preservationists and regenerators of their own land in one of the most biodiverse regions of the world.

Accelerating Appalachia (eastern Kentucky and western NC) is a business accelerator that nurtures natural and entrepreneurial capital to help provide a foundation for a scale-appropriate, post-extractive, regenerative economy in coal country. Tapping into the skill base of the former manufacturing and agriculture economies—food, farming, forests, fiber, and fuels—Accelerating Appalachia connects businesses to impact investing and venture capital programs.

REGENERATING FINANCE

The Bendigo Community Bank Model (Australia), now represented by over three hundred branches throughout Australia, is a unique banking framework in which Bendigo partners with local communities, requiring them to make an initial upfront investment in a branch operation while Bendigo Bank assumes responsibility for staff training, IT, products, capital, and regulatory and compliance issues. Net income is then split between Bendigo Bank and the local community enterprise. A portion of community branch earnings are directed toward local grantmaking, with over $130 million in funds so allocated since the first community bank branch opened in the late 1990s, proving that this innovative model "working at the edges" is scalable. The model has helped recirculate the flow of financial capital into local economies in meaningful, self-directed ways and is giving local leaders the business acumen to become active players in their communities' economic transitions.

First Green Bank (central Florida) was founded by Ken LaRoe, a third-generation central Floridian who was inspired to start up a bank aligned with his values after selling an earlier successful mainstream banking venture and then reading Yvon Chouinard's *Let My People Go Surfing* on a cross-country trip. As a new member of GABV, LaRoe is on a quest to create a lending portfolio that supports businesses that contribute to the regeneration of a local economy dominated by strip malls, condominiums, and tourist-related development. Far from discouraged by the challenges he faces, LaRoe reports that he has reached "something close to self-actualization: the pinnacle of Maslow's hierarchy of needs."

[Note: First Green Bank was subsequently sold, driven by investor desire to realize both profit and liquidity, a persistent challenge for changemakers. LaRoe has launched a new bank, Climate First Bank, also in Florida but this time with investors who are fully aligned with the mission.]

Studying these projects has provided a proving ground for our theoretical explorations, helping us identify regenerative principles through direct observation and engagement. Witnessing the creativity and resourcefulness of our *Field Guide* partners has also been extraordinarily inspiring for us.

In some cases—such as Grasslands LLC, the Evergreen Cooperatives, and the Lopez Community Land Trust, for example—we have encountered projects that have been carefully and deliberately architected by seasoned holistic thinkers from the outset. In other cases—such as Detroit Kitchen and Viva Farms, for example—we have witnessed start-up projects taking on a regenerative life guided by more intuitive leaders who skillfully tap into the essence and entrepreneurial energy of their communities.

In almost every instance we see the evidence of what we can only call the "invisible regenerative hand" at work. We see people whose everyday lives assume a new and nobler purpose as they experience the following qualities in their work:

- Truly "empowered participation" in projects on Lopez Island, Washington; in inner-city Chicago, Cleveland, and Detroit; and in Mexico's Sierra Gorda;
- "Right relationship" to each other and to nature embedded in the very fabric of the Accelerating Appalachia Incubator and UK's GroCycle company;
- The desire to honor and to elevate all stakeholders a business touches, which propels the partnership between McCarty Family Farms in Kansas and the Dannon Company; the strategies of the privately held ("in right relationship with owners") global DNV GL; and the collaboration among members of the Principal 6 Cooperative Trade Movement;
- The restless ambition to create a values-driven financial system while struggling against the constraints of the old, flawed system, a drive that energizes Bendigo's over three hundred Community Bank Branches scattered across Australia, Community Sourced Capital's expanding U.S. network, Central Florida's First Green Bank, and all the member banks of GABV.

There is an identifiable spirit that energizes the regenerative projects our *Field Guide* stories describe and now literally thousands of other ones emerging around the world. It's this regenerative, hopeful spirit, a willingness to believe that unseen possibilities exist, that sets them apart from many other worthy endeavors to address societal and environmental ills. That spirit was perhaps best expressed by Yorman Nunez of the Bronx Cooperative Development Initiative, who, though unaware of our regenerative thesis, articulated the critical distinction between resiliency and regenerativeness:

> Resiliency speaks to what we are doing in response to outside forces that are beating us down. That may be necessary, but maybe building protections is not the best possible use of our

energy. Regeneration makes you think about the activities that get you through a real healing process to a place of wellness. Because of the realities we live with, that is a much harder proposition and process to go through ... but necessary if we really want to get to a point of true sustainability.

IMPLICATIONS FOR POLITICS AND PUBLIC POLICY

The need for regenerative reforms is particularly critical in politics and public policy. No business can transform itself in a vacuum. Policy is what defines the rules of the game at institutional scale and guides the direction of progress, or lack thereof. The long-term cost of economic crises is measured not only in financial losses but in ruined lives, foreclosed homes, devastated communities, slashed public services, and a generation of youth suffering from alarming levels of hopelessness and anxiety that will inevitably manifest in deep societal ills or worse. The time lost trying to redress and reform Wall Street's most egregious excesses and the public debt burden left on public balance sheets only exacerbates these already high costs.

Firefighting the financial system has also distracted the public and private sectors from the need to prepare for the economic transition that will inevitably be forced upon us by Mother Nature and/or social upheaval if we do not initiate systemic change on our own. Yet a multitude of additional crises, ranging from increasing water stress to pandemics, to terrorism and increased social unrest, also appear to be spiraling out of control. If we understand their root causes holistically, we see them as one interconnected, systemic crisis, not as isolated problems to solve. Our global leaders' ability to respond is constrained by the sheer quantity and complexity of the challenges. This, as Dana Meadows observed in 1992, reflects a system operating beyond its limits.[122] Worse yet, we must plan on an acceleration of such crises in the years and decades to come as social and ecological stresses mount. Welcome to the Anthropocene, the new geological era of our own making, with profound geopolitical and social ramifications.

Questions and issues of extreme complexity and consequence now abound. Consider our response to climate change alone and the need to transition our energy system away from fossil fuels:

- How can we mobilize the staggering $44 trillion of new investment in energy infrastructure and energy efficiency that the International Energy Agency estimates will be necessary by 2050 to replace the current energy system?[123] To put that number in context, the market value of all global public companies combined is $60 trillion.
- How can we eliminate the burning of fossil fuels by mid-century?
- What about our ability to absorb the economic write-off of $20 trillion in stranded assets representing the majority of proved fossil fuel reserves that must be left in the ground or not burned,[124] because burning them would blow us through the 2-degree Celsius warming threshold that scientists agree is the likely tipping point to truly permanent catastrophic consequences?
- What about the fact that three-quarters of those fossil fuel reserves are owned not by public companies but by nation-states like Saudi Arabia, Iraq, Iran, Venezuela, Canada, Russia, and via leases, even the United States, whose economies, public budgets, and social cohesion are currently highly dependent upon the continued extraction and sale of fossil fuels?
- How are we going to negotiate a deal with OPEC countries (or Putin) that restricts their ability to sell their oil? Same question for Exxon and Shell. And who could enforce such an agreement?

If we do not address these issues, we will destroy life on the planet as we know it. Yet, if we do not address them properly, we could easily collapse the economy upon which we also depend. This is the "Big Choice," challenge, and dilemma facing our generation,[125] the ultimate double bind of humanity. Consequently, it would be foolhardy to suggest that the choices we must make and the solutions we undertake will be anything but immensely difficult. Technological solutions not yet developed, such as ultra deep geothermal energy, and technologies not yet imagined will certainly play a role, but counting on unknowns for such a massive shift is not prudent. Various studies point to the job creation and investment potential of the energy transition, but the scale and complexity of the required shift, both economically and politically, is unprecedented. Finally and perhaps most difficult to comprehend, as of this writing, there is still not even an open and honest discussion about the unprecedented geopolitical challenge stranded assets represent as detailed above, coming at a time of rising barbarism in the Middle East and the seeming breakdown of the post–Cold War world order.

[Note to reader: It is not hard to recognize in this analysis the idea we now call "the polycrisis," which ten years later has entered our awareness. We shall return to the ambitious public policy agenda necessary to turn the ship around and drive the transformation to regenerative economies in chapter 12.]

IMPLICATIONS FOR FINANCE

The challenge of reimaging finance theory and reforming finance practice accordingly will be particularly critical and exceptionally difficult. Abraham Lincoln could not have understood the prescience of his warning when he said, "I have the South in front of me and the bankers behind me—and for my country I fear the bankers more."

The dual difficulty will be to rein in the antisocial excesses of the financial sector while redirecting the vital flow of credit and investment capital to support the transition to a regenerative economy. Our circulatory system is failing, literally, a systemic necrosis caused by lack of adequate "blood flow" (money in an economy) to all the organs of the system. We must release the obstructive dams and rehabilitate the healthy channels of circulation that have atrophied as a consequence of our flawed thinking and neglect and build entirely new arteries to flow capital in new ways, particularly to repair damages done to our ecosystems and human cultures, both when they do and when they do not optimize the financial return on capital.

This redirection will be particularly challenging not only because it runs counter to the darker culture of banking that has cycled in and out for centuries, but also because it runs counter to the misconstrued "purpose" of banking and finance to which even the many honest and decent financiers subscribe.

Aristotle wrote that chrematistics—roughly translated, "the use of money to make money"—is unnatural.[126] I suspect what Aristotle meant is that chrematistics does not follow the natural order of things (in many ways, Aristotle was an early holistic thinker).

If he is right, and I believe he is, then we have a long way to go to create a financial system that serves the needs of the real economy. Today's financial system—led by dominant institutions including too-big-to-fail banks, and the rapidly expanding hedge funds and private equity funds—is based on one common belief: The purpose of banking and finance is to make money using money, particularly, other people's money. We accept that it is the duty of our bankers, a moral duty to some, to do so as "productively" as possible, by which we mean in our outdated reductionist thinking, in such a way as to generate the highest risk-adjusted return on financial capital invested, provided that it is legal. And by risk, we mean risk to financial capital, nothing to do with systemic health. This is the religion practiced in the Church of Neoclassical Economics. If that means channeling savings to finance the production of dirty tar sands oil, or excessive speculation by giant hedge funds or by the banks themselves, or the short-term extraction of long-run systemic health out of companies and communities and humanity itself by leveraged financial engineering or extractive tech algorithms with the unprecedented, winner-take-all profit margins of platform business models, then so be it.

Many now call today's dominant form of capitalism "finance capitalism"—an unflattering reference to the short-term, extractive approach to capitalism currently led by our Wall Street ideology. Ironically, while most people loathe the inequality this system fuels, and condemn financiers who break the law or act irresponsibly, they generally do not question that the purpose of banking and finance is to make money by using other people's money, preferably at the fastest rate possible. We financiers even use the phrase "extract value" as an achievement, free of any embarrassment or shame. "How much value did you extract from that transaction?"

Transitioning to a regenerative economy will require a profound rethinking of finance ideology and a profound redesign of the global financial system because this extractive approach undermines the need to build long-term resilient enterprises and ecosystems, and even entirely new institutions designed to address the unprecedented challenges of the current context within a regenerative economy. Instead of striving to be master of the world, finance must become a subsystem of the economy that operates in service of the real, regenerative economy, a massive topic for another time.

In other words, the purpose of Regenerative Finance—inclusive of banking and investment—must be to serve the health of the whole system. Or as I often close my public remarks: *The purpose of capital is to serve life—and not the other way around.*

While this purpose is served by investing in regenerative enterprises, it also includes making a sustainable profit for the constructive risks a financial institution takes—like transforming short-term savings into long-term productive loans—and for the services it provides in the process. New approaches to investing beyond current efforts at impact investing such as crowdsourcing, blended capital, and the more radical "Evergreen Direct Investing" will arise to complement our short-term-obsessed public capital markets and the extractive nature of so much of private equity and now venture capital as well.[127] Capital structures and ownership models suited to long-term decision-making while reasserting the responsibility and purpose that goes with real ownership is essential. As always, the fractal nature of healthy systems means that the principles of regenerative health must be applied to all scales of finance, from local to global.

A growing list of financial institutions and financiers who believe it is their responsibility to serve the real economy, rather than extract from it, suggests that the emergence of Regenerative Finance is accelerating, if we have eyes to see it. We see evidence of it in some of the post-2008 financial crisis reform efforts that are pointing us in the right direction, and in challenges to our current beliefs about the superiority of a purely private banking system.

In fact, *the very notion that our banking system is private is a mirage.* Banking already is a hybrid public/private enterprise. The problem is that bankers and the ideologically captured public officials just pretend otherwise.

Here is just a brief preview of what financial system transformation entails and where it is already happening:

- Led by the example of the Dutch bank Triodos, a growing network of banks, called the Global Alliance for Banking on Values, is committed to serving the real economy.

- In the U.S., RSF Social Finance, which extends productive loans to regenerative enterprises following the philosophy of Rudolph Steiner, just celebrated its (now fortieth) anniversary.[128] Many other mission-driven loan funds and community capital vehicles exist and are sprouting up in response to the recognized failures of our banking system.

- Numerous public/private financial institutions, most notably the regional development banks, already exist. Imperfect as they are, they prove that there is and always has been a well-recognized public/private nature of banking, and the public need for a credit allocation process to serve a healthy economic system including the vital circulation of credit where it is less profitable to do so. There are even examples of healthy, disciplined public banks, such as the Bank of North Dakota in the U.S., that provide a stabilizing complement to the private banking system. And in places ranging from Germany to China, the role of the public sector in banking is much more common and accepted. We should expect renewed debate around the role of the public sector in banking and even the money creation process, either directly or in creative hybrid public/private partnerships, as we tackle the multitrillion-dollar financing challenge of the transition to, and maintenance of, a truly regenerative economy.[129]

- Impact investing—where investors seek to align their investments with social and environmental purpose—is burgeoning, particularly among certain wealthy families in the U.S. and increasingly Europe, as discussed earlier. Far from perfect or sufficient, it is a clear sign of an emerging green shoot of the regenerative economy. As mentioned above, the move now into system change investing is moving the field closer to the regenerative paradigm.

- Financial reform policies have struggled to take hold due to the excessive power our financiers now have over our political system and our ideological beliefs. Nevertheless, even here there has been important progress. The excess capital requirements for "systemically important" (i.e., "too big to fail") institutions are directionally correct even if insufficient as we have discussed. With the effect of incentivizing banks to remain *not* systemically important (i.e., remain smaller, less complex), it's an example of the kind of self-regulating feedback loop we need. While it is being resisted strongly in the U.S. and U.K., a financial transaction tax targeting the excessive short-term speculation that plagues our capital markets is broadly supported in Europe and elsewhere and continues to be debated globally behind the scenes.

- We will also need to rethink all the subsidies that corrupt and hamper the development of the financial system we need, beginning with the cost of capital subsidy to our largest banks. The implicit and demonstrated-under-duress government recognition that it cannot and will not let the largest institutions fail if doing so risks taking down the real economy reduces the cost of capital of these banks, their primary cost of doing business. Bank deposit insurance and access to the central bank for funding are subsidies. Each serves a useful purpose, but today's bloated financial conglomerates have exploited these privileges in ways that serve only their own interests while putting the real economy at risk. "Too big to fail" and "too complex to manage" banks like today's JPMorgan and Goldman Sachs require a profoundly different incentive-driven regulatory regime that likely will drive them to break themselves up into manageable enterprises that do not threaten the health of the real economy. The "too big to fail" banks that remain will act in ways that, while profitable with reasonable banker compensation aligned with other professions, truly serve the health of the whole.

It is an absolute requirement that we get our financial system house in order if we are to transition to a regenerative economy, and we are starting from a troubled place. The transformation of our energy, water, agriculture, and transportation systems underway, and the entire built environment, collectively represent the largest investment opportunity in the history of capitalism. We simply need a financial system in service to the needs of economic system transformation, not in service to its (naive) self-interest. Ultimately the interests of the whole are indivisible form the interests of finance.

MEASURING AND MANAGING SYSTEMIC HEALTH IN COMPLEX WEBS

Managing a complex economic web of "capitals" and multiple, competing factors is not going to be easy—particularly because it is new to us. Instead of optimizing one variable, such as GDP growth, "shareholder value," or economic efficiency, as is conventionally done, managing a complex whole requires a harmonizing process that integrates multiple variables dynamically in proper alignment and proportion. Furthermore, since the universal principles are both qualitative and quantitative, creating regenerative health in today's complex human networks will require a harmonization process that is both subjective (seeing patterns, making judgments based on values and first principles) and analytic (measuring what matters).

Many of the subjective aspects of management are being addressed in approaches such as Peter Senge's *Fifth Discipline* and Otto Scharmer's *Theory U* that use systems thinking to create more effective learning organizations.

Nobel laureate Elinor Ostrom's study of how certain groups developed effective economic governance of the commons will become particularly helpful to us as we struggle to learn how to holistically manage multilevel political economies on a greater scale in the future.[130] It will take creative extrapolation to move from the locally managed natural commons that Ostrom was studying—a river system, for example—to local and regional economies, and all the way to the shared common resources of the planet, such as the atmosphere. Emphasizing the multifaceted nature of human-ecosystem interaction and arguing against any singular panacea for all social-ecological system problems, Ostrom nevertheless identified eight design directives found across a wide range of communities that manage common pool resources (CPR) effectively:

- Define clear group boundaries with effective exclusion of external unentitled parties.

- Match rules governing use of common goods to local needs and conditions.
- Ensure that those affected by the rules can participate in modifying them.
- Develop a system for monitoring members' behavior and maintaining accountability that is carried out by community members themselves.
- Use graduated sanctions for those who violate community rules.
- Provide accessible, low-cost means for dispute resolution.
- Make sure that outside authorities respect the rule-making rights of community members.
- Use subsidiarity (i.e., decisions made at the lowest level possible) to build responsibility for governing the commons in nested levels from the immediate local up to the entire interconnected system.

Other approaches to holistic management add a more ecological spin. For instance, Allan Savory's work in holistic-range management won the 2010 Buckminster Fuller Challenge for initiatives that take "a comprehensive, anticipatory, design approach to radically advance human well-being and the health of our planet's ecosystems." Savory's work started with the observation that healthy natural systems function as holistic communities with mutualistic (symbiotic) relationships among all parts. Consequently, instead of single-mindedly obsessing on maximizing short-term financial value, Savory's approach to managing whole systems emphasizes: (1) the importance of managing the relationships among parts; (2) being aware of excesses and limits; and (3) addressing issues of "weakest links." Some of his guiding principles for management that are easily extrapolated to human systems include the following:

- Understand the unique context and define what you are managing in its entirety, what Savory calls "the whole under management," including all the potential products, not just the most obvious, and design your system to take advantage of what exists in terms of all available resources. (As an interesting aside, Savory once said to me that one cannot manage an economy absent the unique cultural and ecological context in which it exists, a direct challenge to the modern discipline of economics, which often takes the view that such issues are outside its domain.) Define what you want now and far into the future. Develop goals and strategies to achieve the quality of life you desire, and learn how to build a system-nurturing environment to sustain it. Be aware that different elements play different roles and that all are necessary. Support the health of each element, and make sure that circulation is robust and balance is maintained.

For instance, while the Kenyan Greenbelt Movement founded by Nobel Peace Prize winner Wangari Maathai was ostensibly about planting trees, it actually improved women's rights, local income, local education, local nutrition, and environmental conservation simultaneously. These simultaneous outcomes emerged from careful consideration of the resources available in the current context; what outcomes were desired; and what strategies would be effective for connecting the two.

- Watch for the earliest indicators of systemic health or lack thereof. Indicators of improved economic functioning would include the widespread sprouting of new regenerative enterprises, improvements in educational systems and physical infrastructure, and increased access to seed capital and finance at the lower levels of economic systems. Indicators of ill health would include rising inequality, shrinking opportunities, growing individual debt, crumbling infrastructure, and poor circulation of credit at lower levels of the economy.

- Be adaptive and responsive to the ever-changing context that is a quality of all living systems. Manage your system proactively and dynamically, before imbalances become critical.

- Assume your plan and even your goals are wrong, not right. Test your decisions, with an eye to whether they are socially, environmentally, and financially sound for both the short and long term. Use a "canary in a coal mine" approach, that is, build in feedback loops for monitoring, readjusting, and replanning as necessary.

- Be aware of timing. Be sensitive to pressures and long-term changes taking place in the environment. Realize that individual businesses and whole economies go through cycles, and that activities that are needed and possible at one stage of the cycle may be impossible and counterproductive at another. An understanding of where you are in a cycle improves the effectiveness of your strategies.

- Finally, my colleagues at nRhythm have reduced the directive to leaders of regenerative organizations to this simple priority: Create the conditions for health, which includes removing obstacles. In other words, act more like a farmer focused on the soil than an engineer focused on optimizing the performance of a machine.

In addition to the subjective elements, our ability to achieve vitality will be greatly aided by analytic tools designed to help us assess the health of each type of capital, as well as the systemic health of "wholes" at all levels of the system. These new tools will include the comprehensive—i.e., systemic and holistic—valuation of business enterprise activities. For example, the International Integrated Reporting Council (IIRC)[131] and the Sustainability Accounting Standards Board (SASB)[132] have initiatives underway to promote greater transparency through "integrated reporting"—that is, by measuring, reporting, and managing multiple forms of capital and stakeholder interests in an integrated fashion—for public companies using industry-relevant standards.

To be effective, however, systemic and holistic measurement and management of complex systems must go further than integrated reporting by individual enterprises, as important as that is. We believe that the rigorous form of holism being developed by the Energy Network Sciences (ENS) can provide the measurement tools we need to turn our newly understood and intuitively pleasing sense of how economies must change into the scientifically sound policies we need to transform our current economic system into a vibrant, regenerative economy and then to manage it as such indefinitely into the future.

ENS research is particularly intriguing because it offers ways of measuring both subjective principles such as certain aspects of "in right relationship," and technical ones such as "circulation" and "balance." The "Top 10 Measures of Systemic Health"[133] summarized below, suggested by a team of researchers from FHI 360, Towson University, and Capital Institute, includes measures of traditionally subjective and traditionally analytic elements. All of these measures have been validated on real-world systems, though primarily on ecosystems and living systems outside economics. The first four are measures of Structure and Flow. The final six are measures of Rules, Roles, and Relationships. While some of the descriptions get quite technical, you can see the parallels to the principles of Regenerative Economics laid out here.

The exciting and somewhat startling thing is that we discovered this convergence after I had deduced the eight principles from more qualitative academic research and intuition, reinforced by our study of real-world initiatives and my direct experiences, particularly in regenerative agriculture. This discovery strongly affirms our confidence in the conceptual framework we are proposing. It's a start. Further developing and then adapting these measures to local and bioregional scale economies, and ultimately using them to help manage the global economy, as well as constructing supportive public policy prescriptions, is the exciting work still ahead.

MEASURES OF STRUCTURE AND FLOW

- **Regenerative Return Flows.** Assesses how much money and other resources the system recycles into building and maintaining its internal capacities, including human capital as well as physical infrastructure. The Finn cycling index, for instance, measures how much of the flow is cycled flow, while others have enhanced our understanding of all the fluxes generated by nutrient cycling.[134] Using a comprehensive cycling index (CCI), we may be able to quantify appropriate dividend rates for different business models before causing damage to the health of the organism. In a similar way, insufficient government reinvestment in economic vitality can be measured as the basis for fiscal policy decisions.

- **Robust Cross-Scale Circulation.** Assesses how rapidly and well resources reach all levels. Such aggradation can be measured by Flux Density, multiplier effects, or Total System Throughput (which is the flow network equivalent of GDP).

- **Reliable Inputs.** Assesses how much risk and uncertainty there are for the critical resource, information, and monetary flows upon which the system depends. This can be measured as a ratio of renewable inputs to total inputs or using an "Emergy" analysis.

- **Healthy Outflows.** Assesses how much damage the system's outflows do externally to the wider system within which the economy is embedded.

MEASURES OF RULES, ROLES, AND RELATIONSHIPS

- **Diversity of Roles.** Assesses both the diversity and the number of players in different activities critical to system functioning, for instance, the number of grocery stores, banks, hospitals, or schools in a given area with a particular population.

- **Distribution of Sizes or Resources.** Assesses where money and resources go. Can be plotted using weighted distribution of stocks or flows.

- **Degree of Mutualism.** Assesses ratio of win-win versus win-lose relationships within the network, currently measured as weighted relationships.

- **Adaptability/Place on the Adaptive Cycle.** Assesses the system's readiness for change and its place in a classical S-curve cycle of development, currently measured using Fath's adaptive cycle measures.

- **Balance of Efficiency and Resilience.** Assesses the balance between levels of diversity and flexibility (resilience) and streamlining and throughput (efficiency). This metric is currently measured using Ulanowicz's "Window of Vitality" or robustness metrics as described in our "Dynamic Balance" first principle.

- **Constructive versus Exploitative.** Assesses the level of value-added and capacity-building activities versus organizational draining or gradient-degrading (exploitative) ones.

SECOND EDITION REFLECTION

This chapter was a far-reaching overview that began with practical examples documenting the evidence that Regenerative Economics is already at work in the real world. On the one hand, as mentioned up front, these examples are now a decade out of date. But I believe that they offer the reader a sense of the long expanse of time over which this transformation is taking place. An updated look at these projects would reveal both continuity and evolutionary change. The lesson in this is that there is no simple answer to the request, "show me the regenerative economy."

I find it interesting that investors and academics always want to see case studies, while entrepreneurs and genuine thought leaders simply create the ideas of the future they seek, sometimes in the face of any evidence that it is possible. This tells me that it is the imagination of "innovative, adaptive, and responsive" entrepreneurs—both intellectual and practical—that will create the regenerative economy we need. Such an economy is both everywhere seeking to unfold, and nowhere yet fully realized at the same time. One can't look at a caterpillar or a chrysalis and ask to see a butterfly!

I will offer additional examples in part 2 of the book, although I must admit I hesitate to do so. By including one, two, or ten examples, what is revealed in the concrete particular at the same time limits our individual and collective imagination. The key premise of the regenerative economy paradigm—as with all life—is that life is inherently intelligent, to quote living systems expert Fritjof Capra. Unseen potential will emerge if we simply create the conditions for health and remove major obstacles standing in the way of the natural process. Of course, concrete examples are useful to help us "see." But my overarching aim is to help us see what everyone already sees, but in a new way. A new way to see what is hidden in plain sight and waiting to unfold, enabled by our regenerative lens. The regenerative paradigm is literally a revolutionary way of seeing, thinking, and being. A change in paradigm. This feels scary to most, as we lose the foundation under our feet. But it is also an exhilarating expression of being alive and part of a process far bigger than we can understand at the same time.

This chapter also included a survey of the macro implications for public policy and even touched on what Regenerative Finance will entail. We will return to each of these essential topics for a deeper inquiry in part 2. Each of these topics deserves an entire book, beyond the scope of this conceptual introduction.

Finally, we introduced a two part framework to conceive of new measures and metrics to monitor regenerative health, based on the work of a group of science advisors led by Sally Goerner and including Robert Ulanowicz and Brian Fath. This framework is based on the science of energy flow networks (both living and also present in the nonliving—reality is fractal—such as lightning). Their work substantially predated my 2015 booklet but found strong alignment with our eight principles.

There is an inherent challenge in developing measures, metrics, and models that seek to guide Regenerative Economics policymaking in a similar way that reductionist and abstract metrics such as GDP and inflation do for neoclassical economics. Since regenerative potential is by definition unknowable in advance, what we need to measure and monitor are not so much new goals, and progress toward those goals, which would be easier. There is an important place for this, but it takes on a secondary role. Rather, we need to monitor the conditions that we believe will lead to regenerative potential and the broadly defined well-being we desire. By analogy, for human health, our doctors don't measure how fast we can run the fifty-yard dash. They monitor our heart rate, blood pressure, and other indicators of systemic health or disease, not simply the outcomes we desire. These interconnected precedent conditions, what I call intrinsic measures, represent a fundamentally different type of metric to monitor. Our principles offer us the vital clue to what we need to care about in order to create conditions for a healthy economy, organization, family dynamic, or our own self, since all are living systems.

The application of both quantitative and qualitative measures will be essential. The challenges, as we learned a decade ago, are twofold. First, the data sets that government bodies and businesses have been collecting for decades were not designed for such a purpose. For example, we know experientially when a business transaction is extractive or mutually beneficial, and even how much so. Consider the difference between Walmart or a big developer coming to town with aggressive lawyers, in contrast to a family business like a restaurant seeking to open on Main Street, sourcing products from local farmers and fishermen and creating a community gathering space for breaking bread together. We know what likely happened, but there is no data to tell us anything about those profoundly different historical development processes and economic exchanges. And it would be unfair simply to say "big is bad." It's much easier to measure the ex post impacts on abstractions such as "jobs," which tell us little about the true impact on community well-being. And second, since this approach represents a paradigm shift, there is little if any funding available to make a serious effort toward developing the necessary data sources and modeling work. Perhaps big data, citizen data on the blockchain, and even warm data combined with AI will change the possibilities and economics of this project soon.[135] I will be keen to return to what the vital insights energy flow network science can offer brilliant and ambitious researchers when combined with next generation tools such as blockchain, and with carefully and wisely tuned AI agents. A holistic approach to economic health measurement and modeling is an urgent next step in the development of Regenerative Economics as a discipline.

In the meantime, there is no reason we cannot continue to make progress through experimentation based solely on the guidance offered by our first principles of regenerative vitality as our compass. By analogy, when one is lost in the forest, one only needs two things. First, knowledge of where one wants to head, and second is an accurate compass. Our destination is to become healthy and whole, that is to thrive in all of its diverse manifestations. It's a state of being, not a checklist. The eight first principles of the regenerative paradigm offer just such a true north and a compass with which we can begin to walk.

There is nothing more difficult to plan, nor more
dangerous to manage, than the creation of a new
system. For the creator has the enmity of all who would
profit by the preservation of the old system and merely
lukewarm defenders in those who would gain
by the new one.

—*NICCOLO MACHIAVELLI*

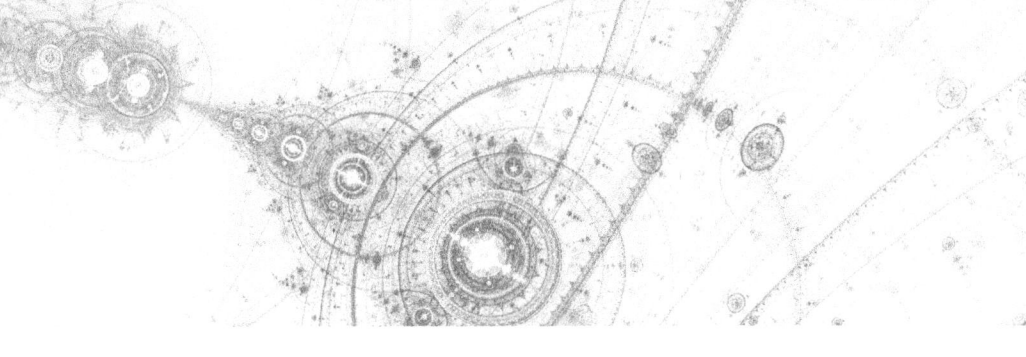

CHAPTER FIVE

CREATING A REGENERATIVE CIVILIZATION

We believe that regenerative economies are the natural next step in economic evolution, bringing economics into alignment with our latest scientific understanding of how the living universe actually works. We already see expressions of regenerative efforts emerging all around us, although they are often invisible to those observers still trapped in the outdated reductionist paradigm. Until now, this transition has been hampered by the lack of an effective story.

We believe the vision of regenerative economies—informed by practical experience, built around evidence-based first principles and patterns of systemic health, anchored in scientific rigor, and reinforced by the insights from universal wisdom traditions and a commonsense moral framework—can provide the foundation for the narrative we need at this critical juncture. Of course, more context-relevant language and nuance will need to be developed for a diversity of audiences that must hear this new story.

The centerpiece of this story is that systems that last in the real world are systems that are healthy, regenerative energy flow networks. They follow a consistent pattern, one in alignment with the eight principles described herein. Such a pattern and principles are not absolute truth. As the Buddhist parable suggests, they are fingers pointing at the moon, not to be confused with the moon.

Sustainability, indeed thriving and abundance, is an outcome or a miraculous by-product of the regenerative process, based on a system design that follows this universal pattern.

Therefore, since human economies are also energy flow networks, we suggest that the best and likely only way to achieve lasting prosperity and well-being is to build healthy *human networks following these same universal patterns*, ones capable of generating widespread social and economic vitality across all levels of society. Today's science of regenerative systems shows us how to achieve such widespread well-being by both identifying the universal principles that support durably vibrant systems and giving us precise measures and targets to guide our steps.

The contrast between this story of how to build a healthy economy and today's dominant neoliberal extreme expression of neoclassical economics is striking. While democratic, free enterprise systems theoretically promote widespread empowerment and well-being, today's laissez-faire version of capitalism is failing because it promotes largely erroneous beliefs about how to create a healthy economy. Comparing this failing theory with the regenerative vision is instructive:

SYSTEMIC VS. REDUCTIONIST THEORY	
REGENERATIVE THEORY (SYSTEMIC)	**CONVENTIONAL THEORY (REDUCTIONIST)**
Focuses on how the system grows as the key to long-run prosperity, not the growth of the system per se.	Focuses on the growth of the system measured by GDP as the path to prosperity.
Acts in ways that support the long-term health of the whole society and planet, with feedback loops designed into the system to ensure systemic health rather than treating the symptoms of ill health after the fact.	Acts in ways that tend to benefit the wealthy and powerful, often at the expense of harm done to other parts of the system, subject only to after-the-fact mitigation by government policy.
Maximizes long-term health by ensuring equitable benefits to all stakeholders.	Maximizes profits to owners by minimizing benefits to other stakeholders and then relying on government programs to fill the gaps (or not).

SYSTEMIC VS. REDUCTIONIST THEORY	
REGENERATIVE THEORY (SYSTEMIC)	**CONVENTIONAL THEORY (REDUCTIONIST)**
Values the long-term vitality of human beings and essential ecosystem function.	Values money and short-term profit ahead of human beings and the environment.
Circulates money/wealth/information robustly.	Concentrates money/wealth/information increasingly, subject only to regulation/redistribution debates after the fact.
Balances the freedom upon which innovation thrives, and the constraints necessary for collaborative community, by building self-regulating mechanisms into the design of the system that are aligned with the principles of systemic health.	Polarized debate over the value of individual freedom (laissez-faire) versus the need for government regulation in response to market deficiencies. Added regulation comes after the damage is done, with all the unintended consequences such a reactive approach entails.
Maintains long-term health by balancing a variety of critical but competing factors.	Increases owner and superstar profits by maximizing scale and efficiency enabled by technology.
Centers on reciprocity, mutual benefit, and common cause.	Stresses selfishness and effective exploitation of land and labor for the benefit of capital.
Invests long term in people and common-cause infrastructure.	Long-term investment (capital recycling) displaced by short-term extractive speculation and manipulation of the system benefitting a small elite.
Argues that addressing social, economic, and environmental crises provides an excellent way to increase both profits and economic health.	Ignores looming social, economic, and environmental crises, arguing that profits and growth must come first because they are the key to economic strength.

The broad shift in vision accompanying Regenerative Economics will be just as profound as the one Copernicus precipitated when the revelation that the Earth traveled around the Sun undermined the infallibility of medieval authorities and changed our view of how the world worked. Our transition will be filled with profound and frightening challenges. To meet these challenges, we have offered a new story, a synthesis of many thinkers' insights with the actions of entrepreneurs manifesting this change on the ground into a coherent and scientifically rigorous economic theory. It provides a hopeful and credible alternative to the pessimism our current and looming global threats can instill, the uncritical techno-optimism we are genetically wired to believe in no matter how irrational, and the naive head-in-the-sand denial that is all too prevalent today.

This scientifically rigorous yet intuition-sourced and heartfelt theory of whole-system economics will enable us to manifest the vast unseen potential for cross-scale vitality lying dormant in human systems. When individuals tap into this latent potential, we say they have activated their innate genius. We are suggesting that a similar genius lies dormant in entire human networks—in the entire global economy—waiting to be activated at systemic scale. This is the promised great hope of Regenerative Economics!

Systems science tells us that systems only truly change in response to pressure. A new awareness of regenerative design principles and patterns coupled with accelerating pressure for change due to accelerating ecological, social, political, and economic crises will make reforms that seem impossible today become inevitable.

When properly articulated, the new narrative will break down seemingly intractable barriers. This, in turn, can help us transcend some of our false ideological divides and make breakthroughs in our broken politics more feasible. For example, the new framework can help both the Left and the Right see that the ideological battle between "free markets with little government" and "big government with regulated markets" is largely a false choice. The real choice is between effective and ineffective tools, and effective and ineffective system design.

My belief is that this new Regenerative Economics framework will change the debate and forge profound public policy changes in the U.S. and around the world. For example, where conservatives and liberals, Wall Street chieftains and central bankers, mayors and labor union leaders currently argue over how best to foster ever-increasing yet undifferentiated economic growth, in the future economic debates will center on how best to foster regenerative development that is aligned with how economic flow networks actually work.

In short, this new narrative illuminates a pathway to transcend our broken national and global politics and get to the urgent work at hand. It is now our choice whether to embark down this path. Our long-run prosperity and our very survival both depend on nothing less than a once-in-the-history-of-civilization transformation to a regenerative civilization based on a holistic worldview. Yet at the same time, it is a return to something loosely familiar to all of us, since we are all indigenous at the core.

This is the Great Work awaiting us in the twenty-first century.

CHANGING THE DREAM

> "Your people dreamed of huge factories, tall buildings, as many cars as there are raindrops in this river. . . . Now you begin to see that your dream is a nightmare."
> [Interviewer:] How might we make things better?
> "That's simple. All you have to do is change the dream. . . . You need only plant a different seed, teach your children to dream new dreams."
>
> —ELDER OF ECUADOR'S SHUAR TRIBE, 1991

Working with enlightened entrepreneurs on real-world projects and discovering a solid empirical foundation for a new theory of Regenerative Economics has given me hope. It has made me confident in the dream of a rich plurality of regenerative cultures, each unique to the context of place. It offers the promise of a regenerative civilization, and an answer to the question, why are we here? While the destination feels clear, the path remains unknowable. The work is just beginning.

But it is more than a dream. In the face of accelerating darkness, I see cracks everywhere and the light of regeneration unfolding, often hidden in plain sight. As Leonard Cohen understood, "There is a crack in everything. That's how the light gets in."

What an amazing time to be alive, filled with both profound challenge as well as unprecedented possibilities.

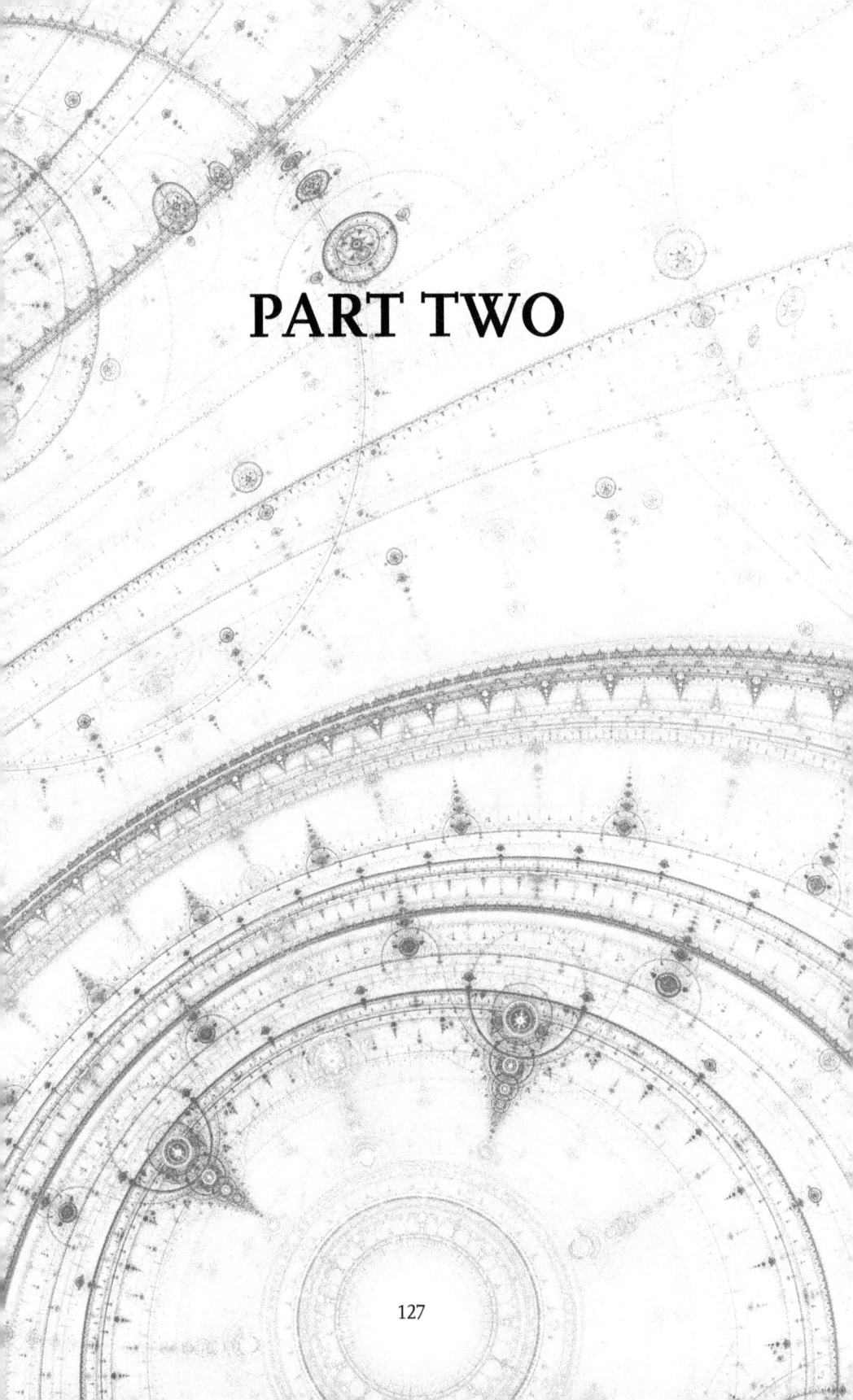

PART TWO

> We shall not cease from exploration
> And the end of all our exploring
> Will be to arrive where we started
> And know the place for the first time.

—T. S. Elliot

CHAPTER SIX

INTRODUCTION TO PART TWO:
A Decade of Learnings and a Theory of Change

Since introducing the idea of a regenerative economy based on living systems science in 2015, I have encountered further learnings and experiences that have only reinforced my convictions. First and foremost, the congruity of the regenerative paradigm with my growing awareness of indigenous ways of being from different parts of the world continues to amaze me. Our latest science remarkably affirms what our indigenous elders somehow had always intuited. This becomes clear when we compare recent evidenced-based science with the indigenous teachings of origin stories and natural laws guiding how to live in harmony with nature and one another. Not surprisingly, the language is different. But the underlying common understanding now between science and ancient spirit of the interconnection and interdependence with a single whole living organism we are all a part of, not apart from, is breathtaking. Similarly, our latest science clearly validates many of our ancient wisdom traditions, including, in particular, neo-Confucianism and the Bhagavad Gita, but certainly not limited to them. Our wisdom is literally coming full circle after all our exploring, and we are arriving "where we started," as T. S. Eliot foresaw. Perhaps, if we are finally ready, we may "know the place for the first time." What an awe-inspiring moment in the long evolution of the human project!

Leading cosmologists Jude Currivan and Brian Swimme refer to the integration of ancient knowledge systems and our latest evidence-based story of how the universe came to be, and our co-creative role in it, as the "Unitive Narrative." We will soon hear more about this worldview that better explains our interdependent, self-organizing, and networked reality than the mechanistic "clockwork universe" metaphor of the Newton worldview, which has defined the narrative of modernity. Remarkably, we are living through a change of era, more profound and with far greater consequences, than the shift from the medieval era to the modern era five centuries ago.

As discussed in the reflection at the end of chapter 3, I'm pleased with how well the eight "first principles" of regenerative vitality have held up to the test of time. It would be easy to add more principles, for example, a principle describing the fractal patterns we notice in living systems. But I've chosen to keep to eight and would shrink the number if I could without losing too much in order to facilitate communication. There is always a trade-off between too much and too little detail. I'm sure we will find new and better ways to communicate, using linear language, about the regenerative paradigm in the context of an economy. As a reminder, breaking down a complex whole into its essential parts—in this case, into eight first principles—is the reductionist method. We do that to enhance understanding. But we must always remember that the parts are interconnected and together contribute to a greater whole. It is the whole that is what evolution teaches us that manifests regenerative potential. The singular interconnected mandala appears again here for ease of reference (see figure 6.1).

In part 2, I'd first like to clarify some confusion over the process of regeneration and my proposal for Regenerative Economics. After expanding upon our understanding of the regenerative process, I will more fully distinguish Regenerative Economics (RE) from Ecological Economics (EE) in particular, a topic that is not well understood and is often confused, even in the field of new economic thinking inspired by ecology. In brief, EE offers the critical leap over the fence represented by the challenge of ecological overshoot. The economy, Herman Daly instructed, is a wholly owned subsidiary of the biosphere and not the other way around. RE, on the other hand, begins

ALIGNMENT WITH LIFE'S PRINCIPLES UNLOCKS REGENERATIVE POTENTIAL

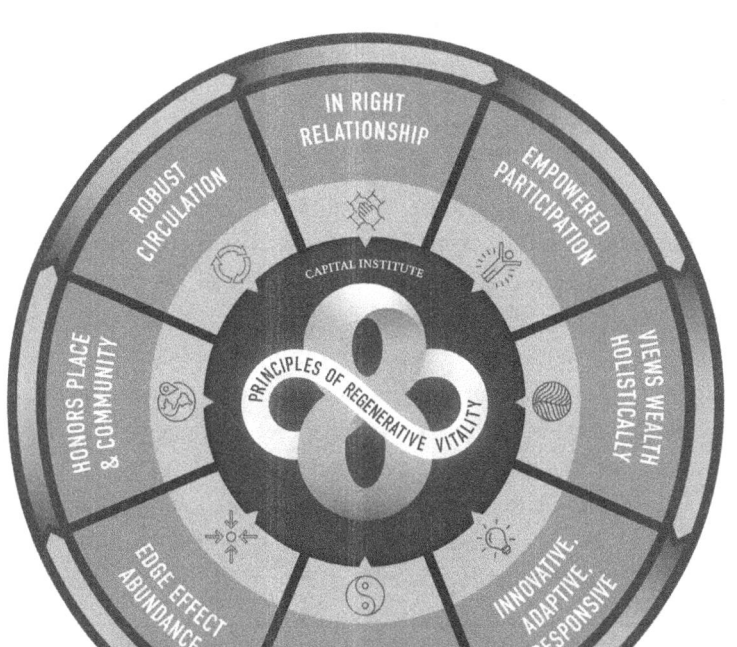

■ **Figure 6.1 Eight Principles of Regenerative Vitality.** *Credit:* John Fullerton, Capital Institute.

on the EE side of the fence and then discovers a second fence on the horizon. A leap over this second fence is a leap beyond the materialist Newtonian paradigm into an entirely new world. It is the world of life inclusive of materialism but not limited to materialism alone, as we will explore.

I could write an entire book on the many intellectual and experiential learnings that have benefited my understanding over this past decade, many of them from seeing, investing in, and collaborating with real projects on the ground. But mostly from struggling—

this is hard work. Intellectually, Sandy Wiggins, Jude Currivan, and most recently Federico Faggin have illuminated for me the primacy of consciousness, out of which manifests everything we consider reality. I have also gained an appreciation for the importance of nonergodic design for ecosystems of enterprises seeking to become antifragile, thanks to the work of Graham Boyd, author with Jack Reardon of *The Ergodic Investor and Entrepreneur*, to the antifragile brilliance of the Mondragón cooperatives in the Basque country of Spain.[136] However, for this book, I choose to significantly expand on the institution of the commons only briefly referenced in part 1. The commons, broadly defined to include both the natural and technological commons, as we shall see, is an entire category missing from conventional economics and vital to both the emergence and self-governance of regenerative economies. Most important, we will discover the systemic solution to ever-rising inequality within a free enterprise system.

I then offer some brief reflections on technology itself, also missing from the first edition. With the rise of AI into our daily awareness, nothing perhaps is more critical than to begin to imagine what regenerative technology might mean, and if it's even possible. I believe that it most certainly is, again if we first develop our perception so that we can see it, and how it differs.

I then turn to where I started on this journey, to the financial system and the obstacle that I call the "finance algorithm." This refers to the ideology, the values, the mechanics, models, and metrics that now constitute accepted practice of finance. I continue to see this finance algorithm with its grip on the mainstream economy as perhaps the critical obstacle holding back the emergence of regenerative economies. What's changed is my conviction about the importance of loosening the grip that the finance algorithm has on the entire system and therefore our lives. Remarkably, in the wake of the 2008 financial crisis, the finance algorithm has completed its embedding in our leading technology protagonists and platforms and has only gotten more dangerous as a result in the past decade. I close out part 2 with a chapter outlining a public policy agenda, and then a call to action for us all. These proposals naturally stem from a theory of change that has evolved during this past decade.

THEORY OF CHANGE

There is a saying attributed to the Marxist political theorist Fredric Jameson that it is easier to imagine the end of the world than the end of capitalism. I'll extend the challenge significantly by saying not only late-stage capitalism but the entire reductionist logic of the materialist paradigm upon which both capitalism and socialism and everything in between are built.

The challenge to change the system is immense, and I have long taken comfort in Dana Meadows's instruction not to allow the lack of an implementation plan to interfere with the articulation of a compelling vision, the essential first step in system change. But I can offer here my best attempt at a credible theory of change. It rests on three pillars.

First, I draw heavily on Dana's seminal article, "Places to Intervene in a System."[137] Hunter Lovins was present in a workshop when someone asked, "So Dana, how do we change a system?" Dana had been growing frustrated at the conversation that was missing an effective change strategy, so she jumped up and spontaneously wrote in ascending order of importance about nine key leverage points. Those later emerged in the article as the twelve leverage points detailed on the left side of figure 6.2.

The key insight Dana was illuminating was that while there are many critical leverage points where we can intervene to change a complex system, too often we focus on the ones with lesser impact than the ones with the greatest impact. For example, you can see that our efforts for more transparent metrics, the theory of change driving the move to require companies to report on ESG measures, is down at number six—information flows. We should not be surprised that this leverage point alone, while certainly important, has failed to transform the system on its own. Even new goals, listed up at number 3, such as the SDGs and the numerous attempts to replace GDP, sit below the most powerful leverage points. It is the paradigm within which the system exists that is the most powerful leverage point, and of course even harder, the ability to let go and transcend paradigms. This is pillar one of my theory of change and underlies all my work on Regenerative Economics. It represents a profound shift in paradigm.

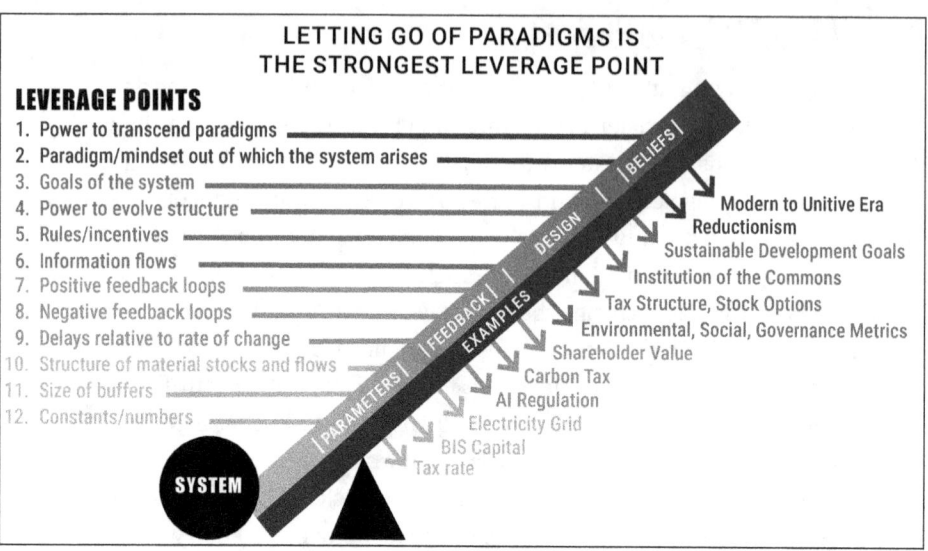

■ **Figure 6.2 Leverage Points: Places to Intervene in a System.** *Credit: Donella Meadows, The Donella Meadows Project, Academy for Systems Change.*

The second pillar comes from Monica Sharma, a systems thinker and a true force of nature best known for her work with the United Nations helping to solve the AIDS crisis in Africa. Monica explains that there are three levels of work involved in making change. First are the problems we are seeking to address, the outer layer of her three concentric circles. Many of us wake up in the morning and work on some problem we are looking to solve. Then there is the level of consciousness, the inner circle. Some people understandably believe that to improve the world, raising the level of collective consciousness is the highest leverage point. Think of a monk meditating for hours every day. Finally, Monica explains, there is a third layer, a circle between the inner and outer circles. This is the systems layer, what systems scientists and system architects are focused on. The level of consciousness is what gives rise to the system we create and allow to persist, and the system design is precisely what creates the problems we find as a result of that system. So, for example, climate change is the result of our consciousness that sees humans as separate from our environment, leading to our reductionist approach to neoclassical economics that fails to see that upsetting the carbon cycle balance has consequences that undermine the health of not only the economy but all life on Earth. And here is Monica's lesson for us. To make real change in the world, we must work across all three of these layers at the same time—no easy task. The inner work of higher consciousness, the systems design focus, and, getting our hands dirty with real practical work on the ground that both keeps it real and, critically, contributes to our ongoing learning.

The final pillar of my theory of change is very empowering to us all. It comes from Ilya Prigogine, the father of chaos theory and a winner of the Nobel Prize in Chemistry. He explains, "When a complex system is far from equilibrium, small islands of coherence in a sea of chaos have the capacity to shift the entire system to a higher order." This means when we build communities of practice, when we learn to learn together through our higher and a more holistic understanding of intelligence, and through practical experience on the ground, we can make a difference. We can and do contribute to shifting the system, even if we can't see the direct cause and effect. All the islands of coherence matter, from the B Corp movement and Conscious Capitalism to Spencer Bebe's "nature states" of bioregionalism. When a system is unstable, as our economic system most certainly is today, our work in these "islands of coherence" matters most, even when we can't quite see how. What caused the Berlin Wall to fall when it did? We may never know. The point is, we are not dependent upon some top-down seemingly immovable power to direct change. This is the science of systems change, and it should be very empowering to all changemakers.

In sum, we must tackle the difficult paradigm shift as job one, for everything follows from that. We must anchor our individual and collective work through an intentional commitment to the higher consciousness necessary to shift paradigms, but at the same time address the system design that creates the problems we care about in the first place. And we need to dig in with real-world challenges, bringing this higher consciousness to the organizations that will define our daily experiences of the real work on the ground rather than stay isolated in some ivory tower. Finally, we must believe in the power of our "islands of coherence" and seek to link up with the plethora of other islands, weaving a web of change infrastructure that can shift the entire system.

It's not how big you grow, it's how you grow big.

— *Jane Jacobs*

CHAPTER SEVEN

MISUNDERSTANDINGS ABOUT REGENERATION

I would like to address three misconceptions about the meaning of regeneration and my work since publication a decade ago. These all have direct implications on understanding Regenerative Economics, and what needs to be properly understood as its servant, Regenerative Finance. More broadly, this confusion undermines the paradigm shift awaiting institutions, organizations, and communities of all shapes and forms, across the private sector, the public sector, the nonprofit sector, and even new sectors that don't yet exist on any meaningful scale, such as the institution of the commons sector we will turn to in chapter 9. And critically, it undermines our ability to even ask the right questions. For example, what would regenerative technology look like, and why is the institution of the commons sector, comparable in scope and scale to the private sector and the public sector, essential if our economy is ever to be truly regenerative? We will examine these questions below.

The first confusion is fundamental; we must clarify the scientific meaning of the term itself. The second confusion is to conflate "first principles" of a system design with ethical or moral principles, from human values such as "truth," or personal intentions such as "excellence," to a political ideology that emerges from such values.

And finally, regeneration is often misunderstood as simply an environmental thing, or an agriculture thing. While both are true, this misses the more profound idea, an idea that if we grasp and fully embrace it, offers reason for hope grounded in scientific reality as we meet the existential interconnected crises we now call the polycrisis, certain to accelerate in the years ahead. It is therefore no mere academic exercise. There is no avoiding the chaos of the transformation that has surely begun. It is vital that we meet it with an accurate understanding of what regeneration means.

THE SCIENCE OF REGENERATION

Let's begin with the science, which has evolved dramatically since Charles Darwin's foundational work on biology and evolution. In fact, while the discipline of ecology also has its roots in the nineteenth century, it's a young, largely twentieth-century science and continues to evolve to this day. The term ecosystem was first used in 1935, but it was not until Eugene Odum and Howard Odum published Fundamentals of Ecology in 1953 that the integrative study of ecosystems with humans embedded in them became a formal discipline within the academy. It's fair to say that modern systems ecology as a stand-alone discipline began with the Odum brothers. We can see the influence of Newton again by observing that the pioneers of biology, including Darwin with all his brilliance and breakthrough thinking, were primarily focused on the parts (species) rather than the whole (ecosystems). I am not a scholar, but as I see the hierarchies of knowledge, biology should sit within ecology, but since biology came first, this is not the case. Here is yet further evidence in my mind of our vital need to learn to see wholes, more aligned with Goethe than Newton. To this day, we remain overly preoccupied with the parts, often without being conscious that we even have a choice to focus first on the primacy of relationships that constitute the "whole" rather than the parts.

In 2024, renowned systems scientist and physicist Fritjof Capra announced a "new synthesis" of his decades of work and multiple books on a systems view of life in a short, accessible article titled "Principles of Life."[138] In it, he summarized in easy-to-understand language what he sees as the four systemic principles of life: First, life organizes itself in networks; second, life is regenerative; third, life is creative; and fourth, life is intelligent. Let's have a closer look.

"Life organizes itself in networks." The web of life description of the structure of how life is organized is Capra's greatest contribution to our understanding and is well-known among ecologists and living systems scientists of all specialties. The network metaphor now extends beyond biological and ecological systems to social systems as well. Indeed, the network is slowly replacing the machine metaphor of our previously understood "clockwork universe" that dates to Newton, most prominently of course in the technology sector of the economy. Critically, the living networks in ecosystems are self-organizing and emergent, rather than being built by an outside force. This makes life and living systems profoundly different than machines, including our human technologies made by toolmakers, engineers, and financiers. The money system, the telecommunications system, the internet, and now AI are technologies, not living systems themselves.[139] As with all human technologies, it is up to us how we choose to use them that determines their impact on our lives.

"Life is inherently regenerative." This, of course, is the foundation of the entire idea of this book. What is worth emphasizing is that this description of the process of life has now risen to one of four first principles in Capra's thinking, deeply reinforcing the logic of a regenerative economy in my mind. If the process of life—meaning how it works—is regenerative, the process of an economy, too, must be regenerative if we are to have an economy aligned with how life works. Beyond mere sustainability, the flourishing we desire for an economy, just as we experience it in the natural world, is the outcome of this regenerative process.

"Life is inherently creative." For me, this principle defines the essence of life. The creativity of life manifests through a process known as emergence. This is how organisms and entire systems change and evolve in response to pressure and possibility. Their essential and ongoing innovation is adaptive and responsive to the changing context to remain living systems and not become dead or collapsed systems. The further implication of this principle is that since humans are part of life, the essence of our humanity is our creativity. Think about that the next time you hear about the singular importance of STEM education. We are losing sight of the all-important balance, but in the end, the primacy of our creativity.

"Life is inherently intelligent." Coming as evidence-based science and not merely an abstract belief, this insight demands that we pause in complete awe. I consider it the miracle of life. It replaces our now outdated Cartesian understanding that the mind is a thing (inside our brain is the typical assumption), separate from our body, matter, and the world around us. Instead, Capra instructs, mind itself is seen as a process known as cognition, the process of knowing. Imagine the web of life as intelligent. And if we choose to believe the latest thinking from cosmology being proposed by Currivan and Swimme, which resonates deeply with me, we live in a living universe, so the universe itself is intelligent too!

I now refer to Capra's succinct synthesis in my teaching. Keep in mind that again we have broken down a single complex whole that we call "life" into four component "first principles" to better understand it and then express it in linear language, even bullet points. But this is our ever-present companion reductionist thinking again. In reality, "life" is all one thing. More precisely, it is *one creative, dynamic, intelligent, and evolving regenerative process, embedded in a fractal structure of interwoven networks*. Whenever we try to dissect it, we necessarily lose some of the magic.

Clearly "regeneration" is a real, evidence-based phenomenon, the inherent process of life itself. Regeneration is life. It is most certainly not just a new name for sustainability, with all the confusion around the meaning of sustainability. This is not, however, a rejection of all the authentic and useful meanings of the concept of sustainability. As I see it, and others may differ, regeneration includes and then steps beyond our understanding of sustainability. In fact, I see sustainability (and much more) as an outcome of the regenerative process.

Misunderstandings About Regeneration

But this is the key insight. To attach this living systems process to our economic system design is, dare I say, a profound break from the reductionist thinking of scientific materialism.[140] It is profound precisely because the discipline of economics remains largely built on the outdated Newtonian logic of a machine that can be "optimized" through ever greater productivity and efficiency, limited to what we can see and measure (materialism) absent possibilities not yet manifest in the material world. Consider one example to illustrate this point. When Einstein's parents first met, the *potential* of $E = MC2$ became real along with all the progress that it manifested. But it was absent from a materialist worldview until Einstein derived the equation. What else is lying in wait, simply as unmanifested potential that will change everything? This is how life has always evolved, and we are part of that process, not limited to the current workings and limited possibilities of a machine.

IMPLICATIONS FOR ECONOMICS

Let us digress here to concretely apply the implications of the science to economics before moving on to the other confusions. To review, I have reduced the logic into three simple premises that now provide the foundation for a theory of Regenerative Economics:

- The human economy is a living system.
- There are patterns and first principles that explain how all living systems work.
- If the human economy is to be not only "sustainable" but genuinely healthy and to thrive over the very long run, it, too, will need to be designed and operate in accordance with these same patterns and principles that explain how all life actually works in the real world.

Let us examine each one in order.

The first premise, the economy is a living system, demands the most attention. Everything flows from it. We can begin by saying that it is self-evident that the economy is a system, what we call the economic system. It is, therefore, either a living system or a nonliving system. Examples of living systems include a tree, a forest, a human being, a human family, and, I would suggest, any ecosystem of interconnected and interdependent living and nonliving phenomena. Remember, a forest is interconnected and interdependent with the minerals in the soil, which have their source in the mountain rock above the forest and the rainfall that washes the minerals down the river system; similarly, the forest creates clouds that in turn create the rain that washes down the mountainsides. This hydrological cycle is essential to the health and "regenerative potential" of the entire ecosystem. In a similar way, for human organizations to thrive as living systems, they, too, must be understood as interdependent and interconnected through a similar regenerative process.

Examples of nonliving systems include a computer, the internet, the phone system, and transportation systems. None of these are self-organizing, self-fueling, or self-regulating. They are tools and technologies. In other words, they are machines, the products of the genius and reductionist logic of human engineering. But they evolve only when we design them and power them to do so, when we change the algorithm. With poor design or loss of power, they simply stop. With living systems, we can have all degrees of health or disease, but they don't require human engineering to run in the first place. An organism with cancer is still living until the cancer subsumes the host, at which point it becomes a dead system, or a system that has collapsed. We can understand the organism with cancer as a living but diseased organism in a stage of collapse.

My argument is that the human economy is made up of human beings and their tools and technologies, manifested by their human ingenuity. Those technologies range from the knife and fork to the wheel and bicycle, from the steel mill to the widget factory, and all the way to the silicon chip and computers, the software that runs them, and now artificial intelligence.[141] If you're not convinced, perhaps hearing this distinction between life and machines, between computers with their software, between artificial intelligence and the human mind coming from Federico Faggin, the man who literally invented the microchip, will persuade you.[142] Importantly, the human economy is also embedded in the far grander living system we (overly) simplistically refer to as the biosphere. One pattern we observe in living systems is that they are fractal, with patterns repeating across scales. Such fractal patterns define holism, which explains how there are wholes embedded in greater wholes across our known reality. For example, there are "wholes" known as cells embedded in larger wholes we call organs, embedded in whole subsystems like our cardiovascular system, which in turn are embedded in entire organisms and all the way up to ecosystems and even the biosphere. Note, we can go all the way down to the atom (and protons, neutrons, and electrons), all in "right relationship," and all the way up to the universe made up of billions of (perhaps more than a trillion) galaxies!

As such, we see one essential and fundamental reality that our modern economics grounded in a Newtonian worldview, and the institutional structures, guiding policies, and resulting practices, totally ignores: The human economy must be understood as embedded in the larger whole of human society, which in turn is embedded in the *process* that manifests the evolution of the biosphere.

More accurately, we should refer to this greater living system as the "Gaiasphere," in accordance with the Gaia hypothesis first introduced by chemist and earth scientist James Lovelock and evolutionary biologist Lynn Margulis. According to this hypothesis, the more conventional spheres (in a reductionist sense) consisting of the atmosphere (air), the hydrosphere (water), the geo or lithosphere (rock/mineral), and the biosphere (living organisms) combined with the four biogeochemical cycles (the carbon cycle, the nitrogen cycle, the water cycle, and the phosphorus cycle) create a complex interacting system of cycles and feedback loops that create the conditions for self-organizing, self-maintaining life on our "living" planet, Gaia. Initially considered a radical extreme idea, the so-called Gaia hypothesis has found increasing acceptance even within the reductionist scientific community. It points to one process, the process we call life as now understood by Capra and other twenty-first-century scientists from evolutionary biology and even cosmology.[143]

The Gaia hypothesis also just so happens to align with the core belief of indigenous wisdom that sees "Mother Earth" as a living being, inseparable from human beings. Isn't it remarkable that our latest Western science is affirming what we have somehow always known, in contrast with the more limited vision of separate parts, what we thought we knew coming out of the "Enlightenment"? In other words, despite the extraordinary advances in science dating to Newton and the entire Scientific Revolution, our discoveries have been discoveries of partial truths for the most part. The more we have discovered, especially at the dawn of the twenty-first century, the more we align with the truths of many of our ancient wisdom traditions. Within this emerging unified view, scientific discoveries continue to boggle the mind.

In summary, our premise is the human economy is a living system, made up of human beings and their technologies. As with all life, the economy is embedded in the larger living social systems of human cultures and societies, bioregions, and ultimately the entirety of the system known as Gaia. It's important to observe the two distinct assertions here. Embeddedness can exist without understanding the economy as a living system, just as a (nonliving) prosthetic limb can be embedded in a living body. We are suggesting here that both are true. The economy itself is a living system—albeit an unhealthy one today—and it is embedded in the larger living system we call the Gaiasphere in accordance with the fractal pattern of holism.

The second premise, that all living systems follow similar patterns and "first principles," is now generally accepted science. It's important to keep in mind that these are patterns and principles that describe how life works, not "laws" reducible to mathematics as we have in physics. Systems ecologist Robert Ulanowicz uses the helpful phrase "tendencies toward" when describing these patterns and principles. For example, human males have a tendency toward being larger than human females. That is the pattern. But that does not suggest that all males are larger than all females. Ecologists (and regenerative economists!) will always struggle to reduce the complexity of life to a finite set of principles, patterns, and a common way to communicate them. That's the nature of complexity. But this does not undermine the premise. There are common patterns and "first principles" (the irreducible things we know to be true to the best of our understanding) that describe the process of regeneration, that is, the process of life, even if we use different frameworks and words to describe them.

Let me illustrate. Biologist Janine Benyus and the Biomimicry Institute have distilled six overarching "Biomimicry Life's Principles" from an earlier set of nine "Life's Principles." These, too, are "first principles," just as our eight "first principles of regenerative vitality" developed for Regenerative Economics. A careful observation will find plenty of overlap, as expected. But we will find, as well, that context matters. For example, since the field of biomimicry has been primarily focused on product and material design, its principles naturally emphasize the key issues associated with this context. As a result, "life-friendly chemistry" is a first principle.

For the larger system of an economy, I see life-friendly (green) chemistry as embedded in the first principle of "robust circulation," which demands not only efficient circulation but also healthy inputs and healthy outputs where waste becomes food, not toxic pollution. On the other hand, since wealth is so fundamental to economics, I added a first principle "holistic wealth" even though it properly could sit within the principle of "dynamic balance." I elevate it given its importance to the context. In sum, any living systems framework must combine patterns and principles together and be relevant to the context in which it is being applied—crossing scales as large as the entire planet all the way down to a microscopic organism. There are no "laws of thermodynamics" equivalent to point to, and according to evolutionary biologist and systems scientist Dr. Stuart Kauffman, there can never be such laws. "It is fundamental to the Newtonian paradigm," Kauffman states, "that the set of possibilities that constitute the phase space is always definable and fixed ahead of time. This fails for the diachronic evolution of ever-new adaptions in any biosphere... Evolving biospheres are outside the Newtonian paradigm."[144]

Through conversations with Kauffman, Currivan, and others, I feel confident in asserting that if evolving (living system) biospheres are outside the Newtonian paradigm, then it stands to reason that the evolving global economy is too. Importantly, Kauffman is suggesting that even the break from classical physics and its simple cause and effect logic to quantum physics with the introduction of probability to explain uncertainty fails to account for what we observe with complex, ever-evolving living systems. Both classical mechanics and quantum mechanics use mathematical formalism to describe and make predictions about physical phenomena. Kauffman and Andrea Roli are suggesting that the emergence we observe in nature, including the emergence of new species to the emergence of life from the oceans onto land, cannot be reduced to mathematics and predicted with sophisticated models.

I take this as scientific validation that explains why what we call regenerative potential, the essence of the regenerative paradigm, cannot and will never be something we can accurately model and predict. Just as Benyus teaches that life creates conditions conducive to life, we must instead focus on creating conditions for life/health in our economies and trust that life—we are part of life—knows how to evolve to survive in accordance with Capra's "life is inherently creative and intelligent." As this applies to a living economy, it suggests focusing first on aligning with all of our eight principles in our system design, and the hard geophysical constraints that we know we must honor to inspire and force our creativity.

The third premise follows directly from the first two. A human economy that is healthy and whole, that is, not only "sustainable" but thriving over the long run, must follow these same patterns and principles just as an airplane design must obey the laws of gravity. Otherwise, someone needs to make the case that the human economy is the only exception to the rule that all living systems we observe in the real world follow these same patterns and design principles. This premise, for me, is a self-evident truth.

The implications demand a new understanding of leadership. Yes, of course, we must plan and create intelligent goals. But importantly, we must hold our goals lightly, monitor for where we are wrong rather than seek to prove we are right, and make room for emergence. The unexpected potential we cannot plan for is emergence. As all living systems have consistently demonstrated over vast periods of time, we know that emergence is not only possible but defines life itself. That is a radical belief, and in complete contrast to our goal-driven, outcomes-defined approach to economics, to policymaking and business (and much else), all grounded in the Newtonian paradigm.

Taken together, the conclusion is quite simple. Living systems distinguish themselves because they are living systems, not dead or collapsed systems. Life is extremely forgiving, but it has limits. The human economy has reached the limits and is now quite sick, and worse, undermining the health of its host. The symptoms are what we now call the polycrisis, and it's going exponential. Naturally, efforts have begun to "fix" the system, notwithstanding ideological distractions and outright denial of reality by some of our so-called leaders. But such fixes, while helpful, are inadequate to meet the challenge because they are engineered by the same kind of (reductionist) thinking that created the problems in the first place, to paraphrase Albert Einstein.

Wisdom would suggest that we learn how life works and align our economy with living systems design to participate in rather than extinguish the regenerative process we call life. Regeneration promises currently unseen, unknowable, and unquantifiable potential as a result of its property we call emergence. Again, drawing on Kauffman, "emergence is not engineering." When we create the conditions for life, and remove critical obstacles, the dance of creative, intelligent emergence flows naturally, in alignment with Capra's principles. Let us learn to dance with complexity.

ON FIRST PRINCIPLES

The second confusion relates to the meaning of principles. There are at least three different kinds of principles, which is the cause of misunderstanding. Only one of these three can be understood as "first principles." In my search for first principles, I am following Buckminster Fuller's lead when he said, "I'm not trying to copy nature. I'm trying to find the principles she's using."

Aristotle defined first principles as "the first basis from which a thing is known." In other words, they're the core essentials, the minimum number of qualities necessary to understand an idea or a larger "whole," the building blocks of true knowledge.[145] It's a reductionist process, in fact, reducing complexity down to its essence. So we can say that in philosophy or science, a "first principle" is an assumption or quality that cannot be deduced from any other assumption or quality.

When I talk about patterns and "first principles," therefore, I'm referring to descriptive qualities of a real thing such as a system. Such first principles may be described differently by different people all referring to the same thing in a way they think best describes the essence of the thing, but they are not subject to human preference or choice. They are our most accurate description of truth, as best we understand it. They are negotiable only when our understanding improves, not based on opinion or preferences.

A second meaning of principles relates to ethical or moral principles. Do unto others. Don't lie, cheat, or steal. Help those less fortunate than you. The list goes on. These are all human values, rules to live by that we can all choose to follow, or not. They may overlap—"right relationship" for example—and thus influence the systemic health of the economy and the biosphere within which it exists, but they are not "first principles" that describe how life itself works.

Finally, a third type of principles could be called prescriptions for action. For example, we strive for excellence. We show up on time. Our word is our bond. We always act with integrity. Overlapping with ethical principles, here again these are human choices, not empirical descriptions.

Often in "new economy" conversations and within alternative approaches to address systemic change, people conflate these moral or ethical principles and or principles dictating behavior with what I'm calling "first principles." This has created great misunderstanding of the concept of Regenerative Economics. The key point is regeneration is a real, scientific process that explains how life works. The first principles and patterns must serve as our guide, our compass we can rely on for genuine systemic transformation. Most important, they provide the secret to creating conditions that will allow potential to emerge, and even surprise us.

Let me offer an other analogy. If our ambition is a circular economy, the assumptions about reuse and recycle cannot conflict with the second law of thermodynamics. There is no perpetual motion machine! Yet we wonder why our efforts have not met with more success. In a similar way, we will and do see a plurality of regenerative economies emerging. But to be regenerative, they will need to broadly align with our first principles of regenerative vitality, even as they manifest in unique context specific ways. In a similar fashion, every snowflake is unique, but every snowflake looks like a snowflake.

RETHINK EVERYTHING: MORE THAN AN ENVIRONMENTAL OR AGRICULTURAL IDEA

"Stop, put your pencils down, and rethink everything." These were my words used from an interview that became the opening frame of *Going Circular*, an award-winning documentary about the circular economy. While that film was primarily about the idea of closing the loop in our linear take-make-waste production system in favor of reduce-reuse-upcycle-recycle, the importance of rethinking everything all at one time through a regenerative lens is the important point.

This leads directly to the third misunderstanding about the regenerative paradigm. As the word *regeneration* has now made it onto stages like Davos, most in sustainable business circles see it as an environmental or agricultural idea alone. The famous McKinsey butterfly diagram utilized in the work of the Ellen MacArthur Foundation showing agriculture products on one wing and manufacturing products on the other has accentuated this confusion. Regeneration is most certainly both an agricultural and an environmental idea. But critically, it is far more than either, notwithstanding the imperative of each. There will be no butterfly emerging out of our overstuffed caterpillar of an economy if we limit regeneration to agriculture alone. The regenerative paradigm consists of applying the process that describes how all life works to all human social systems, including the entire economic system and all the component networks and organizations that together make up the economy. Only by doing so can we change the story from the factually erroneous myth of separation that has defined so much of modernity and begin a new story for a new era. That new story is a story of connection and interdependence with all life. Any separation of agriculture from manufacturing, for example, is a fiction of our reductionist thinking. It's all connected and it's all interdependent.

The regenerative paradigm certainly begins with how we manage large landscapes across our planet, now that the human project has put itself in charge of virtually all large land and seascapes in one way or another. This includes our oceans, our forests, our soils, our grasslands, our watersheds, our mangroves and salt marshes, our coral reefs, and even the frozen poles and nearly lifeless deserts. Unfortunately, our machine age mindset has viewed all these precious bioregions as natural resources for human use and too often plunder. "There are no unsacred places," Wendell Berry instructs. "There are only sacred places and desecrated places."

Bioregional regeneration at the landscape scale must be understood as the responsibility that comes with the privilege of life. It is also the foundation of a regenerative economy. It is objectively true that damaged ecological function implies no healthy economy—notwithstanding the sacred responsibility that comes with human power to steward all ecological function as an end in itself. Note that ecological function is profoundly different than ecosystem services, an idea we will address below. Without healthy ecosystem function, from the rainforests to the grasslands and salt marshes, to our life-giving soils and to all of our sacred waterways, there is degeneration—putting all life at risk.

Most people now associate the concept of regeneration with agriculture, broadly defined. This is a good thing insofar as it goes and an extremely hopeful area of renewed interest as we begin to address the polycrisis. Regenerative agriculture practices vary, some more effective than others. They represent the most obvious application of the regenerative paradigm to the foundational sector of our economic system. Agriculture includes crops, animal husbandry, and natural fiber production, as well as silviculture (forest management), wild fishery management, and aquaculture. All these activities require management of living resources, in contrast with industrial production designed to make stuff. All are designed to meet human needs from abundance while regenerating for the future, rather than unsustainably extracting from our vital ecosystems. We can refer to all these activities as holistic management of living systems in accordance with the process of regeneration.

The key to the regenerative paradigm and understanding the potential of Regenerative Economics is not to stop with agriculture broadly defined. As I learned from Allan Savory, we must learn holistic management for everything we manage because anything we manage is by definition complex, not complicated. We manage our health, so we must learn to develop health care holistically using our same regenerative principles. Same for the built environment where regenerative development is now a well-established field thanks to pioneers such as the Regenesis Group. The education system must be transformed from the industrial model of efficient but potentially destructive silos to a holistic approach that nourishes the unique potential of every student, in alignment with their unique passions and gifts, and continuing throughout their lives as lifelong learners, just as learning and evolution never stops for Gaia.

And of course, we manage our businesses as organisms separate from the products we engineer. Unfortunately, just as with neoclassical economics before it, the formation of the academic discipline of "management science" was under the Newtonian reductionist influence as well. Most notably, Frederick Winslow Taylor's seminal *Principles of Scientific Management* (1911) set out "to prove that the best management is a true science, resting upon clearly defined laws," which led directly to the optimization and productivity logic or organizational management that still dominates our business schools and business practice.

There are revolutionaries, of course. Peter Senge and his pathbreaking book, *The Fifth Discipline* (1990), called for "learning organizations," asserting that continuous learning using a systems approach is the only sustainable competitive advantage. We will see that learning is living, and Senge's early teachers included the great Chilean biologist Humberto Maturana, who together with Francisco

Varela created the term *autopoiesis* to describe the self-generating, self-maintaining structure of living systems. Later Arie de Geus, formerly the head of strategic planning at Royal Dutch Shell, and collaborator of Senge's at MIT, wrote *The Living Company* (1997), in which he explored the characteristics of twenty-seven companies that had survived more than a century—in other words, companies that had managed to remain living. In his book, de Geus highlighted the strong identity and sense of values common to all living companies and declared that managers must shift from optimizing capital to managing companies to optimize people.

Just exactly how do we do this? It is the same for all organizations as for the larger system. We create the conditions for people—the true source of energy of all human enterprise—to thrive, in order to unlock unseen potential. This approach by Senge and de Geus, both pioneers of the regenerative paradigm even if they used different language—learning companies and living companies—is profoundly different than the "optimize the machine to maximize productivity" approach that sees people as cogs in the machine. Unfortunately, this reductionist approach, applying reductionist science not only to the making of things but to the management of complexity, which it is not suited to do, remains common in business today. I've been told that Amazon knows it will burn through its warehouse workers and builds in a recruiting pipeline to replace them because it's cheaper than addressing working conditions. But at what cost to the larger system of which Amazon is a part? Similarly, the hierarchical and rigid nature of many government agencies and bureaucracies of all kinds is ripe for reinvention, with the application of living systems design to better guide management of these complex living organisms. Just imagine the unseen costs of the cruel and lasting trauma that Elon Musk's "DOGE" process of "deleting" workers only to rehire them, mere cogs in the machine. A case study for the ages of degeneration.

In summary, the transformation to the regenerative paradigm has been underway for decades, mostly outside our field of vision. It will impact all human institutions and organizations. If we are wise, it will teach us which institutions and organizations can be reformed, which ones we must transform, and which ones no longer serve us and must be allowed to die, composting their resources into a higher and productive use. It is truly a time when we must slow down, even put our pencils down, unlearn, and relearn a more holistic, truly revolutionary way of seeing what everyone is seeing, and then rethink everything. Only in this way will we manage to wisely and effectively navigate a pathway through the polycrisis that is upon us.

The major problems in the world are the result
of the difference between how nature works
and the way people think.

—Gregory Bateson

CHAPTER EIGHT

THE REGENERATIVE PARADIGM

We have clarified what regeneration means, what "first principles" mean in the context of science and philosophy, and the vital and universal application of holistic decision-making in the management of all human institutions and sectors of the economy. We have emphasized that the concept extends beyond agriculture to all human endeavors that we manage, including to the design and management of our economic system.

The scope of our inquiry is enormous, for the economy is, for better or worse, the water we all swim in. To clarify the regenerative paradigm in the context of economic system design and responses to the polycrisis, we will need to compare and contrast it across the spectrum of economic reform ideas. We will need to distinguish it from the Newtonian paradigm of materialism, the mechanistic thinking that dominates modern life, at least in the developed Western world that is so influential in all our decision-making.

Let me state up front that while I will compare and contrast ideas and approaches to decision-making in economics and business, I am not implying a value judgment about better or worse ideas. Where we have gotten stuck is our lack of seeing different ways of thinking and a lack of discernment regarding which contexts to apply to these different modes of thinking. I hope to show how the regenerative paradigm embraces and includes the best of many other ideas. It is not in conflict with them. Rather, it embraces and extends beyond them into a profoundly different approach, since it is built on a different foundation. By analogy, there is nothing in biology or ecology that negates the laws of physics. Quite the contrary, biology and ecology must build upon these laws. Yet they extend beyond the material to the living. Nevertheless, no ecologist would say ecology is better than physics!

As a result, the regenerative paradigm doesn't easily work within the concept of a "big tent" of ideas. One cannot explain an ecosystem using physics alone. Said differently, there are many pathways to the regenerative paradigm, so long as we use an accurate compass. But without that accurate compass, we will not find the regenerative paradigm. That compass is grounded in our latest scientific understanding and even yet-to-be-tested hypotheses of how life works. It is, let me be clear, a leap.

TWO FENCES AND TWO LEAPS

Before digging into the weeds, let me present a visual of two leaps over two fences. Imagine you are standing on a ridge looking out over a vast prairie. As you scan the reality we experience in the mainstream economy, you spot a fence way off near the horizon. That fence represents the awareness of the limits to growth of the metabolism of the economic system, first introduced to the world by the MIT systems scientists in their seminal 1973 report to the Club of Rome by the same name.

That fence, still not even recognized by most of the mainstream, demanded that we rethink neoclassical economics, which was predicated on the idea that the economy was a closed system, apart from "nature." Instead, nature was merely represented as an input to the closed system. The early economists called that input "land" alongside labor and capital. Today mainstream economics refers to it as natural resources, recognizing the plethora of natural resource inputs fueling the metabolism of the economic system. Seen as a closed system, there were no feedback loops to the natural world, only a presumed substitution of inputs made possible by endless innovation to keep the "machine" efficient and expanding. There are no conceivable limits to growth this side of the fence line.

This is the world most of our leaders in the public sector and the private sector still ignorantly inhabit, although finally this is beginning to change (except for most economists, financiers, and technologists, it would seem!). But there have been great intellects questioning the premise of exponential growth on a finite planet, dating all the way back to Thomas Malthus and John Stuart Mill, both contemporaries of Adam Smith. In 1926, Nobel chemist Frederick Soddy questioned the belief that the economy could act as a perpetual motion machine, inspiring Karl Polanyi and in particular Nicholas Georgescu-Roegen, whose magnus opus, *The Entropy Law and the Economic Process* (1971), is credited by Herman Daly as the fundamental text of the field alongside Soddy's work. Daly's own *Steady-State Economics* (1977) expanded upon Georgescu-Roegen and other important economic system thinkers, most notably Kenneth Boulding making these ideas much more accessible while maintaining intellectual rigor. E. F. Schumacher was in a philosophical/spiritual category of his own, with immense influence on rethinking economics.

The field continued to develop significantly throughout the 1980s and 1990s, led by thinkers including Robert Costanza, who was the first president of the International Society for Ecological Economics and editor of its own peer-reviewed journal, and Joshua Farley, who wrote a textbook with Daly. Many of my important early colleagues and patient ecological economics tutors in addition to Daly include Peter Brown, Peter Victor, Bill Rees, Juliet Schor, Bob Nadeau, Hazel Henderson, and Tim Jackson just to name a few. The point in reviewing this detail is to illuminate the rich and long history of the discipline, today with many additional writers and thinkers building on the foundation including new frameworks such as doughnut economics, degrowth, and post-growth economics. The leading proponents of these ideas include Kate Raworth, Jason Hickel, and Hans Stegeman among others. Ecological Economics is now a rigorous discipline, although certainly not without conflicting ideas and theories of change, most notably regarding the benefits and risks of putting a price on "ecosystem services." At times, we even see ecological economics begin to bleed into Regenerative Economics. And the word *regenerative* is now in wide use and misuse, even by such companies as Walmart. This does create confusion, but that's the nature of new paradigms.

Remarkably, now half a century after the early pioneers (and a full century after Soddy), Ecological Economics remains outside mainstream economic thinking, often ignored and ostracized within the academy. In fact, despite all this history and rigorous development of the discipline, most ecological economists, Daly included throughout his life, find themselves housed outside the economics departments within universities. But five decades of concerted effort have defined what I'm calling the first leap over that first fence.

Beyond this first fence, we remain in the Newtonian paradigm of materialism, where reductionist logic coupled with probability distributions to estimate uncertainty allow us to quantify, model, and define the possibility space. But we are in a new world from the world of neoclassical economics. We are in a finite and constrained material world, the entropy law guiding with its immovable rule. We are in a world that understands the economy is fully embedded in the living world, with a need to respect nature's limits, most often expressed via the planetary boundaries framework, or overshoot before it. There is also an intentional value shift within the discipline of Ecological Economics to reintegrate social goals into the framework, evidenced by efforts such as the Genuine Progress Indicator (GPI) first introduced by Daly and Clifford Cobb in 1994 as the Index of Sustainable Economic Welfare, anticipating the entire field of alternative measures to GDP and measures of well-being that are much in vogue today. Such social objectives had been conveniently and intentionally left out of the neoclassical framework in the naive belief that growth of the pie was the business of economists, while distribution of the pie was the business of political scientists and expressed through politics. The messy and complex distribution issues were also left out of neoclassical economics because they were not easily reduced to mathematical equations and optimization algorithms. Reductionism in plain sight.

Most critically, beyond this first fence, we have brought economics back into the world of the second law of thermodynamics, which remarkably, and without explanation from my research, had been overlooked or willfully ignored by neoclassical economists, seemingly based on the belief of infinite innovation to find substitutes when scarcity arises. Some advocates of the circular economy seem unaware of the implications of the second law, with naive ideas about continuous reuse and recycling. It turns out that the first "R" of the circular economy mantra (reduce-reuse-recycle) is by far the most important one.

The reality beyond this first fence is sobering, demanding a radical rethink of our growth-driven economic system, just as the authors of *Limits to Growth* anticipated in 1972. A call to essentially shrink and share becomes the only logical response, expressed in numerous ways. Calls for "degrowth" sound logical, at least until we shrink to a scale that respects the "planetary boundaries" we looked at in the introduction where a "steady-state economy," as Daly called it, can continue sustainably into the future. Alternative measures of genuine well-being to replace the crude and inadequate GDP metric are common sense to most of us, yet remarkably difficult to embed in our policies and, most important, our behaviors.

And yet if we are honest, the future beyond this first fence feels bleak. Just the language of degrowth sounds unnatural and self-terminating, even before considering the current grossly unequal distribution of prosperity. How to shrink the total pie, more accurately the material throughput of the economy, while enabling the still materially constrained if not impoverished majority of humanity to raise their material well-being feels not only implausible but also physically, logistically, and politically impossible. That difficulty is only compounded by growing divisiveness, conflicting economic interests, and political dysfunction. The project seems doomed from the start, yet those beyond the first fence also know business as usual is unsustainable.

We must understand that the economic system, beginning with the underdeveloped economies in the Global South, to global corporate strategies and incentive systems, to state and local government budgets and their capacity to service growing demands and outstanding debts, to our retirement system, to individual human ambitions and dreams but also imperfections including greed and envy—it's all predicated on growth. Any variation of "shrink and share" as a strategy leaves us with a sense of impending dread. It feels unnatural. And of course, it is. The cycle of life—growth, decay and death, and regeneration—is how life actually works in practice.

Now imagine you trek on, desperate to find a more hopeful alternative, but hope grounded in the rigor of science. You travel across this hot and dry prairie in search of a previously unseen way out of the growth predicament, the double bind of all time. Our system is predicated on growth, yet continued growth is undermining our ability to survive, much less thrive. And the evidence is mounting by the day. As your elevation increases upon a distant plateau, you scan toward the expanded horizon and can barely make out a second, higher fence. It's a fence few have seen, and fewer dare to talk about. Those who have attempted to discuss what they see have been ignored, or worse. That second fence marks the boarder of materialism itself, the entire Newtonian paradigm. It's the edge of modernity.

Regenerative Economics, in its raw and hopeful infancy filled with fresh promise, represents a leap over that second fence. It agrees that exponential growth on a finite planet is impossible, a point shared between the fences. Yet it demands a new way to see what everyone between the fences is seeing. A revolutionary way to think beyond how Newton taught us to think. It demands a shift from relying solely on the reductionist mindset of materialism we have honed so well during the modern age, which delivered great progress. It demands of us that we distinguish between what is complicated and suitable to the use of our reductionist logic, and what is by contrast complex. Complexity is entirely different from the merely complicated. Complexity demands holistic thinking, holistic decision-making rising to holistic management. The clockwork universe metaphor must give way to a networked, living organism metaphor.

This land beyond the second fence is again a new world. But this time, it is an entirely new paradigm as well.

Let's now turn to a more granular look at the spectrum of approaches to economics and the growing awareness that demands we rethink our degenerative economic system. Regenerative pioneer Carol Sanford referred to the following four "paradigms" to help clarify the distinctions between different responses to the polycrisis. I don't see them as four paradigms. I see them instead falling within the two-fence metaphor, as I will explain below. But let's look at each concept in order first, as they are useful categories, even if the categories do not reach the level of paradigm.

Business as Usual—the extractive, degenerative mainstream economic system, built on the neoclassical economics framework. BAU applies to both socialism and capitalism, as both depend upon exponential and, perhaps to differing degrees, extractive economic growth as the source of prosperity. The former with a heavier hand of intervention by the state to address market failures, and the latter with less government intervention based on the genuine belief that regulation is too often a cure that is worse than the disease (notwithstanding ideological games and cruelty that creep up at times like now).

Arrest the Disorder—that is, stop the bleeding. The seminal report to the Club of Rome called *Limits to Growth* is foundational to this paradigm, warning of systemic "disorder" to come based on an understanding of how systems operate. Two more recent examples are the critical planetary boundaries framework developed by Johan Rockström and colleagues, and the ecological overshoot framework developed earlier by Mathis Wackernagel and Rees. Both seek to define ecological boundaries within which we must constrain economic throughput of materials and energy to "arrest the disorder" (ecosystem crises). Similarly, quantifying environmental, social, and governance (ESG) measures for corporate performance and making them transparent for both business managers and investors is a business application of this category if it is combined with context-specific limits that tell us how much is too much. So is the climate change Net Zero by 2050 agenda, and the entire circular economy movement; both are focused on arresting disorder, notwithstanding their disappointing results to date.

The field of environmental economics, with the focus on putting a price on externalities to bring them into economic decision-making, fits here. Finally, philanthropic social programs such as treatment of addiction and poverty alleviation or policy initiatives such as demanding the upgrade of municipal waste systems that overflow into rivers or a tax on carbon emissions all fit into this category. There is much work to do to arrest the disorder of our economic system! This is critical work.

Do Good—moving up the ladder from degenerative business as usual toward regenerative to define activities and models designed not only to do less harm and arrest the disorder but also to create positive impact. Do-good/impact initiatives therefore also incorporate arresting disorder. But importantly, their purpose is to drive change into positive territory, rather than just arresting disorder. This is the essence of impact, including the entire and hopeful impact investment movement, the B Corp movement, and the Net Positive concept first introduced by Forum for the Future and more recently popularized by Paul Polman and Andrew Winston,[146] moving beyond Net Zero into positive territory across a multitude of nonfinancial metrics and a critical bridge to the regenerative paradigm. I would place the United Nations' Sustainable Development Goals (SDGs) in this category as well, inclusive of arresting disorder as the goals are. By the same token, other metrics that are alternatives to GDP, and the Well-Being Economy movement, fit here. In fact, the entire field of Ecological Economics as articulated by Daly and colleagues decades ago, and associated degrowth and postgrowth ideas, all sit here and in the arrest disorder and do good categories above. Finally, numerous philanthropic initiatives fit into this category, often with no clear separation between arresting disorder and doing good. It's all important work, even though it can't be considered regenerative.

Regenerate—this fourth category is radically different. The goal shifts to creating conditions for healthy function, with the understanding that living systems in fact heal themselves and adapt and evolve as needed when the conditions are right. Recall Capra: Life is creative and intelligent. We develop goals and may set interim targets but hold them more lightly given the unpredictability of the emergent process of living systems. Static goals would, in fact, be detrimental to the regenerative process. One could think of this approach as creating conditions for getting lucky in ways we would never anticipate. Venture capitalists understand this far better than bankers, notwithstanding their singular and degenerative focus on exponential growth.

The real goal becomes unlocking presently unseen potential. In this way, the regenerative paradigm is emergent, unpredictable, and unforecastable. Recall Kauffman's contrasting of holism and reductionism: "Emergence is not engineering." Ultimately this means it is not reducible to mathematical equations and accurate forecasting. The leap over this second fence on the horizon does not ignore or negate all of the vital work between the fences. It sees this work as absolutely necessary. Yet it is insufficient to break the double bind. This second leap represents, to our logical minds, a true leap of faith. Our intuitive minds and indeed our hearts, however, feel the relief.

We sense it as a leap perhaps, but a leap into the warm embrace of the time-tested process of life. A leap into alignment with life feels natural, a coming home.

These four phases are summarized in figure 8.1 below. As we contemplate system transformation, it's important to understand that the steps to the right each incorporate and include what precedes it on the left. There is no either-or sorting. So, for example, the circular economy is fully embedded in a regenerative economy, addressing

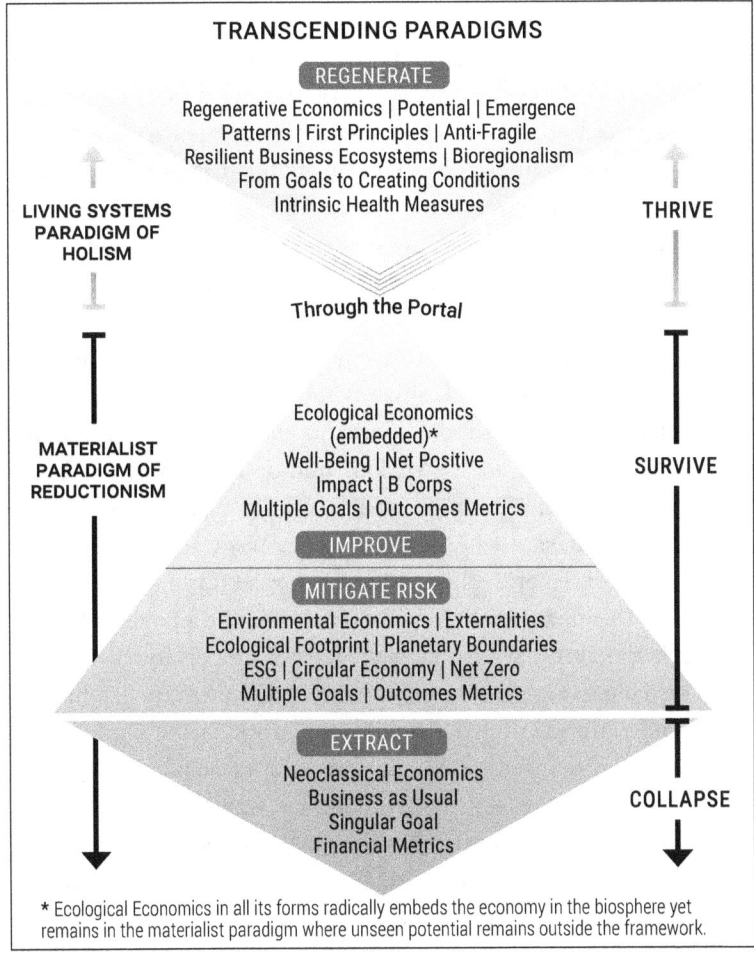

Figure 8.1 From Materialism to Living Systems Paradigm. *Credit: John Fullerton, Capital Institute, inspired by Carol Sanford.*

the matter/energy dimension of the principle of robust circulation, although neglecting the more fundamental information flows.

But as I mentioned at the beginning of this discussion, I don't see four paradigms here. I see two. The first is the Newtonian paradigm of scientific materialism. It encompasses the existing degenerative "business as usual" category, plus the leap over the first fence, which includes the categories of "arrest the disorder" and "do good." Then over the second fence we find the shift in paradigm to the holistic way of seeing and thinking that must encompass what sits before that second fence, just as biology must encompass physics and chemistry. However, the opposite is not the case. Beyond fence two includes what lies before fence two, but what lies before fence two is profoundly different from what lies beyond fence two. By analogy, the principles of ecology and biology must honor and encompass the laws of physics and the principles of chemistry, but physics and chemistry need not encompass the principles of ecology.

We can call the first paradigm that exists on either side of the first fence the materialist or mechanistic paradigm. Over the second fence is the living systems or regenerative paradigm. Jude Currivan refers to this as the Unitive paradigm, where our latest evidenced-based science remarkably affirms and expands the intuitions and teachings of our many wisdom traditions. Science and spirit reconnecting for the first time in half a millenium. Future historians will decide what it will be called, and it may take a while, just as it was a long time before the Renaissance was known as the Renaissance. But this new paradigm will certainly define a new era beyond the clockwork universe of what we today call modernity.

The old paradigm works on incremental improvements through reductionist problem-solving, what legendary sustainability pioneer Ray Anderson referred to as "climbing mount sustainability." The new paradigm represents genuine transformation beyond incremental change, a literal metamorphosis. We are seeking to emerge from the polycrisis with the caterpillar transformed into a butterfly. We just don't know what the butterfly looks like yet. We can't see it yet because it's emergent.

Our challenge is to first see the profound shift that will define this new era. A shift that continues to know how and when to use the brilliance of reductionist, mechanistic thinking to engineer what is complicated and to solve complicated problems. But a shift that at the same time invokes the wisdom to know when we are dealing with complexity and to transform our approach from reductionism to holism, from machine thinking to ecological thinking and the evidence-based, regenerative process that defines the living systems paradigm. This paradigm, as we have seen, is grounded in first aligning with living systems patterns and principles in order to create conditions and remove obstacles for the ongoing healthy function of the organism, an approach quite distinct from the problem-solving and goal-setting approach of reductionism.

Holism and living systems science are required to work with complexity. And the polycrisis is a complexity challenge, not a complicated problem to solve. As a shortcut, Allan Savory nicely observes, anything we make is complicated, while anything we manage is complex. To manage complexity, we must acquire new knowledge and then, critically, develop new muscles in our minds to recognize when to shift gears and practice holistic decision-making.

The outcomes we experience flow directly from how we make decisions. How we see and how we think drives our decision-making. Like any new habit, holistic decision-making is hard work at first. With practice and perseverance, it becomes second nature, but only after extended repetition. It's a discipline, like going to the gym.

But make no mistake. This is a revolution in how we think. It is a revolution in perception. And as the great holistic thinker Leonardo da Vinci taught us, *"All our knowledge has its origins in our perceptions."*

Together with the patrimony of nature, there is also an historic, artistic and cultural patrimony which is likewise under threat. This patrimony is a part of the shared identity of each place and a foundation upon which to build a habitable city.

—*Pope Francis,* Laudato Si': On Care for Our Common Home

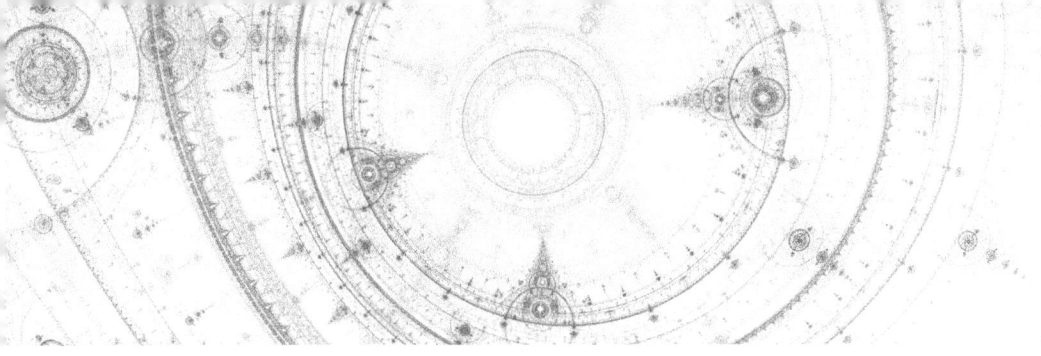

CHAPTER NINE

EPIPHANY—THE MISSING INSTITUTION OF THE COMMONS

Let's begin by returning to the work of Elinor Ostrom, whom we met in part 1. Recall that she won the 2009 Swedish Central Bank Prize in Economic Sciences (the "Nobel Prize in Economics") for her work on governance of the commons.[147] She defines common pool resources as "natural or human-made resources where exclusion is difficult and exploitation by one user reduces the resource availability for the others." Overfishing and overgrazing are the classic examples, but note that she includes both natural and human-made resources. I might modify the definition slightly to say "reduces or degrades the resource availability and quality" in order to capture, for example, what has happened to the internet as a result of the social media algorithms.

The concept of the commons dates to medieval Europe's land management practices under feudalism. Sheep grazing pastures on open land in England were managed collectively by peasants prior to them being privatized through a process known as the enclosure movement. More generally, the commons refers to any shared resource that is collectively owned, managed, and used by a community. There are many examples of a commons, from grazing lands to fisheries, to the rainforests and radiating arctic ice, to the vast atmosphere. More recently, we also think of technological commons such as the internet.

Within the overall commons concept that is now manifesting both in the natural world and the digital world, we can break down the ideas into the practice of commoning and the system architecture of the commons. The practice of commoning is represented by the work Ostrom researched on the management of common resource pools, and now the creation and management of new common resources such as the open-source software movement or Wikipedia. In addition to Ostrom, thinkers like David Bollier and Michel Bauwens are key figures in this space.

Here I intend to focus on the system architecture implications of the commons concept, since it relates profoundly to the global architecture of our economic system. Peter Barnes has been singularly focused on the idea of the structural idea of the commons, what he calls our "co-inherited wealth," since the publication of his important book *Who Owns the Sky* in 2003. In his work, he makes the case for an "institution" of the commons, separate from both the private sector and the public sector. Such an approach is profoundly distinct from managing the commons within the public sector or the private sector, notwithstanding the enclosures that persist.

It was with Barnes's latest book, *Ours: The Case for Universal Property* (2021), that the epiphany hit home for me. The commons is the missing "sector," not just an abstraction outside the workings of our economy! In the discipline of economics, we are structurally ignoring the largest source of wealth by far, as well as our sacred inheritance. We are left fighting over scarcity rather than celebrating and wisely managing our abundance. Nothing in economics could be more important than seeing that we've got the pie all wrong.

The proper management of any commons demands first valuing it and then enforcing restraint to protect it. And by valuing it, I am *not* proposing to monetize it, as it will become clear. The effective management of the commons requires making hard choices, something we are not good at doing. Garrett Hardin brought focus to this societal challenge with his influential 1968 article, "The Tragedy of the Commons," right around the time that the environmental movement was gaining momentum. Quite simply, individuals acting in their own self-interest will ultimately deplete these shared resources. For example, Americans' obsession with driving large cars rather than taking the train serves our immediate self-interest, but climate chaos is the result, among other causes, that affects all of us catastrophically.

New technologies may change the details, but they have not managed to change the story, largely due to what is known as the rebound effect, first identified by—yes, it's true—one of the founding fathers of neoclassical economics, William Stanley Jevons, in the eighteenth century.[148] When we invent new technologies, in this case cheaper and more fuel-efficient cars, we don't bank the efficiencies. We tend to expand demand instead. So we get more driving, requiring more and wider roads, and we get larger cars. And even when we do bank some of the efficiencies, the surplus cash gets spent on or invested in something else that has its own ecological footprint. Even the explosion of world-class electric cars in China is misleading in its implications. The energy required to make the cars, mine the minerals for batteries, and charge the batteries is a primary reason that China's coal usage continues to accelerate in absolute terms at the same time that China leads the world in renewable energy. Absolute decoupling from fossil fuels is a far higher bar than relative decoupling. And only absolute decoupling is what can reverse the level of CO_2 emissions.

Here's the key insight about the commons: Neither the public sector, with its short election cycles (and, it must be acknowledged, difficulty in making unpopular choices, but also corruption), nor the private sector, with its design and rigid ideology of maximizing shareholder value (with the finance algorithm enforcing this discipline), can effectively manage the commons for the long-term health of the whole. We have learned that modifications such as the concept of stakeholder value is no match for the drive for ever-increasing profits when our choices are difficult, when it's not pure win-win. The so-called invisible hand of the market fails to achieve shared prosperity, and the public sector has proven itself to be incapable of providing the necessary restraint.

Ostrom contributed significantly to understanding how we can avoid the tragedy of the commons based on her empirical work studying largely indigenous practices of local land stewardship and governance. There are important lessons for us to learn, but these practices take time, are built on trust, and get more difficult and complex as the scale necessary to work expands. There's a reason that we don't yet have a global commons institution to manage the atmosphere, and the results speak for themselves. As a species, we have reached global scale and impact, yet we are still in the adolescent phase of learning effective "management of the household," from the Greek *oikonomia*, the root of "economy."

What I'm suggesting is no mere philosophical argument for a shift in perspective. We literally don't have the necessary institutional architecture in place to cope with, much less manage, the polycrisis. Our failed attempts at policy-led reform and business-led change are evidence of this truth. The reason is a failure of our imagination. We don't have the necessary world order architecture.

HISTORICAL CONTEXT

The post–World War II world order was established at Bretton Woods in 1944. Forty-four nations agreed to establish a system of fixed exchange rates centered on the U.S. dollar, which would be pegged to gold. The goal was driven by the postwar context: to promote stability, cooperation, and international trade. The defining context after two horrendous world wars was simple: prevent another war. The United Nations was established the following year to address the shortcomings of the League of Nations, which failed to keep the peace.

Bretton Woods led to the creation of the International Monetary Fund (IMF) and the World Bank. These global institutions would seek to manage the stability of this new global economy woven together through common interests of healthy international trade. Stable exchange rates and, when necessary, financial assistance, all overseen by the IMF, were intended to pave a path to vibrant international trade based on a mistaken belief in David Ricardo's "law" of comparative advantage that was based on the assumption that capital would not cross national borders.[149] While this may have been a reasonable assumption in Ricardo's day—Why would the Brits trust their savings to be invested in France and vice versa?—that assumption would not hold up in the modern age of globalization. Win-win was the plan, and importantly, with strong incentives never to go to war again. But comparative advantage turned to competitive advantage largely without acknowledgment from the economics profession pushing ever more open trade from both sides of the political aisle. Globalization created winners and losers, as we now know, with profound consequences. One must hand it to Trump for making this point when so many others across the political spectrum missed it, but of course in his own way.

Finally, the World Bank was set up to fund development projects, to rebuild in both Europe and Japan, but also extending to the Global South. The intention was to ensure that nations would recover and that the benefits of global trade would be widely shared.

That those seemingly good intentions did not play out as planned is evidence of the need to rethink the core assumptions of macroeconomics. Capital Institute has begun to reimagine macroeconomic institutions, building on a foundation of the first principles of regenerative vitality. Here I intend to focus on one key revelation.

The postwar context of war fatigue and the need to rebuild was what understandably defined the Bretton Woods architecture for a new world order. While war has resurfaced as a reality in the twenty-first century, that former context shares little in common with the previously unimaginable context we face eighty years later, defined by what we call the polycrisis. To manage the polycrisis effectively, we need both a new worldview—the living systems paradigm argued for here—and a new global institutional architecture informed by that worldview.

The world population was 2.3 billion people at the end of World War II, a small fraction of today's 8 billion. China remained a sleeping giant. Much of the global industrial economy outside the U.S. was destroyed by the war; it has grown by a factor of ten since. The institutional design suited to the postwar context is incapable of addressing the radically new and challenging context of the polycrisis. But with some modifications—most notably the drop of the gold standard, the rise of China, and the formation of the BRICS as an emerging trading block—the institutional design of the world order has changed little since Bretton Woods. We have a design not fit for purpose. No wonder our attempts to address the crisis through existing institutions are not working.

The best time to begin to develop a comprehensive global institution of the commons, a diversified, interconnected web of organizations to complement the institutions of the private and public sectors, would have been a quarter century ago, or earlier. The second-best time, and the only realistic option, is today. We have some working models managing various common assets to learn from for specific forms of co-inherited wealth. They tend to be regional in nature, from our fisheries in international waters to indigenously managed rainforests. Even the state of Alaska manages its vast oil reserves as common pool assets via the Alaska Permanent Fund. Distinct from either the public sector or the private sector, with its own trustees to guard its legal governance mandate, the fund provides all residents a share of the "co-inherited" fossil fuel wealth in the form of dividends flowing directly to all citizens born in the state.

UNIVERSAL PROPERTY RIGHTS

Let us now analyze the logic of understanding all forms of the commons sector as co-inherited wealth, and the mechanisms to manage them via universal property rights. But first, it's important to point out that this approach is profoundly different than putting a price on nature via a tax such as a carbon tax, or through monetizing "ecosystem services," as we can now observe via the carbon credit market. Both approaches work from the logic of the existing market-based system we live in. They are designed to bring nature into the private, public, and civil society systems and the existing public policy framework options. Done properly, these can be constructive steps to begin to turn the ship, and we should continue developing such tools effectively and carefully. But I'm suggesting a far more radical approach. Radical in the literal sense: meaning getting to the root of the matter.

What Barnes is talking about is the institutionalization of the commons into a fourth sector, complementing the private, public, and civil society sectors. Such a commons sector with a unique purpose would offer a meaningful counterbalance to the dominant private sector, the supporting public sector, and the balance and gaps filled by the civil society sector. Any suggestion that the commons could be managed within the NGO sector that can be effective in fill-ing gaps, yet with its own governance and enforcement limitations, is underestimating the scope and scale of the challenge. We cannot view the management of co-inherited wealth simply as a "gap." In fact, it dwarfs private wealth economically, as we will see. Furthermore, much of our co-inherited wealth is sacred, as our indigenous elders understand, and deserves to be treated as such.

While estimating the value of such abundance is fraught with challenges, we can get a sense of the relative magnitude by breaking it down into the biological and the human-made. We shall refer to each commons domain as the biosphere and the technosphere.

BIOSPHERE AND TECHNOSPHERE

In 2014, Dr. Robert Costanza and his colleagues published an updated estimate of ecosystem services provided by the biosphere,[150] which revised their 1997 estimate of $33 trillion up to $125 trillion *annually*, a nearly fourfold increase. These studies estimate seventeen different ecosystem services, ranging from nutrient cycling and climate regulation all the way to food production and recreation. These are "essential services" performed by nature that we rely on but pay nothing for in conventional economic thinking. By comparison, global GDP was $76 trillion in 2014, only 60 percent of the certainly still undervalued ecosystem services.

We can put a very rough estimate on the stock of wealth from an annual flow of wealth the same way we value a company as a multiple of annual income with a price earnings ratio. Note that GDP is analogous to revenues, not income. Notwithstanding all the complexity and issues associated with valuing ecosystem services, the value of $125 trillion of "free services" per year into perpetuity is certainly at least ten times the cost-free annual flow of "income" in the form of free services, or $1,250 trillion. That is to say, $1.25 quadrillion of value! Certainly a "PE ratio" much larger than ten could be justified, and this analysis ignores all value associated with ecosystem services we don't yet understand. Most important, it ignores the intrinsic sacred value of nature, which is literally priceless.

Second, let's consider the technosphere. There is the cumulative built capital and intellectual capital of human civilization that greets a baby when he or she is born into our world. Nobel economist Herbert Simon, who some call the "father of artificial intelligence," has posited that if we are generous with ourselves, we have "earned" only about 20 percent of our wealth. The rest, according to Simon, "is patrimony associated with being a member of an enormously productive social system, which has accumulated a vast store of physical capital and an even larger store of intellectual capital." Note that Simon anticipated Pope Francis's reference to that same patrimony in the quote from his encyclical that opened this chapter.

To clarify, if there were no universities and no microchips and no computers, there would be no Microsoft. If there were no books, no microchips, no computers, no software and no internet, no roads, no planes and trucks, there would be no Amazon (the company). If there were no liquid stock and bond markets, in addition to computers and universities, there would be no hedge fund industry as we know it today and none of the financial wealth created seemingly out of thin air. Yet whose balance sheet do all those "co-inherited" assets show up on today? No one's. We'll take Simon's estimate that the private wealth we actually count—money, stocks and bonds, real estate, and so forth—is only 20 percent of the total, and we'll add his "patrimony" suggestion of an additional four times "earned" financial wealth to our table below, which seeks to put an order of magnitude estimate on total co-inherited wealth.

Furthermore, we are ignoring entire categories of what I'll call cultural wealth, such as the arts, mathematics, science, the rule of law, libraries, and the vast array of government functions that support modern civilization such as law enforcement that we typically do not count as "wealth." The lines between cultural and other forms of wealth get blurry for sure. More challenging, what of the value we experience through spiritual practices, through awe, and from working in service to a cause larger than ourselves? All these categories and more contribute to our sense of well-being, to our true wealth, holistically understood. The reader can put a relative estimate on these cultural forms of wealth for themselves and add it to the estimates below. Perhaps they, too, are simply priceless.

But even ignoring cultural wealth and other categories I've certainly neglected, and even using a very low multiple of ten to put a value on our free annual ecosystem services, the results of our simple analysis are stunning, as displayed in this table:

Category	$Trillion	%Total
Financial Wealth As Measured	$500	13%
Built and Intellectual Capital	$2,000	$53%
Natural Capital	$1,250	33%
Total Co-Inherited Wealth	$3,250	87%
TOTAL WEALTH	$3,750	100%

In summary, current estimates of total financial wealth, consisting of stocks and bonds, money, and real estate of all forms, is about $500 trillion,[151] about four times the global sum of annual GDP by country. These are very big numbers. But the sum of co-inherited wealth as we have analyzed it very crudely here simply to get a sense of scale, wealth that sits outside conventional economic analysis entirely, is estimated at $3.25 quadrillion, 87 percent of total wealth based on my assumptions above.

In other words, the conventional discipline of economics is focused on a small slice—in this analysis a mere 13 percent of our total wealth. It ignores 87 percent of the total, not counting much of our cultural wealth and the sacred, which is priceless. The point is not the precise numbers which are only gross estimates. The point is the order of magnitude. No small omission!

We are taught about the abundance of life in school and in places of worship, yet for so many of us, our lived experience is different. In economics, we are taught about scarcity, and we have designed a mechanistic system we call "economics" around allocating scarce resources efficiently. Yet we pay none of the fair costs for either appropriate use, free riding on, or even desecrating, our abundance. It's no wonder that so many experience scarcity rather than abundance. It's no wonder we are facing a polycrisis, threatening all we hold dear.

We love the entrepreneurial spirit in America and our entrepreneurial heroes, many of whom are indeed admirable. But let's be honest. To become wildly "successful" in our modern economy means to become expert at expropriating critical aspects of this co-inherited wealth for personal gain as much as it means expressing a certain genius for innovation and a drive for success.

Such thinking will draw scorn. It challenges the narrative we tell ourselves particularly in the United States, in this our land of individualism, freedom, and opportunity. It's an affront to our very identity as a country of explorers, innovators, and achievers, a meritocracy (we tell ourselves) where everyone has a chance at success.

The polycrisis demands that we question our well-heeled narratives, especially the ones the powerful like to tell themselves. Note that I am not making a moral judgment about individuals here. Most of us wake up accepting the system we are required to engage in as a given, beyond our control or even our responsibility. Anything else, we are told by followers who put themselves out as leaders, is impractical. I'm simply describing the reality of the system as we have designed it to work, intentionally and unintentionally. The rules and even our accepted ethical behavior allow this expropriation of co-inherited wealth so long as we don't break the law (or get caught doing so).

Here's the thing. We can actually enjoy the game if we create a healthier form of play with a different objective. Barnes has us consider the game of Monopoly, which, by the way, was designed to warn us of the dangers of allowing monopolies to persist. Imagine if "the game" had built-in constraints to unfair and unhealthy expropriation of our co-inherited wealth, with negative feedback loops to moderate disparities, and recirculation algorithms ensuring continuous circulation of private and co-inherited wealth built into the design of the game. In other words, what if the game delivered a more balanced *pre-distribution* of wealth as a design feature. There would still be meaningful private wealth disparities for all kinds of good reasons. But with our vast co-inherited wealth integrated into and managed within the system, private wealth extremes would be radically softened and perhaps, if we chose, eliminated. Crucially, we would finally cease to despoil our co-inherited wealth.

In my ideal vision of a regenerative economy, brilliant entrepreneurs applying their genius and energy to innovations responsive to the profound challenges of the polycrisis would become "rich" beyond their dreams, but their individual financial wealth might top out under $1 billion, while the system architecture would flow extraordinary financial wealth back into the system. Addictive algorithms that have caused a mental health crisis, particularly among the young, and have put our democracy at risk would simply be prohibited by the trustees of the internet commons—no price is worth the cost to systemic health. And yes, that might wipe half the value off Google's and Meta's market capitalization. Extractive and parasitic multibillion-dollar so-called activist hedge funds would find that the rents they would need to pay into the capital markets commons would force them to shrink down to a size where their function would actually be healthy for the system, yet unable to create the systemic damage they do today.

We are left with two critical questions. First, is this 87 percent estimate of all wealth reasonable, at least to an order of magnitude? Because if it is, how could we be so blind? How could the discipline of economics somehow ignore 87 percent of the pie that is fundamental to its purpose, that is, the nature of wealth, wealth creation, and the robust circulation of wealth necessary to an economic system?

Second, and critically, if such vast wealth exists outside the formal economy that we study and organize polices around, how can we reintegrate this extraordinary abundance into our economic system, and into the models, measures, and mechanisms we use to understand, operate, monitor, and govern the system?

We have two options really. First, a partial approach would be to deal with the unaccounted-for costs such as pollution. This is the core idea of environmental economics, to put a price on so-called externalities. If the trash littered outside a ballpark after games is unfair to the community, then the ticket prices for the game should include the cost to clean up the trash. So far, so good. But when we apply this approach to a "cost" like excess carbon in the atmosphere, we run into trouble. Yes, the cost should not be zero, so a carbon tax would seem a good idea, so long as the distributional consequences are managed fairly—easier said than done. But is there a "right" price to put on carbon emissions when the cost is not a cost that can be fixed with money, but a wrong that money cannot fix, as my colleague with a PhD in philosophy Peter Brown asks? And if the atmosphere is our co-inherited wealth, why should some people have the right to pay to destroy it while others (the majority, no less) have no say? Profound ethical questions are unavoidable. The externalities framework of environmental economics seeking to bring these so-called externalities back into the neoclassical model fails to address the hard questions.

Based on the scientific consensus, four degrees (or higher) warming above preindustrial levels is certainly a wrong that cannot be fixed with money. Suddenly we see the limitations of our favorite mechanism—the market, even with costs "internalized"—to allocate scarce resources. The market is a tool that is ill-suited to managing something as complex as the atmosphere. And national governments, each with their own self-interests, ideological or ignorant predilections, and short-term electoral time frames, are similarly ill-equipped to manage the difficult allocation decisions. This is why fisheries require a special oversight body with both expertise and enforcement power to manage the fisheries sustainably. The tool that the oversight body uses is a quota, not a market and not a tax. Anyone who wants to use the commons must purchase a license, and the number of fish that the license allows to be caught is controlled based on the dynamic context of the fisheries, even if that means shutting the fishery entirely for an extended period of time to allow it to recover—hard decisions cannot be avoided or kicked down the road. The commons governance oversees the respective common resource pool, and when a conflict arises, overrules the free market to prevent a tragedy of the commons.

A THOUGHT EXPERIMENT

It's important to get clear on our destination, the essential design, and the necessary institutions of a regenerative economy before we can construct a clear and viable path to get there. The implementation challenges of this proposal will be enormous. But unless someone can make the case that the private sector and public sector combined are up to the challenge—notwithstanding a half century of evidence to the contrary—we must dare ourselves to imagine what a genuine design solution could look like.

I see no alternative to an institution of the commons that will complement the private and public sectors. Together, the architecture of our economic system design must manage all our wealth sustainably, not the mere 13 percent that the current system is designed to address.

Let that sink in for a moment. We have unconscionable inequality that is not only morally repugnant but is giving rise to forces that are destroying democracy. Recall genuine democracy is a condition of regenerative social systems because without empowered participation, there cannot be a healthy system. This reality is not based on any political or ideological belief. Rather, it is based on our understanding of the systems science. We are desecrating the planet because there is a profit in it. And yet we are not even counting, much less managing, for the shared benefit and health of all, the bulk of our co-inherited wealth. It's not even a category in our thinking, for the most part. We have simply handed it all over to the enterprising very few to expropriate fair and square in accordance with the rules we have set for the game.

Marx argued that labor was the fundamental source of economic value, although he was also quite aware of the foundational contribution of "nature" to the economic process and wealth creation. But his focus was on labor and the relative power between labor and capital. This made total sense in a context of abundant "natural capital" and the mismatch in power between capital and labor that he was focused on. Had there been an institution of the commons in our minds when Marx challenged the system, as there was a private sector and a public sector, we might have seen a distant three-way tension from the beginning. Unfortunately, of the three primary drivers historically associated with wealth creation—"land, labor, and capital"—the primary one was missing a seat at the table for the entire span of the debate. And there was a fourth category not even imagined in that early industrial and premodern technology era, the cumulative wealth of human intelligence and technology plentiful as the air is to breathe for current and future generations.

The true source of our shared prosperity is staring us in the face—the full abundance of co-inherited wealth inclusive of the biosphere and what I am calling the technosphere. As we have seen, it represents several multiples of our inequitably distributed private wealth. This whole arrangement is simply absurd. It's also an enormous opportunity to reimagine and redesign the game in alignment with the self-governing and self-fueling qualities of all healthy living systems. Remember, "self-governing" for complex human social systems must be carried out by institutions, since at eight billion humans, we have long outgrown tribal councils of governance.

Let's now imagine what such an institution of the commons to manage the multitude of co-inherited resource pools might look like.

First, we will break down the commons into our two broad categories: natural and human created. We will refer to these two categories as the "biosphere" and the "technosphere."[152] What's important is we are asserting that they are both part of the commons, notwithstanding the fact that some significant parts of each are currently privatized or government controlled. We are interested in first clarifying our thinking, in seeing what everyone sees, but in a new way. Then we can struggle to find a practical path to an institutional design for the management of the commons sector with all of its complexity, given the present reality.

We can then further break each category down into subcategories. So, for example, with the biosphere, we can consider space, the lower atmosphere, the oceans, the sea beds, the forests, the grasslands, soil, artic ice, marshlands, watersheds, the tundra, the coral reefs, and more. Plus, we must add the entire subsurface of the planet that includes aquifers, mineral deposits, and even deep geothermal energy potential from molten rock. Finally, there are the four geochemical cycles: carbon, water, phosphorus, and nitrogen. It's a lot. Few with leadership or governance responsibilities in either the public sector or the private sector even understand the earth science that explains this marvel of a "living system" first proposed as the Gaia hypothesis by James Lovelock.[153] And for the most part, it is managed with a hodgepodge of semi-effective regulations (or no regulations at all, in many cases) that have marginal effect at best in slowing the colonization of the planet by humanity. Meanwhile, we observe the accelerating degeneration of all life, despite it being the source of our abundance.

It's worth putting some numbers on the scale and scope of this degradation, for they are chilling. The WWF's flagship Living Planet Report documents a "catastrophic 73% decline in the average size of global wildlife populations in just 50 years," with the steepest declines happening in Latin America (95%) and Africa (76%).[154] Freshwater populations are showing the steepest declines globally, at 85 percent. Indeed, scientists are calling this the sixth mass extinction, the last one being when an asteroid hit the Yucatán Peninsula, wiping out the dinosaurs. The science of universal entanglement is clear, that everything is connected to everything. Humans have no reason to think that we are exempt from the sixth mass extinction. The economy, what Nate Hagens calls the superorganism created by humanity, is the culprit. Yet we don't even have an institutional-scale sector of the economy responsible to manage the complex web of life as part of the twenty-first-century economic architecture.

Let's now consider the technosphere, growing in scale, scope, and complexity by the year. As with the biosphere, its evolution builds upon prior developments. However, the pace of complexification runs exponentially faster. Unlike the biosphere, which is in decline, the technosphere is growing exponentially, as is the associated abundance we can expect from it, if we manage it wisely. We can begin by breaking it down into three categories: information, networks, and material assets. Philosophically, one can understand all these categories as manifested from human consciousness, but a consciousness commons is beyond my pay grade!

Within the category of information, we could further break it down into intellectual property and data. And all kinds of categorization within each. Networks include, of course, the internet and other communications networks, the various financial system networks from stock markets to the payments systems. We must also include the global goods trading network of transportation systems and the laws and treaties that make up the global free trade regime. As I write these words, the world is seeing the value destruction being caused by the launch of a global trade war by the United States, notwithstanding the legitimate need to redesign such trade networks so that they serve the health of the whole rather than the most powerful global corporations. Material assets include the physical infrastructure of our cities, our factories, our capital buildings, our housing stock, and even Disneyland. Of course, much of this is in the hands of the private sector and public sector. But perhaps it's not as simple as that? Consider, for example, the energy and vitality of New York City, or the beauty and romance of Paris, each considered not as a sum of buildings (parts) but as a singular whole. Is that not a form of co-inherited wealth to anyone born in the twenty-first century? But should real estate speculators or developers extract so much of the financial value from such cities without a mechanism to circulate some of that wealth among all the co-inheritors? You get the idea.

Not surprisingly, this all adds up to a lot to wrap one's head around. I'm not attempting to make sense of it all here, simply to point out the enormity of what somehow has largely escaped the focused and prioritized attention of the economics profession and policymakers. As a result, we are losing the struggle to manage a household that lacks a sound architecture, and the household is crumbling under our feet.

Any approach toward the creation of an institution of the commons, to balance the institution of the private and public sectors, will require a well-developed theory of the commons, a set of proposals about the management of the complex web of interconnected and transnational commons in all its forms, and finally a plan for how we get from here to there. It's a massive intellectual and practical challenge, far beyond the scope of this book. Peter Barnes's work and that of other commons scholars, including Nobel laureate Elinor Ostrom, author David Bollier, and the many leading digital commons thinkers and entrepreneurs, offer us plenty of sound thinking to begin. To be clear, my view is not that the commons will replace the private or public sector. Rather, it is the missing sector called for by a living systems paradigm that will complete the architecture of a viable regenerative economic system. It is therefore not some utopia or back-to-the-land idea. It is essential to contemplate if we are serious about economic system transformation away from an entropy-accelerating economy benefiting for a brief time (in the scope of the human project) a small minority while imperiling us all in the long run—no bunkers will save you—to a complex living systems network of genuine regenerative economies.

Such a metamorphosis, aligning with the regenerative process that explains how all life evolves in order to both survive and thrive, demands that we integrate the abundance of our co-inherited wealth into the architecture of the system itself. Our present path of endless and losing battles patching the holes after the damage is done is not viable. In fact, it's self-terminating.

TWO EPIPHANIES

At the heart of Barnes's proposal is the concept of universal property rights. He defines such rights as "a set of non-transferable rights backed by a subset of wealth we inherit together." It's important to say right up front that while we are talking about a human economy, we understand its indivisibility from the larger life system in which it is both embedded and inextricably linked. These rights come with responsibilities to the health of the whole that supersede any individual rights.

There are two epiphanies we encounter when we contemplate the implications of universal property rights in the context of a regenerative economy. Let's first recall a slightly expanded definition of regenerative economics as the application of nature's laws, principles, and patterns of systemic health, self-organization, self-governance, self-regulation, self-renewal, and regenerative vitality to socioeconomic systems. Prior to encountering Barnes's work, I struggled to imagine how the qualities of "self-governing, self-regulating, and self-renewal," and particularly what Jane Jacobs called "self-fueling," could be truly embedded in the design of a human economy.

The quality of self-regulating has tremendous appeal given the public sector's difficulty with first designing, then imposing, and finally enforcing intelligent and effective regulations, and regulations that can also evolve as fast as the innovation of technology. Corruption further undermines effective regulation. With an honest appreciation of the many challenges, it's difficult not to have some sympathy for the conservative political perspective that regulations are often a cure worse than the disease.

We are trapped in a serious dilemma. All but the most ardent, and I would say naive, if not mad, libertarians would concede that we need some regulations to steer commerce in a healthy direction. Yet we find it's easy for regulations to fall into the trap of bureaucratic red tape, stifling innovation. Regulation is often ineffective for numerous reasons, ranging from the inherent and dynamic complexity of the economy to the powerful interests corrupting the process. And regulations often do come with material unintended consequences. We are trapped in a double bind, a debate between the Left and the Right in which both sides have a point, and no satisfactory solution seems possible. Oscillating winds of political power shift the nature of the compromise in which neither side is happy, dynamism suffers, and the economic system is increasingly unhealthy to our shared prosperity regardless.

Introducing the missing institution of the commons allows us to transcend this double bind. It allows us to unleash regenerative potential neither those on the left nor those on the right can presently see, trapped as they are in this divisive and long-standing ideological debate. Free markets versus regulation is what E. F. Schumacher called a divergent problem. Such problems cannot converge on a right answer but must be transcended with wisdom. Schumacher warned that the clever fool who confuses divergent problems with convergent problems—i.e., how to design a bicycle—is likely to destroy himself.

The necessity of revising the world economic order with a new institution is completely logical. The context has shifted radically from the post–World War II era. Institutions need to evolve, but the institutional architecture of the system itself must first adapt to the new context. We are stuck with a flawed design because we lack imagination that a living systems view provides.

There's a second, equally profound, epiphany that comes with the introduction of the institution of the commons. We can convert some of the enormous surplus of our shared inheritance to income derived from its responsible use. Just like the way a trust fund works for the lucky few, or an apple tree provides for the deer and squirrels, we can all share in the abundance of life, provided we do so in accordance with the first principles that describe how life creates the conditions for life to sustain itself.

Thomas Paine was the first to introduce the idea of universal income derived from jointly inherited property, what he called our

Epiphany—The Missing Institution of the Commons

"natural inheritance." He was referring to our natural inheritance of land that had been privatized. Imagine if we extend the concept to the entire 87 percent of wealth we have just defined as co-inherited wealth currently ignored in our estimates of private wealth. Again, the precise percentage is not the point. It's the order of magnitude.

Before we see how this might work, let's pause to let the implications sink in fully. We have grotesque and accelerating inequality, with all the adverse consequences to our well-being and the health of the whole system it implies.[155] As inequality grows ever more extreme, history teaches us that revolution is the expected outcome. As extreme as it already is, inequality is set to accelerate exponentially with the rise of AI on top of networked business models, a grade of monopoly so pure it would make Rockefeller blush. The uber elite, clever as they may be, have been licensed by our system architecture to capture a grossly disproportionate share of that 87 percent of our co-inherited wealth for the very few. And by few, I'm suggesting literally only hundreds of humans, perhaps thousands if we are generous with our assessment of windfall allocation. Today, for example, one man controls over 60 percent of the satellites in the lower atmosphere, a common asset pool we all co-inherited but that he pays nothing to occupy with his satellites. Nor is anyone governing the use of the lower atmosphere to ensure that it is not desecrated in ways we have not yet even imagined. It's simply the wild west.

At what cost do we sanction such unfair taking and inequality in the face of all our collective abundance? It's a long list, as you well understand. Let's just say it's everything we hold dear—our mental and physical health, peace, beauty, truth, dignity, nature, love, the sacred, life itself. What the hell are we doing?

It doesn't need to be this way. But we must dare imagine genuine alternatives, and alternatives not constrained by what appears "practical" today, and of course alternatives that don't involve violence. Most important, we need an evolutionary design solution, not a temporary win in a losing battle to the death of what is sacred. Let's see how the institution of the commons might be constructed.

COMMONS SECTOR ARCHITECTURE

First, we identify a series of legally enforceable universal property rights. Second, we decentralize wherever possible, dictated by context. For example, we can manage watersheds, foodsheds, and mineral deposits locally, whereas the atmosphere must be done globally. The internet and stock markets? Tricky, of course. Begin with some easy wins to build upon. For each category, we create a trust with a duty to preserve the underlying asset and thus protect those rights for future generations (human and other than human). Each trust would be set up with a legally enforceable duty to future generations of all life. It would then establish a context-specific mechanism to allocate and charge for the responsible and sustainable usage of only some of the surplus benefit while ensuring equitable benefit.

Notice the profound implication. Suddenly, we are talking about the source of wealth for an equitable universal basic income. Such a UBI would not replace work. Rather, it would supplement income, adding economic resiliency, enabling greater choice for individuals to pursue their vocation and resurrecting the dignity of work in the process. And it would provide a credible response to the disruption of the workplace racing toward us as a result of AI.[156]

Critically, the source of this universal income is derived not from taxpayer-funded government largesse, with all of the negative implications that would entail, but from all our shared inheritance. In this design, we are all trust fund babies! The failing economic system we have today has robbed us of that abundance, our natural inheritance. And the source of our rightful inheritance is not trivial. It is the same 87 percent of all wealth we estimated above that is currently being expropriated by neglectful design into private wealth by the very few while we desecrate the very source of that wealth in the process. Not only a tragedy of the commons, it is also a violation of our most sacred duty.

Let me stress that I don't believe that this was a willful design to benefit the very few. I believe the design is rooted in a lack of perception: a perception blinded by the limitations of reductionist thinking. To paraphrase William Blake, we must cleanse our doors of perception, in order to see our economy as it is, Infinite—or at the very least, richly abundant beyond our current imagination.

Let's look at one example from both the biosphere and technosphere to see how this might work in practice. Such trusts already exist for what we call "natural resources," such as the numerous fisheries of the oceans. Depending on where they are located, there can be multiple oversight bodies responsible and even international treaties for international waters. But the concept is the same. There is a scientifically determined quota established to determine the responsible use of the fishery, harvest without depletion. There is an associated ongoing monitoring system to adjust the quota as needed depending on the changing context. Next there is a permitting mechanism whereby permits are sold for the right to fish a certain quota per year. And critically, there is an enforcement mechanism in place to ensure that the quotas are adhered to, even when the fisheries need to be closed entirely to allow them to recover. Closing a fishery entirely is very unpopular with fishermen and fisherwomen, causing widespread repercussions across their communities. But the oversight body has a duty not to the fishing community alone, although their interests must be considered as well. The primary duty is to the greater ecosystem—human and nonhuman—of life. Special interests can't influence the quota decision. The commons trustees must have independence, their decisions science driven.

We need to make two critical adjustments to how fisheries and quotas are managed today. Rather than the governance being handled by a government body with its short-term vulnerabilities, the common resource pools of the commons sector would be managed by newly established trusts, bioregional in scale, transcending national borders as the context requires, with an enforceable legal fiduciary duty to preserve the fishery in a healthy condition over the long term. And second, the usage fees derived from the sale of permits would be redistributed directly to all of us rather than to the government, a dividend from our co-inherited wealth based on the sustainable surplus. Defining "us" for each common resource pool is of course tricky, but a reasonable decision-making framework is achievable. In the case of the Alaska Permanent Fund mentioned earlier, "us" is all Alaskan-born citizens. One could certainly argue that "us" should extend beyond those living in the state, just as "us" in Norway should extend beyond the Norwegian citizens who got lucky that oil was discovered on their side of an arbitrary line when the nation separated from Sweden. Perhaps in the case of fossil fuel abundance, "us" should really be all eight billion of us? Hard questions abound.

Note the inequality-neutralizing mechanism embedded in the institution of the commons. In the case of the Alaska fund, major oil companies pay for the right to drill under controlled conditions, and the citizens all benefit, not just the shareholders. The funds do not get tangled up in the messy business of the public sector. If politicians need money to fix roads (or wage war), let them ask for funding through a democratic process apart from our shared inheritance.

With this example, we can begin to imagine how numerous commons of the biosphere could be institutionalized with two clear objectives: first and foremost, their permanent protection utilizing our best science, and second, the intelligent and responsible use of their surplus in exchange for user fees, which would be immediately distributed equitably to all of us co-inheritors. To be clear, this is not monetizing nature; it is recirculating a cautious estimate of nature's surplus abundance to be shared equitably. It's the equivalent of selling half the apples that fall from a wild apple tree, leaving the rest for the deer and the birds, and to be composted back into the soil. The price of goods using that surplus would increase to those using it, and everyone else would benefit from the distributions, thus putting an appropriate price on usage and incentivizing thrift where scarcity exists, just as nature does.

As we expand the concept from individual fisheries to global natural commons such as the atmosphere, tremendous complexity is introduced in terms of the "how." I ask you to hold these challenges—for example, the negotiation of international treaties—in suspension for now and remember that what we are currently doing is a failure, leading us down a dystopian path. The first UN-sponsored Conference of the Parties (COP1) on climate change took place in Berlin three decades ago. Since then, despite billions spent on meetings and reports producing endless talk of pledges and progress, emissions have only climbed steadily higher as global temperatures continue to break records.

Instead of asking how is this possible, let's first consider what the outcome might look like. Very briefly, an institution of the commons to manage the global atmosphere today would be in code red, demanding and enforcing urgent action. Usage fees for further pollution would be high and escalating. It would be difficult to imagine an oil company securing new rights to develop coal, or oil and gas reserves, beyond some phase-out period. The economics would not make sense, and as a result, the economics to accelerate renewables deployment and advanced battery technologies would be staggering, allowing the market to do what it does well. Governments would be negotiating for carbon emissions allocations for basic needs. There would be riots in the streets if any of the allocations—effectively a quota system—were offered by governments for private superyacht usage or private jets at any price while ordinary citizens couldn't afford to heat their homes. Incentives to conserve energy and convert to electric heat would be overwhelming.

The atmospheric trust would be a serious institution, comparable to a major central bank, professionally staffed with top management talent, an extensive research capability with many of the best minds in atmospheric science. It would have creative dealmakers facilitating responsive innovation. It would be investing usage fees to enhance the health of the commons. For example, some usage fees would initially be recycled to finance natural carbon sequestration in the soil and the oceans until the code red situation was addressed. Only then would the usage fees be distributed based not on the political winds but on the judgment of the experts governing the institution. But once distrusted, those practicing thrift would benefit, while the gluttons would pay (as is fair), economically resembling our earlier crude attempts at a cap and dividend public policy. You get the idea. Yes, it sounds complex and chaotic, but that's because we are decades late ensuring that the carbon cycle remains in balance. There are consequences for our inaction and for lacking the prescience to see that our institutional world order is not fit for purpose.

Now let's briefly examine how the institution of the commons could be used to manage the technosphere. Again, let's suspend the question of how for this thought experiment. As a reminder for the why, consider the internet, arguably the most profound regenerative technology of our lifetime, manifesting the potential enabled by the robust circulation of information. Yet the lack of an institution of the commons to govern its use has allowed a few companies to misappropriate it and leverage the network effect for massive private gain at the expense of the common good. It is not hyperbole to suggest that data-manipulating and attention-stealing social media and search algorithms combined with a highly extractive advertising business model has decimated the mental health of our children. It is likely destroying democracy, too, if it has not already. It didn't need to be this way. But without institutional change, AI promises far worse. Let's not forget, the internet enables AI.

Imagine if we treated the internet as the technological commons it was conceived to be, overseen by a trust to ensure its safe usage and charge for such usage. No one can argue that Google's and Meta's extraordinary profits and especially profit margins are not derived in part from their clever but unfair free usage of this commons. There are no historical precedents for large-scale businesses with gross margins in the 70–80 percent range as Google search and Facebook command. No one can deny that their algorithms have created real costs to society, even while benefits also accrued. A proper commons governance institution would impose fees or outright prohibition to discourage the destructive algorithms while equitably distributing some of the benefits of the networked business models enabled by the internet, all of our co-inherited wealth, beyond the founders and early investors in these companies.

What might this mean for Meta and Mark Zuckerberg? Gross margins at the company might shrink from an extraordinary 80 percent to, say, "only" 40 percent. The company's valuation might also drop in half or lower, and Zuckerberg's net worth would drop accordingly. At the same time, literally billions of dollars would be recirculated as dividends to us all every year as inheritors of this wealth creation made possible by the invention of the silicon chip, the computer, and the internet.

Now consider the advent of AI. What better example of a commons than the cumulative human intelligence in digital form made freely available on the internet? This is the raw ingredient for the large language models we call "artificial intelligence." Why is there no fee to use all this intelligence to create a business? Do oil companies get to drill in someone's backyard without paying a lease payment or royalty to the landowner or the state? Of course not. There is a reason for the unprecedented valuations of the AI startups. With an institution of the commons, not only all content creators—the first priority—but then all of humanity would have a mechanism to share in this co-inherited wealth now about to be exploited by a few engineers, venture capitalists, and the same mega tech companies that have already exploited and abused the free technosphere.

As a final example, consider the world's stock markets. Initially the exchanges were owned by their members to ensure their integrity above all other concerns. But with the rise of trading volumes and the need for large technology investments (coupled with opportunist managers), they converted to private businesses. Had the exchanges been governed by a commons, the desire to facilitate massive trading volumes would have triggered hard questions.

In reality, a stock market is a commons, not "just" a business. I understand that's a controversial statement in the context of the story we tell ourselves. But anyone born into the world today is born into a world with liquid stock markets, just as they are born into a world with fresh air to breath. Yet there are a relatively few hedge funds that disproportionally benefit from this commons without paying disproportionately for the privilege. At the extreme, a small handful of high-frequency trading firms account for over half the trading volume in stock and futures markets yet pay nothing beyond marginal costs for the privilege of using (and abusing) this commons. There are much worse forms of leveraged speculation that clearly harm the health of the commons and the economy at large for the rest of us who chose to do something different with our lives than stare at screens all day, program computers to do so, or pick fights with companies for a quick "greenmail" buck, now couched in the narrative of activist shareholders. An institution of the commons would be staffed with experts, free of political influence. It would set rules and usage fees like a fishery that serve the health of the markets, not the limitless profit desires of a few trading firms that have confused means and ends, as is the case today.

So, too, does this financial market commons facilitate the enormous valuations of public companies. The recent insanity of so-called meme stocks, with Tesla at the top of the insanity list, valued at more than ten times its peer group relative to sales or earnings, takes this to an entirely different dimension. Think about it. Again, no silicon chip, no computer, no internet, no electronic stock exchange, no smartphone trading apps and thus meme stocks, and Tesla might be worth less than a quarter of its current valuation, and Musk could likely never have bought Twitter. And don't get me started with crypto. A sophisticated institution of the commons could manage the commons of the financial markets for the long-term health of all its beneficiaries, free from the corruption of special interests we see today. As with the atmospheric commons, this would be a serious institution employing some of the best and the brightest analytical minds in meaningful work with a purpose.

Putting a value on the potential shared dividends from all the commons combined is beyond the scope of this thought experiment. But given the scale of the commons, 87 percent of total wealth by our earlier estimate, we can say it is very material, measured in tens of billions of dollars per year and likely much more. It would dramatically reset the scale of inequality we see in the world. Imagine the distributions being structured as an initial distribution to every child born in the world, followed by a growing annuity that begins quite modestly but then steps up first perhaps at age thirty, and then into a meaningful retirement benefit at, say, age seventy-five to supplement private savings.

Properly structured, after a generational and complex phase-in period, we would have a dynamic and purpose-driven sector of the economy comparable in scale to the private sector or the public sector today. It would create new leadership roles for holistic thinkers who understand complexity; it would employ millions of citizens often in multinational and multicultural organizations in vital and meaningful work, and create demand for transdisciplinary and specialty scientists. It would employ our best minds and latest technologies. It would have the power to say no, sitting above national interests where the context requires. Yet much of the work would be highly decentralized. What would have to be centralized, such as the commons for space, the atmosphere, and the internet, would be centralized. The key objective would be the preservation of these commons while serving as a trust to distribute surplus abundance equitably.

Who would pay the cost of these benefits paid out to society, you ask? The individuals, companies, governments, or any organization who is the primary user of each commons, paying its fair share based on usage. Parts of the private sector would be less profitable, proportionate to today's free use of the commons, but the dynamism would be unaffected and in fact complemented by the dynamism of the commons sector. There would be more incentives for businesses to cooperate and find innovative niches to survive in rather than compete to the death for unlimited windfall profits, since their availability would be sharply constrained. In other words, it would work just as it works in the ecosystems of nature.

Let's have a closer look. Exxon and Google would pay a lot, their earnings would be harmed. Solar energy companies and open-source technology companies not using advertising algorithm business models would pay very little, making their products and services more competitive. Individuals with superyachts, private jets, and multiple houses would pay a lot, and likely have to change their lifestyles. Teachers and trail guides, potters and poets living in modest homes would receive a lot, perhaps increasing their income by up to a third, enabling them to pursue their creative passions while enhancing their retirement security. There would be more potters and poets, too, and writers and sculptors, and perhaps fewer and lower-paid coders and traders. In the process, this economic architecture would enable humanity to celebrate its natural creativity—recall that creativity is one of four principles of life—manifesting true transformation. Homelessness and poverty would be substantially curtailed. This is good for the most vulnerable, of course, but critically, good for the health of the whole system as well.

Naturally, this thought exercise raises many difficult questions regarding how to implement such a vision. I hope that this short introduction inspires many of us to get to work figuring it out. For I have no doubt that an institution of the commons is the critical missing link in the architecture of a new world order. It is the missing link that can enable regenerative economies that are self-governing, self-regulating, and self-maintaining. It can enable the flip from our present system designed around the concept of scarcity to the true reality of abundance we are all born into.

> The left hemisphere, ever optimistic, is like a sleepwalker whistling a happy tune as it ambles towards the abyss.
>
> —Iain McGilchrist

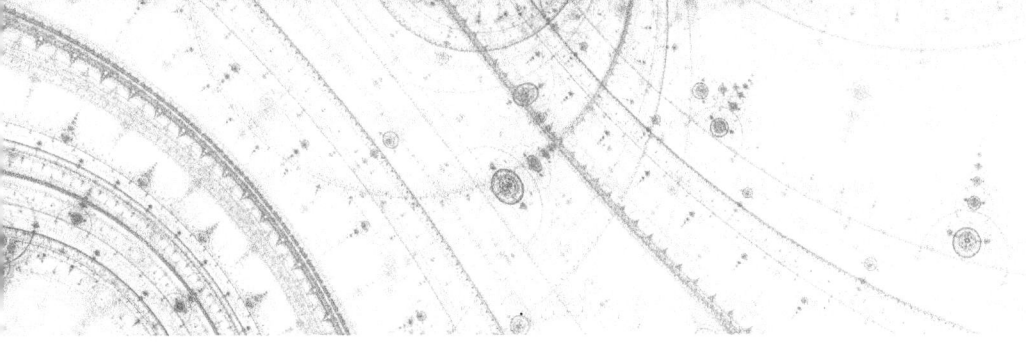

CHAPTER TEN

REGENERATIVE TECHNOLOGY—AN OXYMORON?

In his brilliant book *The Master and His Emissary* (2009), British neuroscientist and philosopher Iain McGilchrist's "emissary" refers to our left-brain-dominant, competitive analytical mind, good at "getting" and seeing the parts, but lacking the holistic vision and intuitive wisdom of the right-lobe-centered "master." In other words, McGilchrist's central warning was to guard against allowing the techno minds, brilliant as they are with the reductionist machine logic of technology, to take over a society. His warning should give us pause.

I'm not sure what I was thinking a decade ago when I failed to address the role of technology in the design of and transformation to a regenerative economy. It was certainly an oversight, as technology has always been a defining character in the evolution of our economic system. With McGilchrist's warning, our experience with reckless finance and then reckless and insidious social media algorithms, and now the rise of distributed blockchain technology that facilitated crypto, and the explosion of artificial intelligence onto the scene, we must ask an urgent question: What might regenerative technology look like, and what does it even mean?

The subject has a scope and importance far beyond my core expertise. I'm delighted that Jessica Groopman and Danielle Lanyard, two

Capital Institute alumnae who have the breadth of expertise and now a regenerative worldview, have taken up the challenge with the launch of the Regenerative Technology Project, which seeks to address exactly these questions. In their seminal white paper on the subject, just as I believe a regenerative economy is an economy in service to life, they define regenerative technology simply as "technology in service to life."[157] Since technology is inseparable from innovation, I hasten to add the importance of one of our eight first principles of regenerative vitality on the subject. Living systems survive only if they innovate to evolve in such a way that benefits the whole.

In other words, we need adaptive and responsive innovation —a first principle. This is very different from innovation for the sake of innovation, or the sake of "breaking things," both of which describe the culture of Silicon Valley today. Regenerative innovation has a purpose greater than maximizing profits or feeding humanity's addiction to convenience. We need innovation in service to life that is adaptive and responsive to the changing context. That context today is defined by the polycrisis.

Technology innovation is also at the heart of what it means to be human. From the taming of fire for human use, to the printing press, the steam engine, and the silicon chip, technology has continuously shaped both the human experience and humanity's impact on the Earth, our home.

Echoing two generations of Batesons, Groopman describes an "Ecology of Tech" as the multitude of contexts and systems affected by our technology choices, from our health and education systems, to entire economies and of course our culture. Such an Ecology of Tech sits on the top layer of a reimagined tech stack, as shown in figure 10.1. The conventional tech stack—infrastructure, hardware, and software—is depicted as Layer 2 in the middle. And most critically, at the foundation—Layer 1—sits the paradigm or worldview out of which our technology designs and uses will emerge. Keep this in mind when we turn to the technology we call finance in the next chapter.

No, tech is not an isolated sector—a "part"—of our economy as our reductionist minds have been taught to see it, any more than finance is merely a sector among many. Both have been proven fully capable of transforming and upsetting the whole apple cart of

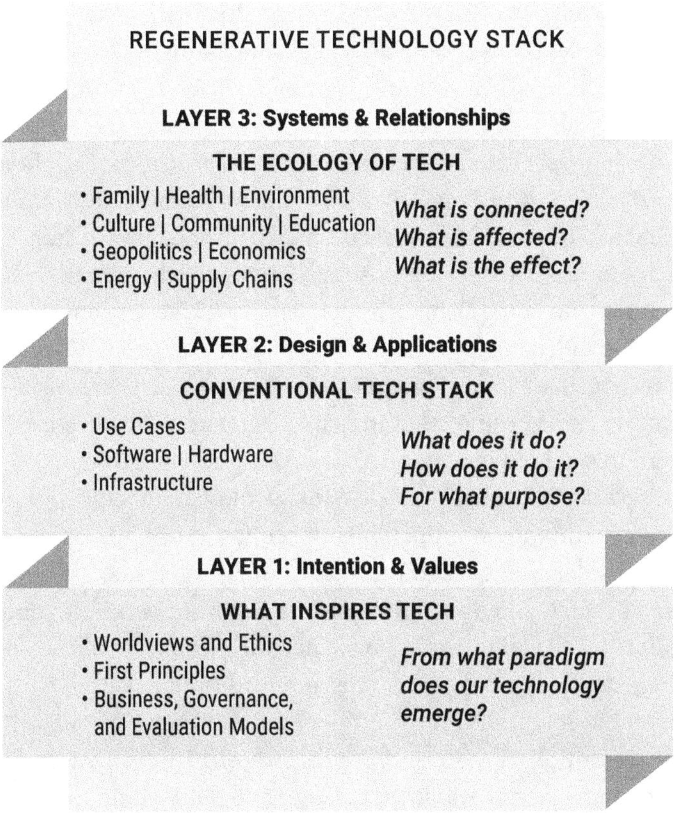

Regenerative Technology—an Oxymoron?

REGENERATIVE TECHNOLOGY STACK

LAYER 3: Systems & Relationships

THE ECOLOGY OF TECH

- Family | Health | Environment
- Culture | Community | Education
- Geopolitics | Economics
- Energy | Supply Chains

What is connected?
What is affected?
What is the effect?

LAYER 2: Design & Applications

CONVENTIONAL TECH STACK

- Use Cases
- Software | Hardware
- Infrastructure

What does it do?
How does it do it?
For what purpose?

LAYER 1: Intention & Values

WHAT INSPIRES TECH

- Worldviews and Ethics
- First Principles
- Business, Governance, and Evaluation Models

From what paradigm does our technology emerge?

Figure 10.1 Technology Nested Within a Larger Whole.
Credit: John Fullerton, Capital Institute, adapted from Jessica Groopman/ Regenerative Technology Project.

our economic system, catalyzing profound and continuous evolution of that system. Holistically understood, technology inventions and choices are rooted in a worldview or paradigm. The paradigm informs intentions and values, which in turn determine technological design. Since we now understand that everything is connected to everything, our technology design therefore affects, well everything! This was the lesson of the printing press and the steam engine, and it is the effect of the microchip, and now AI.

Isn't it remarkable that technology is not considered in conventional economics beyond a "part," like housing or agriculture, to be added together into a "sum of the parts" analysis, and to be fair, through estimates of its influence on "productivity." The complexity of the feedback loops reverberating throughout the economy, geopolitics, our health and our culture overwhelm whatever impacts technology has on productivity, although this too is connected. This narrow and dangerously ignorant perspective is the consequence of allowing Nora Bateson's "whirling blades" of reductionism to guide our thinking and as a result, guide our decision making and how we design and manage entire economies. It is simply impossible to rethink economics without including technology in the project. Like so many things in our dance with complexity, technology represents a profound paradox. It is responsible for great progress, of course. It is also responsible for great loss and in some cases irreparable damage. This has been the pattern throughout history, often in ways we don't even see.

For example, what possible damage did Gutenberg's invention of the printing press in the fifteenth century cause, one might ask? Let's consider this question through our living systems principles lens. The first thing we must grasp is the importance of communication to all living organisms, including human culture. Basic biology understands that accurate communication at a cellular level is essential for health, for life to continue in any organism. Prior to the invention of the printing press, most historical and cultural information was passed down through oral storytelling, a dynamic, living form of communication, filled with appropriate context. While printing democratized knowledge, an overwhelming good, it also standardized knowledge, making it less adaptable and more canonical. Contextual and trans-contextual interpretations became harder or often got lost altogether.

As a result, we are left with concepts such as "strict constitutionalists" in the United States interpreting the Constitution to mean no limitations on Americans for the right to bear arms. Never mind the radically different context in the United States today compared with what the founding fathers experienced in the eighteenth century. The printed word makes it so. Furthermore, knowledge became the providence of a literate elite, fragmenting society and making learning more individualized than the more communal approach of oral traditions. We can see the consequences all around us. So, of course, the printing press brought overwhelming advances for human civilization. But it also created new challenges and divisions, with profound consequences.

A regenerative approach to technology holds the promise of transcending binary good/bad ideological divisiveness. Too often we find ourselves forced into either the techno-optimism tribe or the Luddite tribe. The former is naive and reckless, the latter shuts off much promise for growth and development as a species. But as we move through the twenty-first century, and now in particular with the sudden explosion of AI on the scene, it is the naive and reckless we must contend with by discerning and empowering a more enlightened worldview.

We must acknowledge, the odds are strongly against such an enlightened approach, and here's why. As we have been exploring, the Western materialist and mechanistic way of seeing the world is as a machine that we can analyze by studying the parts, as a "clockwork universe." This (misguided) worldview placed a premium on analytical, reductionist, and what we call rational left-brain-centered ways of knowing. At the same time, it undermined faith in more holistic, creative, and intuitive "right-brain-centered" ways of knowing while dulling our imaginations.[158] Two disciplines represent the extreme of this analytical left-brain-centered kind of thinking, technology and finance. In fact, we can view finance as a technology. It is this tech/fi strain of human thinking that sets the terms of engagement and now dominates the global economy. In other words, we are "left brain led" to oversimplify.

CAN THE MASTER RESUME THE THRONE?

In *The Master and His Emissary*, McGilchrist lays out a stark warning to civilization. His argument is simple and persuasive, even if still controversial given our limited understanding of the human mind. McGilchrist explains how our brains are made up of two interconnected asymmetrical lobes, each complementing the other. But they are not equal. The right lobe, he explains, perceives reality as it is, a dynamic, evolving complex whole that is far more magnificent than the sum of the parts. Its purpose is to see far and wide. The left lobe, in contrast, understands the world as mechanical, static, and abstracted. It evolved to address our immediate needs, suitable for hunting, focused in the moment, competitive to survive, in other words, for "getting." McGilchrist explains this left-lobe aptitude is well-suited for manipulation, for apprehending—but not for comprehending. His obvious conclusion, as the title suggests, is that for human civilization to thrive and even survive, the left brain must remain the emissary, while the right brain must be the master.

The title *The Master and His Emissary* comes from an old parable of a wise king whose kingdom flourished under his rule. As the kingdom grew, he instructed an emissary to rule the expanding periphery. The master's wisdom told him that he had to delegate rule over the parts to keep his focus on the more important whole. The young emissary, however, grew cocky with his achievement overseeing a part. He challenged his master and took power in a coup. Lacking the master's wisdom, the kingdom fell into ruin.

McGilchrist argues persuasively that this explains what modern civilization is doing today. The emissary—manifesting in the "ever-optimistic" arrogance and bravado of our tech bros, hedge fund peddlers, and private equity/banker elites—has been allowed to usurp the master. They have proved their mettle in their "getting." They have indeed "app-rehended, but do they comp-prehend?" Our right-brain-centered, holistic, intuitive, artistic, more humble citizens in comparison have been relegated to struggle on the periphery as we cede power and control over our lives, and life, to our collective emissary. Our leaders lack the wisdom of the master. McGilchrist's warning is clear. If we do not restore a living, intuitive, open, humble, embodied form of knowing, of seeing the greater whole beyond the reductionist parts, of stewarding rather than optimizing, of collaborating while channeling our competitive instincts productively, we are as a species seduced by naive optimism "like a sleepwalker whistling a happy tune as it ambles towards the abyss."

Thus, my question: Is regenerative technology an oxymoron? And my answer is simple: only if we let it be. Like everything else, if we are serious about responding to the polycrisis, we must begin with the urgent need for paradigm shift. Only if we see our technologies as embedded in a holistic, living systems context do we have a prayer in keeping them in service to the higher emissary role, enabling us to manage them for our shared benefit.

It seems to me that AI will be the defining challenge. Think about the "knowledge" that AI is drawing on—anything digitized and on the internet. The vast majority of this information has arisen in the relatively recent past. In other words, it's a product of modernity's reductionist (left-brain centered) way of seeing the world. So left to its own devices, AI risks amplifying and accelerating exponentially exactly McGilchrist's concern. It's quite sobering to ponder. Fortunately, wiser minds than those who dominate the media's attention are rising to perhaps the greatest ethical challenge to face humanity since the invention of the atom bomb.

In her seminal paper, "Regenerative AI Ethics: Aligning AI with Life," Caroline Chubb Calderon writes, "Whether or not AI is considered a living system is beside the point—it is increasingly becoming a participant in Life. Aligning it, and all emerging intelligences, with Life's objective principles is both our surest safeguard against existential risks and our greatest opportunity: unlocking a new frontier of planetary intelligence through the fusion of human, natural, and artificial minds devoted to the flourishing of all Life." I agree! This is the important conversation we need to be having about AI, not just how fast, who wins, and how much power will be required. While interesting and titillating, these questions are trivial in comparison.

But all is not lost, as well documented by the Regenerative Technology Project. For example, Grant Storry, another Regenerative Economics alum, has pivoted his AI company Kiiren to focus on creating customized AI agents drawing on, let's call it, customized "holistic intelligence" to serve the needs of society's future "Masters" seeking transdisciplinary, and cross-cultural and cross-contextual wisdom, not just information. It prioritizes the kind of knowledge we want as master while accessing all "emissary LLMs" (large languate models) as servants. Similarly hopeful, the AI collaboration tool CrowdSmart enables groups to quickly engage and reason together to co-create solutions, regenerative potential currently hidden by our reductionist silos. There are undoubtedly thousands of exciting initiatives underway below the radar of the mainstream media's preoccupation with Nvidia, DeepSeek, and ChatGPT. These early green shoots offer a glimpse of a different future than the dystopian path we appear to be on now.

> Our economy has become an anti-economy, a financial system without a sound economic basis and without economic virtues.
>
> —*Wendell Berry*

CHAPTER ELEVEN

THE FINANCE ALGORITHM

It would be foolish to talk about economics or an economic system without talking about finance and the feedback loops between the financial system and the real economy. Remarkably, our leading economists neglected to examine that interaction until the Great Financial Crisis in 2008 shook them to the core. When visiting the London School of Economics in 2008, Queen Elizabeth famously questioned a group of economists about their failure to foresee the global financial crisis. She asked, "Why did nobody see it coming?"

It turns out one reason, among many, is that the equilibrium models of the real economy used by most mainstream (neoclassical) economists intentionally ignored the entire financial sector. How was that possible? I suppose thanks to an almost religious belief in Adam Smith's invisible hand—the simple but wrong assumption that the markets for goods and services tend to revert to equilibrium. But in truth, it was also because eliminating the complexity of the financial markets and their feedback loops into the real economy made the modeling and predicting easier and neater.

The most notable of these feedback loops is the self-perpetuating boom-and-bust credit cycle that Hyman Minsky warned about in 1992 with his (radical at the time) Financial Instability Hypothesis,[159] a direct challenge to the equilibrium assumption of mainstream economics. By looking at history, Minsky showed that the idea that economies naturally move toward equilibrium, as Smith and later the neoclassical economists assumed, is simply wrong. As we discussed in chapter 2, the real economy in fact does not naturally seek equilibrium as we learned from the Great Depression. This reality gave rise to Keynesian economics and the call for governments to fill demand gaps with public spending when needed. But there also seems to be a sinister force at work moving in the oppositive direction of this equilibrium condition. Good economic times breed complacency among financiers, Minsky explained, which leads to increased risk-taking and thus more destabilizing debt in the system, creating the systemically brittle conditions for the next crash. Finance, it turns out, seems to operate as an automatic destabilizer. Minsky's ideas gained notoriety in the wake of the Russian and Asian debt crises, and the subsequent collapse of the Long-Term Capital Management hedge fund in 1998, deemed a "Minsky moment" since it demonstrated exactly what Minsky had warned about.

Unfortunately, and inexplicably, most mainstream economists would not pay attention until a far worse crash had taken place a decade later in 2008 with the fraud-induced, subprime loan crisis in the United States that would metastasize into the global Great Recession. The costs of this crisis were massive in scale and generational in scope. But perhaps the greatest cost, and the legacy of the entire debacle, was the total and understandable loss of trust in the institution of finance. The roots of the crisis were many, but the inevitable instability was exploited and amplified by Goldman Sachs in particular, with cunning so diabolical and dark it shocked me. Rather than rise to the call of financial statesmanship or exhibit even a modicum of industry self-policing, JPMorgan and others deepened the darkness with replicating trades of their own. When a modern society loses trust in its banking system, the rot multiplies and spreads. The consequences only reveal themselves over time. But for sure, those consequences have undermined our ability to respond to the polycrisis as it demands.

Today, few economists doubt the validity of Minsky's Financial Instability Hypothesis. The credit cycle is real; excess leverage (debt being the primary form) in a company or the entire system is a destabilizing force. Looked at through the lens of our regenerative framework, leverage enhances financial efficiency, but at a cost: a lack of financial resiliency. For a company, or the system overall, we must first conceptualize and then seek out the "window of vitality" with respect to financial leverage (among other attributes) as depicted in figure 3.6 for the system to remain in dynamic balance, in accordance with first principles.

Beyond lost trust, and beyond the destabilizing credit cycle, there is a less visible but more pernicious aspect of modern finance. The ideology, logic, and exponential function embedded in all of finance, what I will here collectively refer to as the "finance algorithm," though working according to design I hasten to add, is undermining the health of the entire economic system, and with it, social stability and ecological health. It acts like a cancer cell, slowly and invisibly at first, but then multiplying increasingly in accordance with its exponential function, killing the host. The symptoms of this disease include grotesque and exploding inequality, an addiction to consumerism and to our phones, chronic illness, an epidemic of anxiety, political corruption of all kinds, a push to hyper-scale artificial intelligence before we know the risks, escalating climate change, and yes, we have been warned, the sixth mass extinction.[160] It shows up as corrosive political division, authoritarianism, and hopelessness among our youth. It is ruthless in holding the economic system firmly in its grip—not out of evil intent, although arrogant and reckless greed is all too common. Nor is the algorithm's grip a bug. It's a design feature. As a financier, the result is clear as a bell to me, and it is chilling if we summon the courage to see it. Leonardo Da Vinci had it right: *"All our knowledge has its origins in our perception."* Modern civilization is trapped in the growth double bind of all time we referred to earlier, mercilessly enforced by the power of a human artifact, the finance algorithm.

For this reason, we will focus primarily on the finance algorithm in this chapter. It's the first order of business to grasp and fully process its implications. The many interesting and important subtopics in finance—from money systems and banking architecture to investment frameworks, the recycling of financial capital at scale, and finally to imagining an institution of the commons to complement the private and public sectors as we have discussed—demand that we rethink what we even mean by ownership. It's a lot, worthy of a follow-up sequel to this book! All of these topics must be rethought in the context of degrading and then redesigning the finance algorithm. In fact, I believe our failure to understand and address the grip of the finance algorithm explains why we have so far failed to make meaningful progress in transforming our economic system. In addition to the need for a new shared vision, I am suggesting that the finance algorithm is perhaps the key obstacle standing in the way of the emergent diversity of regenerative economies throughout the world.

Before we explore how to think about addressing the finance algorithm, let us take stock of the amazing progress on our regenerative journey so far in spite of the obstacles. In the decade since I first published *Regenerative Capitalism*, I have traveled the world and witnessed the nascent yet clearly emergent regenerative economy, often hidden below the radar. It can be seen in the thousands of unique bioregional-based restoration and cultural/economic development initiatives such as Salmon Nation in the Pacific Northwest, not a "nation state but a nature state," the culmination of Spencer Beebe's life work. What began for Spencer, a co-founder of Conservation International and later Ecotrust, and the inventor of debt for nature swaps, as a commitment to "conservation" has evolved profoundly. Salmon Nation can best be understood as bioregionally based and bioregionally sourced, human participating in nature, ecological/cultural/economic regeneration. Yes that's a mouthful, I invite you to chew on it for a moment.

A rich diverse tapestry of distinct bioregional context-specific regenerative initiatives is emerging around the world with new infrastructure such as the bioregional financing facilities envisioned by the BioFi Project,[161] facilitating the flow of enabling financial capital to nourish this critical activity, a vision for an entire new financial "sector" at the foundation of the regenerative economy. Early expressions of this patient relational work is already happening on the Osa Peninsula in Costa Rica; in bioregional learning centers like Sinol de Vale in Brazil, and in South Devon, United Kingdom; and in community-centric economic development initiatives such as Regen Melbourne. It's also happening in inner cities led by pioneers like Rising Tide Capital, and across entire islands such as the Hawai'i Investment Ready initiative, with Shorefast on Fogo Island off Newfoundland, and in what I witnessed emerging on the Island of Andros in Greece. The work takes on all shapes and forms and under multiple descriptive names, but if looked at through a living system lens, one can see the pattern that connects them all.

It can be seen in cutting-edge regenerative purpose-driven B Corps such as Guayakí Yerba Mate and with numerous emerging enterprises designed to operate in alignment with the principles of life such as my partner firm nRhythm, focused on bringing this living systems paradigm to leadership and into organizational design. Early expressions of the regenerative economy finding its legs can be seen in the B Corp movement, and especially in its business ecosystem expression of Sistema B in Latin America. There are now nearly ten thousand registered B Corporations employing close to a million people in seventy counties around the world, and many more companies set up as public benefit corporations in the U.S. and similar structures around the world that are all seeking to balance multiple stakeholder interests.

The steady if uneven emergence of the regenerative economy is revealed with single bold decisions like the Chouinard family's decision to place the iconic Patagonia company into a purpose trust, whose sole beneficiary is now planet Earth. "Instead of going public," Yvon Chouinard said, "we're going purpose." There are many counterintuitive lessons and insights to glean from this one decision. For years, I have wondered about the fact that none of the ownership in Patagonia was distributed to the employees. Not one stock option was ever granted—which seemed to violate my principle of balance or empowered participation. But Yvon anticipated the consequences of such shared ownership. It would create natural internal pressures to focus on the stock price, rather than purpose. Those pressures would be powerful in good times, and potentially divisive in tough times, like when Chouinard decided to shut down the fulfillment warehouse entirely during the pandemic to protect his employees while they continued to earn their full salary. And it would make it difficult, if not impossible, to place the entire company into a trust with Earth as the sole beneficiary. Instead, he and his family bore the responsibility and the burden—billions of dollars of financial wealth foregone, millions of dollars of cash burned during the pandemic—on their own shoulders.

But no single company will ever be a true exemplar of "the regenerative economy" any more than one tree can be regenerative on its own. The proper unit of analysis is no longer the corporation or the nation-state, both artificial human constructs born in the Western modern age, and both a reflection of the dominant reductionist mindset of modernity. This is the scale and scope of transformation we have embarked upon.

The regenerative economy waiting to unfold will be seen clearest in vibrant integrated ecosystems of businesses managed as a single whole. This is profoundly different than current supply chains of global companies such as Apple or Toyota—interconnected business ecosystems in which each part of the ecosystem recognizes the advantages and often necessity of interdependence but is still seeking maximum opportunistic advantage for itself.

Could such a regenerative business ecosystem, one that seeks to optimize the health of the whole, actually exist within our capitalist system you may rightly ask? It already does. It's called Mondragón in Spain's Basque region that we discussed in part 1. While most people look at Mondragón and see cooperatives, many in industrial sectors such as auto parts and construction materials, when we look through a regenerative lens, we see an ecosystem of over eighty autonomous cooperatives generating together €11 billion in annual sales, yet networked like a mature forest, with its own bank and university training, pooling profits, sharing resources, creating resiliency for individual members and for the whole, working across the edges to unlock potential for the benefit of the whole. When you ask what is the purpose of it all, you will hear a one-word answer. Legacy. Or note the miracle of SEKEM in Egypt, a fifty-years-young initiative that has literally greened the desert while creating an example of regenerative economic and cultural development grounded in the collaboration among hundreds of small farms, businesses, and community development education centers in the process.

The regenerative economy is rising! It is an emergent property of an unhealthy economic system, reeling in fits and starts, led by courageous system change entrepreneurs fighting against the odds yet driven by purpose. It's an economic system straining to heal itself, at times convulsing in fever, at other times just suffering from lethargy as people simply struggle to keep food on the table and the bills paid. The transformation is in direct response to the stresses and pressure. Remember, systems change only in response to pressure; that's the science. To accelerate transformation, we need to facilitate this pressure-catalyzed process. We do this by creating the conditions for health to naturally emerge. In life, health is the natural state if we remove the obstacles to health.

We can do the same with economic system health: We create conditions and we remove obstacles. This is far more hopeful and effective than efforts to impose new goals on a system top-down that meet with fierce resistance from the interests of those holding power who have little interest in changing the system.

Our challenge at this late hour is to see the polycrisis as something deeper, what some are calling a "meta-crisis" with a single root cause: our myth of separation. Separation from each other, and separation from what we call nature. Oneness is the true reality after all, evidenced by the 2022 Nobel Prize in physics for our understanding of quantum entanglement, as well as all the world's religions.[162] Yet neoclassical economics and its offshoot finance remains anchored to the limitations of a Newtonian world.

The meta-crisis, serious as it most certainly is, is an opportunity for transformation. In fact, it represents the pressure that will force transformation. As previously stated, systems only change in response to pressure, so this is actually a good thing. Our job is not to "save the world." Our job is to constructively influence—to creatively participate in the process of how the inevitable transformation unfolds. Tactically, there will be much to resist in the moment. But strategically, our first order of business is a developmental task. We must learn the limitations of reductionism, and to dance with the dynamism of complexity, which creates the openings for profound change, the cracks where the light gets in, to borrow from Leonard Cohen. It's more jujitsu than boxing. We must reframe the meta-crisis to metamorphosis, as cosmologist Jude Currivan likes to say, the natural evolutionary path at this pivotal moment. We can and must tap into the energy flow of life's evolutionary path. We must learn to go with the flow, even if that means, metaphorically, a death and rebirth-like experience.

METAMORPHOSIS

Metamorphosis is neither death nor collapse. It is not "shrink" or "degrowth" either. The word is derived from the Greek *meta*, meaning "change," and *morphe*, meaning "form." Metamorphosis means to change form.

Just like the church elders refusing to look through Galileo's telescope that would have revealed the foundational error in their worldview centuries ago, few modern leaders controlling our elite institutions have the courage to break from the comfort of their tribes and their cherished identities to see an alternative worldview. We have invested two decades into relatively trivial (relative to the scale and scope of the challenge) incremental change as the Keeling Curve measuring carbon dioxide in the atmosphere continues its unrelenting rise. We were scolded that the perfect is the enemy of the good when we suggested that we needed to get serious and talk about systemic transformation. The corruption of the fossil fuel industry made it both worse and a moral travesty. Too few have yet to look seriously at what such a metamorphosis demands given our precarious state. Too few in positions of power have looked through the metaphorical telescope. To again quote a former CEO of JPMorganChase over a decade ago after listening intently over lunch, "It's too big, John. I can't go there." And he is one of the good guys.

As we have seen, the entire edifice of neoclassical economics and its twenty-first-century master, the left-lobe-powered finance ideology that drives most decision-making in business and in government, is built on a foundation of sand. It is completely maladapted to deal with the present far-from-equilibrium context of ecological overshoot, unstable and ever-growing inequality, insecurity, a general state of physical and mental disease for perhaps a majority, and rapidly accelerating social division. In fact, to a large degree, we can trace these very "problems" to the reductionist logic of the system design. We just can't see it because again, as Einstein wisely understood, "it is the theory that determines what we are able to see."

The result is the dangerous rise of deeply twisted and fear-based authoritarianism speaking rubbish, which sounds soothing to people in fear. Metaphorically, we remain largely trapped in Plato's cave by our own ignorance, unable to see the possibilities of abundance just outside. The caterpillar has gorged and gorged and gorged. Now, it must transform or die. From its narrow perspective, it cannot possibly imagine the lightness and freedom of flight. So it resists, and it regresses. Barbarism is a possibility if we break down without breaking through.

IMMUNE SYSTEM

With all this as context, let's finally turn to the finance algorithm. The reason we are stuck, and our attempted responses are revealed to be trivial when set against the challenges of the polycrisis, is quite clear. Hardwired into the present economic system is an "immune system," as aptly described by Currivan, that protects and defends to the death the identity of its "body" in its current (unhealthy) form. This is what immune systems do: They protect the current form, that is, they defend against metamorphosis! Let me suggest that the immune system of our economy is what is otherwise known as the financial system. It protects not only its own identity against harm but the identity and form of the broader economic system it now controls.

The mechanism of control is what I shall call the "finance algorithm" anchored in an ideology that values money above all else, by design. I say that not as a judgment about greed but as a simple objective and descriptive fact. It was designed this way for seemingly logical reasons—misguided logic as it turns out, and a logic that nicely validates the selfish will of the powerful who are more clever than wise.

Financial capital is a scarce resource (less so today), the logic goes, and vital for economic development. Its efficient allocation is a laudable, if reductionist, goal—recall that it is but one of our eight forms of capital, a single part of a much greater whole. But reductionist goals often prove disastrous when dealing with complexity, as we have seen. Unfortunately, the finance algorithm's understanding of "efficiency" is a naive and overly simplistic goal born out of reductionist, Newtonian logic, as again we discovered in our discussion of first principles. Efficiency is in direct conflict with the first principle of balance in the real, living world, which seeks to balance efficiency with resiliency, as we discovered in part 1. Reality is a world defined by complexity and interdependence at its core. This matters. It matters a great deal. As Nora Bateson explains, "The opposite of complexity is not simplicity. The opposite of complexity is reductionism." And reductionism is at the heart of our economics and finance, which drives our decision-making; the polycrisis is the outcome.

This finance algorithm, as I am calling it, has been developed and perfected only in the past half century—a toddler in the scheme of human culture and technologies. It is now a sophisticated and ruthlessly effective set of analytics with supporting metrics to ensure that its value system is honored, at all costs. The finance algorithm expresses itself through a left-brain-inspired portfolio of concepts designed for "getting," as McGilchrist would agree, what its value system dictates. They go by such names as net present value, internal rate of return, optimize shareholder value, earnings accretive, compound interest, exponential growth (in profit), earnings multiple expanding, exit premium, option adjusted value, time value of money, discount rate, forward curve, cost benefit analysis, payback period. Most simply, it consists of two money-centric core values: more, and never enough. You can learn it all at the Harvard Business School.

And here's the thing. The finance algorithm is now time-tested and refined. It works. That is to say, it works by its own flawed reductionist logic and value system. Note that this is not a critique of financiers per se, although some deserve harsh criticism. Yet we miss the more profound systemic issue when we scoff at greedy or obnoxious bankers.

What matters and what we are called to do at this late hour is to engage in a *serious* critique. We must engage in a sophisticated analysis of the system and reveal the underlying values that drive our economic decision-making, both in the private sector and in the public sector. It is how we make these decisions that determines the outcomes we experience. We all share responsibility for understanding the finance algorithm at a conceptual level, and its pernicious assault on all life including our own. It's also an assault that gets more vicious when it doesn't get what it wants, when the so-called low-hanging fruit has been harvested. Now is that moment. For the collective good, we must demand not merely reform as was partially delivered post–financial crisis, but genuine transformation. The metamorphosis is upon us.

It bears repeating that what I'm referring to as an immune system is not what we normally associate an immune system with—health. In this case the finance algorithm is protecting and preserving the identity and form of the system as designed, notwithstanding its dire deficiencies. It is blocking the economic system's ability to change its maladaptive form. It is blocking metamorphosis.

More than we realize, the finance algorithm guides most important decision-making of our modern society, from the macroeconomic strategy of nations to the monetary policy of the world's leading central banks, from the straightforward capital investment decisions (coal vs. renewables, steel vs. wood) of the private sector, or the complete conflation of speculation with investment, to the less straightforward decisions in the private sector on whether major newspapers endorse candidates for the most powerful position in the world (conflicted by their overriding financial interests). The bigger the stake in those financial interests, the more powerful and therefore dangerous is the finance algorithm, irrespective of the human being and their values and character involved. It's just the effect of the impersonal algorithm. This has a chilling implication. All else equal—and of course there are always exceptions to prove the rule—it's the proverbial billionaires and the largest and most powerful corporations that are the most dangerous decision-makers. And yet these are the people we too often refer to as our "leaders."

In the regenerative paradigm, seasoned practitioners see the necessity to create conditions for health, first at a cellular level, that is, from the bottom up. Recall Benyus again, "Life creates the conditions conducive to life." In addition, we focus on the necessity to remove obstacles (to the natural healing process), which often can only be addressed top-down. In fact, when thinking about the health of any complex system, we should properly see identifying and removing critical obstacles as part of "creating conditions."

Public policy generally works the other way around. It seeks to solve problems top-down rather than removing obstacles. We are left with a morass of regulations, and always add layers upon layers in a hopeless game of whack-a-mole until it triggers a revolt from a frustrated private sector. While these regulations may not be cures that are worse than the disease, as free market advocates suggest, more often than the Left likes to acknowledge they are incapable of dealing with root causes, so they are ineffective. Again, theory determines our perceptions.

In the context of personal transformation, Heidi Sparkes Guber points out that in the Yoga Sutras, Book IV (Sutra 3) instructs:

> Instrumental causes are not transformed into the creative energy of nature, they merely remove the obstacles (to Enlightenment or Freedom) as a farmer removes a barrier when irrigating a field.

In other words, "instrumental causes" such as our desires, better goals and metrics, and force of will are not what directly cause transformation. What they enable is for us to "remove the obstacles." Quite remarkably, we see once again the regenerative paradigm aligned with the teachings of our ancient wisdom traditions, in this case the Yoga Sutras. We can presume as our hypothesis that the transformation/metamorphosis at the system scale will follow similar patterns as at the individual scale, in keeping with the fractal nature of all life.

This wisdom clarifies for us the difference between movement building with its (often angry) demands for change and the transcendence required for transformation/metamorphosis. We don't will our way to metamorphosis, the way we may will a social movement for a cause. Instead, what these "instrumental causes"—our will and intentions—must do is to identify and remove obstacles. This insight should and does affect our theory and strategy for change, if lasting change (transformation) is what we seek rather than an endless battle of competing interests for a wholly inadequate reform agenda of incremental change. In summary, we create conditions, remove obstacles, and hold our goals a bit more lightly than we are accustomed to, manifesting unexpected emergence—regenerative potential—as the outcome.

Perhaps the arc of Dr. King's moral universe bending toward justice will appear as an arc from some future distant point. But today it seems clear that we will need to pass through what systems scientists call a phase-shift transition, like when a pot of water begins to boil. In a word, we will and already are experiencing what we call a disturbance in complexity science. A metamorphosis is for sure a "disturbance" requiring the weakening and ultimate liquifying of its immune system, thus enabling the organism to change form. This is not a gentle and smooth arc of change. Just ask a caterpillar.

Not surprisingly, our attempts to weaken this immune system called the finance algorithm have proved quite challenging. To begin with, regulation is fiercely resisted by finance, even in the wake of the worst financial crisis since the Great Depression. Political leadership was not up to the task, particularly in the United States, the nexus of the crisis. Nor did even the leaders with integrity, both in the private sector and in government, understand the profound change that the polycrisis context demanded. They had yet to find the courage to look through the telescope. Meaningful improvements to the resiliency of banks and the financial system have been accomplished postcrisis, I must add, although with many unintended consequences that harm the health of the good actors and in the process harm the health of the real economy. But such regulations are primarily a response to abuses and may in fact harden the immune system in the process. Such resiliency reinforcement of the system as it exists is quite different than incentives and regulation designed to transform the system at its foundation by seeking to remove obstacles to transformation. We bailed out the banks and put the worst offenders under the protection of the Federal Reserve. We did not even remove the most blatant obstacles to health such as sociopathic leadership, incompetent boards, and broken incentive systems.

Second, the blowback from the ESG movement is instructive. As I discuss in depth in *Finance for a Regenerative World*,[163] ESG (environmental, social, governance) reporting is at the heart of what the financial sector calls "sustainable finance," despite its wholesale deficiencies even in its core assumptions and theory of change.[164] It has now attracted harsh attack from the antiwoke political Right, especially in the United States. Conservative politicians, trapped in the outdated narrative of capitalism versus socialism, have repositioned their historical role as protector of free market capitalism. This time they are striking out not only against invasive government bureaucracy and burdensome regulation but also against the so-called woke capitalists who have seemingly lost sight of the purpose of business, all in the context of a deepening culture war. For every action, even if inadequate to the challenge, there is an equal and offsetting reaction. No paradigm shift, and the immune system is again hardened in the process. It's a step in the wrong direction when we don't have the time to waste.

Objectively, and not being critical, the progress at weakening the grip of the finance algorithm, that is, weakening the immune system, has been very slow. This is the reality, despite decades of efforts and good intentions of many. One could easily make the case that the continued growing influence and scale of private equity and hedge funds run by the most adept at applying the finance algorithm, and that operate largely outside the purview of regulators, have only strengthened the immune system. Then there is the rise of unregulated, reckless, and often brazen crypto traders, led by a snake oil salesman named Michael Saylor who previously settled a tax fraud case for $40 million. He is pushing the pump and dump of all time disguised as a company named, of all things, "Strategy." The strategy is a multibillion-dollar leveraged bet on Bitcoin, now so overvalued by the bitcoin and meme stock day traders on their Robinhood apps that it has attracted professional short sellers, all while the board members have entered the dump phase, walking away with millions. Not even Goldman would dare try this, although the sitting secretary of commerce, Howard Lutnick, couldn't help himself while pressing for loose or no crypto regulation in the U.S. It's appalling.

Not to be outdone, there is the Trump-majority-owned social media stock with sales totaling less than two Starbucks stores and hemorrhaging cash, valued by the MAGA meme stock day traders at $10 billion?! Before Trump's one-time pal Elon Musk imploded his own personal brand, Tesla's price/earnings ratio (P/E) reached a ludicrous 200, making Musk the richest man in the world, while Toyota and Ford's P/E are both under 10. Even if we grant Tesla a valuation multiple of twice Toyota given its Musk factor, technological prowess, and possibilities of driverless cars, it's still overvalued by a factor of ten (a first approximation of the overvaluation of Musk's personal financial wealth). This is not the real world. Collectively these developments have overshadowed any genuine progress at weakening the immune system. Instead, they have further inflated the dangerous speculative bubble that would shock even Minsky floating above the finance-algorithm-controlled real economy.

Returning to our immune system analogy, Currivan suggests that we can see our present-day speculative financial system, the "whirlpool of speculation" that Keynes warned about, as an autoimmune disease. The body's immune system is unable to distinguish between the body's healthy tissues and foreign invaders, so it creates autoantibodies that attack and destroy healthy tissue. Autoimmune disease (finance attacking the healthy tissue of itself and the real economy) is a fitting description of the global consequences of the financial crisis, the brazen, Goldman Sachs–financed 1MBD Malaysian fraud that followed,[165] the staggering FTX crypto fraud, and the many minor "gettings" such as what we blithely call bank "mis-selling" and "junk fees" that happen on a daily basis out of sight in modern finance. As I recount this story, the adjectives at my disposal fail to do justice to the corrosion of responsibility and morality that has metastasized across our financial system. Perhaps the finance algorithm is in the process of liquifying into soup on its own, and its imaginal cells are busy nourishing themselves out of sight, in preparation for the emergence of something new and quite beautiful. I've had a glimpse in my travels on clear days, but too often the clouds return.

"*Our economy,*" Wendell Berry notes, "*has become an anti-economy, a financial system without a sound economic basis and without economic virtues.*" Hard to say it better than that. As such, finance—that is, the finance algorithm—is a primary obstacle, if not the primary obstacle, to the emergence of a regenerative economy. Recognize that it is the finance algorithm's rules that drive Silicon Valley as well, from the addiction algorithms of Facebook and Google to the arms race for artificial intelligence. And the same algorithm drives the fossil fuel industry and the petro-states in their decision-making. The ethic of the precautionary principle gets overridden by the finance algorithm, even when its wisdom is as obvious as it is when dealing with another technology, nuclear weapons. In keeping with our "create conditions" imperative, weakening if not replacing the obstacle of the finance algorithm is therefore fundamental to the metamorphosis that awaits us.

This is no trivial challenge, to state the obvious. The immune system will defend to the death the identity of the body. And it is very powerful. How then to degrade and ultimately remove the obstacle we are calling the "finance algorithm" may well prove to be the ultimate challenge of the polycrisis. That is the subject of the sequel to this book, *Finance for a Regenerative World*, building on the series of white papers published in 2018 at Capital Institute. But please don't look for any easy or simple answers.

I will leave the reader with two interesting facts about the metamorphosis of a caterpillar to ponder. First, the caterpillar's eyes do die in the process, and it develops new eyes to see the new context of flight. This suggests, and I wholeheartedly agree, we, too, need to develop new ways of seeing. We must put the master in charge of the emissary and learn to see holistically.

Second, the caterpillar's immune system also dies, in order that a new one suitable to the form of the butterfly can emerge. If my analogies are correct, this affirms that the finance algorithm must be degraded and ultimately replaced if our economy is to successfully metamorphose into a new form. On my optimistic days, I believe the antiwoke blowback against ESG may have been a gift disguised in wolf's clothing. Just perhaps, it is a necessary step in degrading the immune system in an unexpected way. ESG was never going to do the trick. As the thoughtful Allen White, co-founder of the Global Reporting Initiative and considered the "Godfather" of sustainability, once said: "ESG does not, by nature, carry a true sustainability gene."[166] Perhaps it was even a distraction rather than incremental progress? I believe that we need to hold open the possibility in our minds. Perhaps with ESG in cautious retreat, the obvious deficiencies in our economic system will be impossible to ignore in the coming years, and we won't have the false pretense of solving the problem. To be clear, making investment decisions with better information is just smart investing. But we cannot confuse a better investment portfolio with economic system transformation.

And finally, I learned from a friend who had a heart transplant that the most dangerous aspect of the operation is that the body's immune system rejects the new organ. To counter this risk, the doctors inject stress hormones into the body. Why, you ask? Because stress degrades and can even shut down the immune system while the body adjusts to the new organ.

Recall Capra's fourth principle. Life is inherently intelligent. Perhaps there is good reason why our financial system is under stress, and why we are all feeling the stress at this transformative moment in human evolution. We are preparing to remove critical obstacles to metamorphosis. Perhaps life is intelligent enough to offer help in liquifying the finance algorithm, in order to regenerate it. Perhaps there is even a method in the madness of Wall Street's abhorrent behavior that made the Great Recession far worse than it needed to be? Perhaps undermining trust in the system with a faulty design was the only way to degrade the algorithm? It's too early to say, and no doubt there will be more darkness before a dawn.

But here's reason for hope. What will emerge if the evolutionary process continues with past patterns is a new immune system adapted to the new context, and therefore fit for purpose in this profoundly new context!

Imagine that.

Nature is a totally efficient, self-regenerating system. If we discover the laws that govern this system and live synergistically within them, sustainability will follow and humankind will be a success

—R. Buckminster Fuller

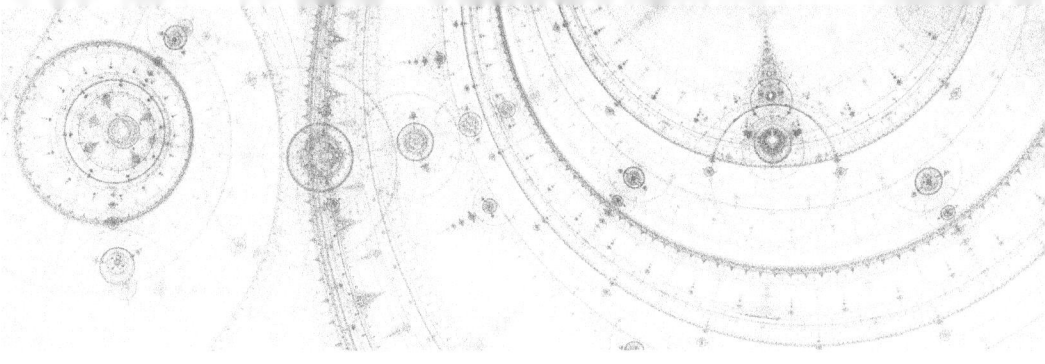

CHAPTER TWELVE

REIMAGINING PUBLIC POLICY

Economics is ultimately about decisions regarding policy choices. Yet policy choices are limited by the design of the economic system architecture, which in turn is limited by the prevailing paradigm. Therefore, any policy recommendations I can make here remain conditioned on the shift in paradigm before they become possible. Some will critique this approach as pie in the sky and "not practical." But so-called practical solutions are destined to be incrementalism disguised as progress. Treat this discussion as the direction we must collectively find a way to head, if our goal is system transformation. My best strategy, which will not satisfy many, is to rely on the three pillars of our theory of change: paradigm shift; work across all three levels—consciousness, system design, and practical work on the ground; and finally, build and nourish our islands of coherence, and then link these networks together.

As we have seen, the global economic and financial systems operate on a foundational architecture developed in the aftermath of World War II at the Bretton Woods Conference. It was a gathering of all forty-four allied nations at the Mount Washington Hotel in Bretton Woods, New Hampshire, to negotiate a stable international monetary system with the intention of avoiding the international economic tensions that led to two world wars. With the United States emerging as the world's dominant economy and military power, and the one Western economy not destroyed in the war, the world looked to the U.S. to play a stabilizing force.

What emerged was a U.S. dollar–based global trading system, with all currencies pegged to the U.S. dollar, and the dollar pegged to the price of gold. Bretton Woods also called for the creation of the International Monetary Fund as a stabilizing institution and the IBRD to focus on reconstruction in Europe. The IRBD would become the World Bank to promote economic development for reconstruction more broadly, including development beyond the war zones and into the Global South. The rise of China as an economic powerhouse was not yet on the horizon. Looking back, the context clearly drove the architecture. After two dreadful world wars, harmony and cooperation among nations was the goal, and stable trade was the strategy. A dependable yet quite rigid architecture (neoclassical economics and its desire for a machine-like system that would maintain equilibrium) was the intention, but the hoped-for stable equilibrium was an illusion for a system that was inherently complex. But complexity science was but a figment of the imagination of its early pioneers and was not present at Bretton Woods.

Of course, unanticipated "exogenous shocks," as the economists would call them, would put pressure on the rigidity built into the system. A more dynamic global economy with rising trade had emerged with the recovery of Europe and Japan in the decades since Bretton Woods. With inflation also rising and a sense that the dollar was overvalued relative to its trading partners' currencies and thus hurting U.S. domestic industry's competitiveness, Richard Nixon suspended the convertibility of dollars to gold in the face of declining gold reserves and mounting pressure from foreign governments. French president Georges Pompidou even sent a battleship to New York harbor to retrieve France's gold deposits from the vaults at the New York Federal Reserve Bank. Bretton Woods's success had created a new context in which the rigidity of fixed exchange rates in a growing dynamic international economy was unsustainable. The world would gradually move to the current freely floating exchange rates and fiat currencies, that is, still government-issued currencies, but no longer backed by gold. In hindsight, this was what systems scientists call an unplanned "phase-shift transition."

Then, after years in the making, the Maastricht Treaty was signed in 1993 among European countries seeking to create economic and monetary union throughout Europe. In 2002, the euro would replace European domestic currencies in many but not all European countries in an effort to improve efficiency across the Eurozone, in a drive for competitiveness. If only they had realized they would be giving up resiliency at the same time, they might have had the wisdom to bring in the euro as a complementary currency rather than an alternative currency as first envisioned by Bernard Lietaer, who first conceived the idea of the euro currency. Countries like Greece and Italy would pay a steep price in the euro crisis following the 2008 financial crisis for this lack of resiliency, all rooted in the reductionist flawed logic of neoclassical economics. Had they kept their domestic currencies while adding the euro as a complement, they could have depreciated their domestic currencies as in the past, and provided urgently needed stimulus to their domestic economies in the form of increased foreign demand. But instead, they were trapped in the rigidity of the Eurozone.

In all, the Bretton Woods system has evolved quite a bit since 1944, but much has remained the same. In particular, the World Bank, with its hard currency debt-based development paradigm (lend dollars to developing countries in South Asia, Africa, and Latin America), forced debtor nations into locally extractive activities such as mining minerals to meet the demand from the developed world for advanced manufacturing and telecommunications networks in order to service their hard currency debt rather than developing resilient domestic economies that could create shared prosperity. The next phase is when a crisis arrives, as it always does—economies are complex—and the IMF comes in and imposes its austerity medicine on countries to squeeze them to service this debt. A vicious cycle of boom and bust debt crises in the emerging economies is the result, a pattern we have seen repeat again and again, destroying the underlying development in the process.

The point here is not to do an exhaustive analysis of the current world order, or the weaknesses of the development paradigm. The point is, first, to expose how the architecture was flawed from the start based on the neoclassical paradigm, and second, to highlight how dramatically the context has changed since Bretton Woods, and since the "Nixon Shock" in 1971. The original "machine design" was flawed, incapable of dealing with complexity. To make matters worse, the global architecture has not adapted to the radically new context, the context of the polycrisis. The combination of rapid globalization and accelerating technological innovation has been both the source of great progress and the source of great instability and grotesque inequality. Whatever modifications to the world order we've seen have been primarily designed to address and facilitate this "progress."

Yet at the same time and most critically over the longer run, the human population has grown fourfold while the global economy's material and energy metabolism has grown twentyfold since Bretton Woods, all while the planet has remained fixed in scale. Yet our institutional economic architecture has not responded hardly at all. One unanticipated seismic change has been the dramatic rise of China, now an economic superpower together with the United States, effectively ending the unipolar world economic order. But China is not playing by the same rules as the Western world order. It seeks its own vision of a world order, more centered on its own influence and state-subsidized competitive advantages, particularly throughout Asia, as one should expect.

Given the profound shift in contexts, it's shocking that there have been so few calls for a newly negotiated world order, an architecture that would better reflect reality and better serve everyone's shared interests for a design fit for purpose in the new context. It took two world wars to force Western leaders to sit down at Bretton Woods. We now have a trade war that Donald Trump launched against the world raging as I write these words. The reimagination of a new economic world order could not come soon enough. Perhaps, just perhaps, the "disturbance" caused by Trump is just the catalyst to reimagine a healthy trade regime in service to a broadly shared prosperity rather than powerful corporate interests. Such an outcome, again, is predicated first on a shift in paradigm to a living systems worldview. Our paradigm shift work remains the same.

What might such a new architecture look like as this new paradigm emerges into the light of day, as someday it will? And what might the supporting fiscal and monetary policies look like if the

Reimagining Public Policy

ambition were to transform to a new world order, grounded in the living systems principles of Regenerative Economics? Let's have a look.

We can begin with the good work underway with the "Beyond Bretton Woods: Finance for a Regenerative Future" initiative founded by James Vacarro and Frank Van Gansbeke.[167] After several successful gatherings, the initiative calls for ten bold modifications to the global financial architecture as follows:

1. Implement a global price on carbon.
2. Incorporate climate into monetary policy.
3. End the $7 trillion (80% of which are implicit, not explicit) fossil fuel subsidies immediately.
4. Take a nature-centric approach to well-being metrics.
5. Regulate the shadow banking sector.
6. Rebalance representation in international financial institutions— the IMF and World Bank in particular.
7. Develop novel institutions for overseeing climate finance.
8. Reimagine and redistribute mitigation, adaptation, and loss and damage financing.
9. Establish a new debt-restructuring mechanism.
10. Design novel nature-based currencies.

This is an excellent list that I warmly endorse, and I encourage readers to go to the Beyond Bretton Woods website to learn more. These are practical, actionable steps demanding urgent attention in a world where attention has become scarce.

As you will understand after reading chapter 9 on the missing institution of the commons, I believe that we need to allow our imagination to think even more expansively and more systemically first at the level of institutional architecture. We need to allow ourselves to imagine not only concrete proposals for new policies and even institutions within the current global architecture such as the novel institutions and currencies described above. I am convinced that we must also address the missing institution of the commons, a meta "institution" in the sense that the private sector is an "institution" made up of thousands of individual organizations. Proposal 1 above, a global price of carbon, should be seen as a vital stopgap measure pending the establishment of an institution of the atmospheric commons. While having no price on carbon is clearly wrong, we must remember that there is a difference between a cost that can be fixed with money and a wrong that can never be fixed. The necessary tool is a science-based quota, enforced by an objective body without the conflicts of interest of the private sector or susceptibility to political pressures of the public sector, just like what works with a fishery.

As described in chapter 9, this collection of institutions, each focused on specific categories of co-inherited wealth, would serve as the essential restraints and money pumps to keep money associated with our co-inherited wealth circulating throughout the system rather than being siphoned off and hoarded at the top, as happens today. Such institutions demand cooperation across state and national borders, and occasionally they demand global cooperation. There simply is no way to compete to the death in a game of destruction without ending up where we are now headed: collapse. How we achieve such an ambition is a fair question to which I do not have a satisfactory answer beyond our theory of change. But we must embark on a dual path and learn as we go.

First, we must begin locally where it is relatively easy. Emphasis on relatively; nothing is easy. Practice on your local fishery, farmland, or open space. Conservation-driven models exist to study and learn from.[168] We must begin the urgent task of creating the thousands of such commons trusts with independent and enforceable governance having a fiduciary duty to the future.

Large-scale and strategic international philanthropy should create a twenty-year commitment to building a community of practice with a bold ambition to stand up such a meta institution of the commons. We then must learn and practice a collective form of governance of our co-inherited wealth, new to the West, but indigenous to the core. Such initiatives are underway around the world today, often within indigenous cultures that have responsibly managed our co-inherited wealth all along as part of their culture. We must learn from them and learn how to scale them out, and scale them up where necessary. Always practice the rule of subsidiarity, keeping decision-making as local as possible, but pushing it up with representation as the context demands, such as a global commons for the atmosphere.

But we must at the same time be bold, for time is not on our side.

Global citizens, representing a diversity of interests and perspectives from North and South, must demand that the United States, China, and the European Union, collectively representing nearly half of the global economy, agree to negotiate for our collective self-interests the design and governance of such a global commons for the atmosphere. With these three economic blocks in broad agreement, the difficult task of building a global consensus, including phase-in timelines and equitable burden sharing, can begin. Given the reality of global politics, this work is best initiated in the civil society sector, thinking systematically rather than reactively.

Fortunately, we are not beginning from scratch. Elinor Ostrom studied these practices extensively and brought important teachings to the Western world on how to effectively manage these common resource pools, calling into question the conclusions in Garrett Hardin's famous 1968 essay, "The Tragedy of the Commons."[169] Interestingly, Aristotle wrote about the same challenge in his *Politics*, observing "that which is common to the greatest number has the least care bestowed upon it."

Let's refresh our memories on Ostrom's insights. Ostrom identified from her research the governance principles necessary for the successful management of common resource pools, as she shared in *Governing the Commons: The Evolution of Institutions for Collective Action* (1990). They will serve as our companion as we contemplate the task of creating a diversity of institutional commons-sector trusts across scales from local to bioregional to global, and across resource types, both natural and technical.

1. Commons need to have clearly defined boundaries.
2. Rules should fit local circumstances.
3. Participatory decision-making is vital.
4. Commons must be monitored.
5. Sanctions for those who abuse the commons should be graduated.
6. Conflict resolution mechanisms should be easily accessible.
7. Commons need the right to organize separate from external authorities.
8. Commons work best when nested within larger networks.

The co-inherited wealth that our cumulative technology represents presents a different level of challenge. The mere concept flies in the face of our unquestioned assumptions regarding private ownership. Here a longer-term education effort will be required. Peter Barnes's book *Ours: The Case for Universal Property* and the Capital Institute's cohort-based course on Regenerative Economics are a good place to start.

At the same time, we now live in a world where the U.S. and China, with nominal GDPs of $28 trillion and $18 trillion, respectively (China larger on a purchasing power parity basis, and still growing faster), tower over the next largest economy, Germany ($4.5 trillion). It's hard to think of a more important project than to entice these two superpowers to sit down and negotiate a framework to establish a global institution of the commons for two of the most important common pool resources: the atmosphere in the biosphere commons and the internet, inclusive of the data on it powering large language models, in the technosphere commons. Sounds like a dream, especially now. But the nightmare that awaits if we don't is what we need to focus our minds on. If Trump wants a Nobel Prize for his "art of a deal," here's his chance. More likely it will be enlightened citizens that begin this process. Students from my course have begun to explore the possibilities.

Rather than repeat the ideas from Beyond Bretton Woods, allow me to add ten bold and essential proposals to their excellent list above for our collective imagination and consideration. My choices are not governed by what is politically feasible today. Rather, they are driven by what I deem to be essential if we are to see a regenerative economic system manifest before it's too late. The challenge of "the how" can be tackled only when the vision is clear. And the vision I am proposing is grounded in nothing less than the patterns and principles that describe life itself.

Where there is no vision, the people perish.

—PROVERBS 29:18

TEN-POINT REGENERATIVE POLICY PROPOSAL

1 Stand Up the Institution of the Commons

Launch a global initiative for the creation of the Institution of the Commons. Begin with a finite number of the world's largest economies to keep the process manageable. Despite its noble intentions, the United Nations is the wrong body for such an effort to be effective. The key is to first do the essential education. Then move toward some quick wins to get a process started while wrestling with the thorny issues such as the internet and AI. At the same time, it would be ideal for bilateral talks with China and the U.S. to begin in parallel.

2 Shrink and Rewire the Financial Sector

Finance has confused means and ends. It does not operate in right relationship with the real economy, nor is the finance algorithm that controls financial decision-making fit for purpose in our embedded interconnected world. The purpose of finance must be established to serve the needs of a regenerative economy, in service to life, and not seek endless new methods of speculation and extraction as an end in itself. The irresponsible rise of cryptocurrencies that serve no purpose beyond speculation and illicit commerce must be curtailed, while allowing for innovations, including complementary digital currencies, that are responsive to our great systemic challenges. Speculative excesses throughout the global capital markets must be severely reined in, which will take a unified global approach and a package of carrots and sticks beginning with a global financial transactions tax.[170] Success will require a radical shrinking of what is the current financial industry as well as innovative growth of new financial infrastructure and institutions to meet the demands of this new context.

3 Expand the Mandate of Central Banks

Convene an emergency conference on central bank leadership. In addition to incorporating climate into monetary policy as proposed by Beyond Bretton Woods, we must also enlist the world's leading central banks, most important, the U.S. Federal Reserve as the steward of the world's reserve currency today, into the North-South dialogue regarding energy transition finance, agriculture transition, and mitigation and adaptation costs. Central banks can break the ice on the "where will the money come from" challenge that plagues these discussions. Facilitating the capitalization of regional, special-purpose development banks with a clear mission and strong governance is a more logical approach than direct investments. The only question is, what are the limits, not whether there is a role to play. If the U.S. central bank can print trillions to bail out the banking industry to protect the real economy, it can and would be wise to play a role here as well to ensure the health of the biosphere upon which the human economy depends. This will demand the domestic political will to recognize that for certain issues, there is no us and them. All of human civilization literally will sink or swim together. Such an approach will necessitate redefining central bank mandates through legislation.

4 Eliminate Adverse Incentives

Level the playing field by ending adverse incentives. Expanding on the Beyond Bretton Woods call to end fossil fuel subsidies, we must restructure all fiscal incentives beginning with the elimination of fossil fuel and chemical subsidies, but also the subsidies for less obvious "bads" such as consumer advertising, excessive corporate and private debt, and leveraged speculation of all forms. Create positive incentives such as targeted tax credits, as we saw with the poorly named Inflation Reduction Act, and feed in tariffs to accelerate the shift to renewable energy, and other critical priorities such as regenerative agriculture, controlling biodiversity loss through avoiding deforestation and desertification, and restoring ocean and freshwater health.

5 Restructure the Tax Code

Bring the tax code in alignment with a Pigouvian approach. This can be most directly achieved by relieving the tax burden from "goods" like work while increasing taxes on "bads," such as market activity that is generating negative "externalities" (costs like pollution that are passed on to somebody other than the business that created them). Such reforms would include income tax relief for the working class, transaction taxes on excessive financial speculation, and a steep and rising carbon tax as noted above, along with other Pigouvian taxes such as an extreme tax on private jet travel and luxury yachts, whose fuel consumption is both wasteful and immoral in light of climate chaos.[171] Most obviously, a wealth tax is the primary way to address soaring inequality after the fact, which, as we've seen, is systemically unhealthy, whatever one's views on the ethics of inequality. We must at the same time explore novel mechanisms to restrain the creation of exponential fortunes in the first place. As discussed in chapter 9, I believe that the creation of an institution of the commons should be the primary tool for this objective, but also various targeted windfall profits taxes can be used to help the transition. Tax reform can be designed as a tax shift, not a tax hike, and can be revenue neutral if desired.

6 Align Public Procurement and Investment

Use the power of the public purse to catalyze the shift in demand to renewable energy and sustainably grown healthy food. The U.S. government is the largest single energy consumer in the world. Its energy demand must lead the transition. Other countries must follow suit. Similarly, public investment in essential R&D is a must given the scale, risk profile, and pace of breakthrough technologies that are essential. While other priorities and agendas have appeared, smarter spending and investment by public bodies should be the easy part.

7 Recirculate Surplus Wealth

Design feedback loops for excessive surplus-wealth circulation back into natural and social capital on an unprecedented scale as a policy priority. Excessive wealth is the target, and it is actually now being studied as a disorder.[172] This is a question of both individual health and systemic health, not moral judgment. Who is to define excessive family wealth? Let the debate begin. Whatever the answer—mine would be anything above $25 million, or $50 million to make the debate easier—there are a number of policy options to address it. I favor tools to pre-distribute wealth such as the money pumps described in chapter 9 on the commons, effectively reducing the slope (above some threshold) on the wealth creation curve in the first place.[173] Some combination of a universal wealth tax and an estate tax would ensure that the surplus is recirculated rather than serve as an overpowering force driving up asset values and the cost of living for all of us with them. I would favor circulation if this wealth recirculated into various designated institutions of the commons at the wealth holder's choice. In this way the surplus would cycle systemically from stocks of abundance, through flows in the economy, and then back into nurturing the stocks. Capital composted at scale. Let the public sector make the compelling case to tax the now "wealthier" public for good schools, improved roads, and safety, rather than harvest the people's co-inherited wealth and then be left to deal with the many consequences of doing so.

8 Reimagine Philanthropy

Related to the point above, we need a new word for philanthropy to elevate its essential recirculation function in the metabolism of surplus financial capital. The tax deductibility of charitable giving is aligned with the need to recirculate wealth, but the payout minimums should at least triple from the current 5 percent in the U.S. The perpetual private foundation should be eliminated as a legal structure given the urgency to recycle financial capital into the most urgent social and ecological needs. Finally, we should begin a dialogue on the surplus wealth tied up in the world's leading sovereign wealth funds, much of it sourced from fossil fuel windfalls, co-inherited wealth not shared equitably. In the context of regenerative economics and co-inherited wealth, it is reasonable to ask the question, Whose money is that really? I can think of no better legacy for vast stocks of sovereign oil wealth to be composted back into natural capital. It also happens to be a systemic health requirement if we are to take our first principles seriously.

9 Develop New Metrics of Systemic Health.

Adding to the Beyond Bretton Woods call for nature-centered metrics, and drawing on energy flow network science and other methods, develop *intrinsic measures* of systemic health for bioregional and national economies and for single enterprises and enterprise networks to augment well-being metrics. Intrinsic measures, like a human's blood pressure, allow us to see if conditions for health are present. Collectively, such measures represent alternatives to simplistic and often misleading GDP measures, and complement more useful outcome measures. A number of systems scientists are busy developing just such tools, measuring regenerative qualities of healthy flow networks such as system intricacy, balance, and circulation.[174] But to become useful, a more robust approach to defining and capturing critical data must be developed and a taxonomy of universal standards applied. This is a serious research project and then a massive data collection project with scope and scale beyond what a major central bank does today for employment and inflation measures.

10 Study the Limits to Investment

Most challenging conceptually and philosophically, if there are limits to growth, then that implies that there are limits to investment.[175] Growth of GDP is a function of growth of consumption, government spending, and real investment (not related to financial speculation). This suggests that we must face the reality that there are trade-offs in what we invest in and how we do it, and long-term implications of our choices. If we want AI on demand, who makes that decision if the energy implications affect everyone? Of course, this has been true since the colonial roots of capitalism, but we can no longer ignore the implications. An Institution of the Commons with enforcement power may serve as one of the key choke points to restrain unwise or wasteful investment, understood holistically.

My experience discussing such policy proposals with government officials has been largely pointless, since the first step, per our theory of change, is to shift the paradigm in order to have an intelligent conversation within a shared worldview. I'll give one example, relating to my proposal for a financial transactions tax (FTT) in the wake of the financial crisis.

As you may recall, government officials and regulators were looking for a way to make Wall Street pay for the damage of the crash, and a small tax on all financial transactions, or perhaps a subset of them such as on stock trading, was very much front and center on the agenda. Given the enormous trading volumes, a tax of a small percentage of 1 percent would add up to billions of dollars per year, and curtail speculation to a degree in the process. A vicious and energized debate ensued, ideological, political, and mechanical.

Naturally, the U.S. was the primary holdout, while a strong consensus arose across Europe in favor. But such a tax on global capital markets works best if everyone plays ball.

I met with a mid-level but very sharp official in Obama's Treasury Department to explain the FTT logic from a living systems perspective. In contrast to most of the arguments in favor, I was not making a case for where we could spend the money (Bill Gates was in favor of the tax as a source for fresh aid to the Global South). My argument was in favor of systemic health. A small tax was a slight cost to efficiency, with a huge pickup in resiliency, was the gist of my argument, aligned with the principle of dynamic balance. I argued that all the high-frequency trading that would be most affected was essentially legalized front running, purely extractive, and not at all "in right relationship." There is probably no simpler and more easily justifiable policy reform to create a meaningful positive alignment of our overly speculative capital markets with the principles of living systems.[176]

You can imagine the look I got. What flowed from his mouth (a former Lehman Brothers trader, it turns out, nice well-meaning fellow) was textbook neoclassical economics dogma. "But John, any tax will harm efficiency, and efficient capital markets lower the cost of capital, which is good for growth." Dead end.

I am convinced that the path to taming and ultimately degrading and transforming the finance algorithm has no shortcuts. Easy wins within the paradigm will have little meaningful impact. The challenge we must face is to shift the paradigm first. Only with an "aha" experience that once seen cannot be unseen do we have a chance to do the radical reform that awaits.

So we are in the paradigm-shifting business, full stop. It's a revolution, not of some new discovery, but a revolution in how people see what they already see. The rest will follow naturally once we manage to shift the paradigm. Just like the Copernican flip that ushered in the modern era, we await our own Copernican moment. A moment when the truth becomes clear that the economy is a human economy made up of human beings and our tools and technologies. It is, therefore a living system. It is, in fact, a highly complex organism structured as fractal networks embedded in larger networks, all interconnected and interdependent. It is not a machine as our theory implies, often without us being conscious of this fact, made up of separate parts that can be optimized for money. That unquestioned assumption is what we must confront, with all the uncomfortable implications it holds. It will be the moment when we realize that our economics is not only out of step but also hiding from us the simple truth that we are destroying ourselves and the planet because there's a profit in it.

Our greatest ally in this most difficult challenge is actually the rising pressures within the system resulting from our ignorant ways. Yes, we must search for a new story, and we must keep trying new strategies to affect change. But one thing is for sure from the study of systems science: Systems only change in response to pressure. They either transcend to higher levels of complexity, or they collapse.

The pressure is rising. The pathway through the polycrisis is to recognize the urgent need to transform our system design to align with the higher complexity of life.

> When a complex system is far from equilibrium, small islands of coherence in a sea of chaos have the capacity to shift the entire system to a higher order.
>
> —Ilya Prigogine, Nobel laureate

EPILOGUE

As I close this second edition, the world is experiencing the shock therapy of Trump's first hundred days in office in 2025. The consequences are as yet unknown. They are certain to be far-reaching and long-lasting, affecting everything from our rule of law to the stability of our democracy, our standing in the world, and the fate of the United States and the dollar as the foundation of the global economy. As we have learned, in the parlance of systems science, we call this a "disturbance," in true understatement.

Disturbances apply to (living) social systems just as they do to the ecological systems throughout the living world. Like a forest fire, a disturbance is necessary from time to time to allow recourses to break rigid bonds of entrenched patterns that may no longer serve the evolutionary health of the whole. Disturbances root out decay and enable resources and energy to reorganize in new ways, better suited to the always dynamic context, and thereby manifest fresh potential in a new cycle of growth. Ecologists call this the release phase of the adaptive cycle, shown below. If we believe human economies are living systems just as human enterprises are living systems, we must assume that they, too, will follow the adaptive cycle as well. Joseph Schumpeter's "gales of creative destruction" from over a half century ago understood this phenomenon at work within our economic system. The cycle begins with birth, followed by an exponential growth phase, a slowing growth phase, then conservation/maturation, followed by release, and then reorganization with fresh innovation to begin the process all over again. This is the cycle of life.

Such renewal comes with real costs, real loss, and struggle in the release phase. We are in the release phase not simply of individual enterprises or even entire industries. We are in the release phase of the entire exponential-growth-based system that has overshot its limits because it was built on the false theoretical foundation of reductionist logic that does not apply to complex adaptive living systems. It is and will be chaotic, but it is not the end of times. It is not the rapture, but it is an apocalypse of sorts. Apocalypse literally means a "lifting of the veil" so that we can see reality in a fresh and more accurate way.

From the perspective of the emergence of regenerative economies, this current "disturbance" appears dire. It appears that we are

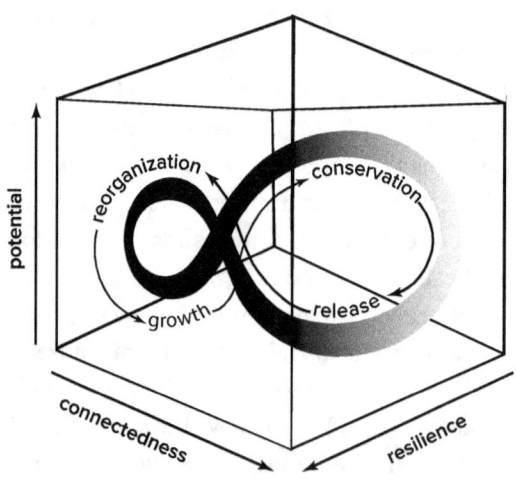

■ **Figure E.1 Adaptive Cycle.** *Credit: Modified from Adaptive Cycle, by Lance Gunderson and C.S. Holling.*

going in exactly the wrong direction. Launching a trade war is hardly working in "right relationship," canceling wind farm projects while attempting to restart coal is bad economics and disastrous climate strategy. And then there is the assault on the rule of law, essential to restrain our darker shadows.

But perhaps this is the natural course, the portal we must pass through if metamorphosis to something far healthier and higher in the evolutionary spiral is required, where incremental change would never cut it. Our proverbial forest fire to weaken the bonds and patterns that no longer serve. Perhaps our disturbance is the collective set of disorienting experiences beginning with 9/11 at the World Trade Center that I bore witness to, triggering a twenty-year so-called war on terror premised on a lie. Soon thereafter came the subprime mortgage fiasco in the United States that would trigger the financial crash of 2008 and the Great Recession that could easily have been a depression. The betrayal of Main Street and households while the bankers were bailed out made it all disgusting. Popular trust in the institution of finance, already on shaky grounds, was destroyed. When you undermine trust in the financial system of a modern economy, you undermine trust in all institutions, as we have seen. That is the true legacy of Wall Street's reckless and arrogant greed, reflecting an institution that has lost its moral compass, its leaders never held to account. As a result, our governments gave up vital capacity to respond to the ongoing economic malaise as they socialized Wall Street's financial wreckage, which was compounded by poorly conceived government housing policy[177] (good intentions but in conflict with living systems principles), it must be said.

Then the pandemic hit, altering our lives in ways that we still don't fully comprehend. Throughout the ordeal, our lost trust in institutions became clear. Will we ever know the source of the pandemic in order to mitigate the risk of it happening again? Will history conclude that Dr. Anthony Fauci was a hero or a villain whose judgment was clouded by association with the pharmaceutical industry that in turn is controlled by the finance algorithm? We simply don't know.

Finally, the violence rages on, with the Russian invasion of Ukraine, unbearable atrocities in the Middle East, and other wars. No doubt future historians will look back and condemn the violence of fossil fuel industry leaders for their willful deceit and our collective lack of will to address climate change as the greatest violence of all.

Now here we are with the return to the White House and the most powerful position in the world of a convicted felon unfit for the station, who led an insurrection, and was never held to account for his actions. That all sure feels like a forest fire to me. But could it all have a purpose?

Recall, Fritjof Capra teaches that life is intelligent, one of four principles of life. Is this an act of intelligent life to force a course correction of our diseased political economy managed by a decaying elite wed to a theoretical construct—neoclassical economics—that uses verifiably false assumptions about how the reality of sustainable life works?

Perhaps. I suggest that we hold out the possibility that, yes, this is part of a mysterious metamorphosis-like process we will never understand but are called to have faith in. The alternative is to conclude that humanity is fatally flawed, and life is short, brutal for most, and meaningless. I choose to believe the former, to believe in the mysterious intelligence of life, our human ingenuity, and our collective ability to wake up and let go of our failing worldview. Beneath all the horrendous headlines, I believe that we are witnessing humanity transcending to a higher level of consciousness, one that releases shame and fear in favor of courage and love, and with that the emergence of a living systems paradigm that we already know is real. Since the interdependence of all is now settled science, the implications are breathtaking. It means that we all have agency in this historic moment. What we do, or choose not to do, even the intentions we set, will affect the outcome. That's what the science says. It's what many of us intuit, indeed know to be true. It's profound and empowering, evoking confidence and courage, infused with awe and wonder. Feel it. So how can we make sense of this moment, and where do we go from here?

First, let's not sugarcoat it. The world is in a hot chaotic mess. People are damaged from trauma and poor mental and physical health. They are afraid, and rightfully angry. They feel betrayal and they were betrayed. Our minds are being actively manipulated by technological forces we don't fully understand. As a result, authoritarians are on the rise, as fear covets the strongman. While the causes of this reality are many and exceedingly complex, one cannot help but see a clear fact among the chaos: the decline of the United States as the leader of the free world in the first quarter of the twenty-first century. Yet our politicians on both sides of the aisle continue to celebrate American exceptionalism, "the greatest country in the world." The U.S. is an exceptional country and a wonderful experiment in democracy. But the data on well-being is damning, particularly regarding all aspects of our health. Shockingly, we now rank dead last in life expectancy among developed economies, suggesting that we would be wise to exercise a bit of humility at this time.

There are lessons for us from the historian Arnold Toynbee's exhaustive study of the causes of decline of over twenty civilizations in his twelve-volume *A Study of History* that runs some seven thousand pages. In brief, Toynbee found a pattern that explained the decline of civilizations. It was the "decay of the elite from a creative minority to merely a dominant minority which imposes its will without deserving obedience." His observations taught him that civilizations begin to collapse when their elites do the following:

- Lose their moral authority and become merely exploitative.
- Pursue narrow self-interest rather than the common good.
- Abandon the virtues and values that initially enable their success.
- Become disconnected from the needs and realities of the general population.

It's a damning list. Can you hear me now, Wall Street? Silicon Valley? Reading Toynbee's characterization of elite decay should cause politicians of all stripes to pause and reflect. Same for the media, epitomized by CBS CEO Leslie Moonves's cynical statement regarding the 2016 presidential race of Donald Trump: "It may not be good for America, but it's damn good for CBS." It's disgusting.

And now we are confronted with the emergence of a hyper elite unlike anything we have seen before, the tech masters of the universe running enterprises of unimaginable scale and impact across all aspects of human civilization and our relationship with the Earth, our home. Based on the messianic zeal of several of the leading protagonists, coupled with an invigorated and even antidemocratic libertarian ideology, we can safely assume that Professor Toynbee would be sounding his alarm at full blast.

The truth is that Trump has a point when he rails against the elite, and the message resonated to many across the country for good reason. It's a dangerous moment in the United States and around the world, compounding the unprecedented challenges posed by the existential ecological crises that are rapidly spinning out of control as denial mentality continues to undermine the urgent response necessary while CO_2 parts per million continue to rise in our atmosphere.

But we must not despair. We cannot succumb to hopelessness. Instead, we must wake up, undergo deep reflection to make sense of this pivotal time, and collectively rise to the moment.

We the majority citizens, not the failing and decayed elite, are being called to collectively lead. There are no heroes coming to save the day. We all constitute the collective hero in our story, through radical empowered participation in the next evolution of life on this planet. The "disturbance" became inevitable when the decay of the elite set in. A grab fest for money and power fueled by ego and greed secured unprecedented privilege for the elite, without any acceptance of the responsibility that goes with it. Jeff Bezos built a $500 million yacht too large to get into a harbor. Ken Griffin is building a $1 billion personal estate in Palm Beach. The media fawns. Actions have consequences.

Let me close with a clear call to action to the Cultural Regenerators among us.[178] We no doubt represent millions of evolutionary leaders, the imaginal cells of cultural metamorphosis amounting to nothing short of a New Renaissance for a new age.

The Italian Renaissance marked a cultural shift and a rebirth of human potential. It led to the Scientific Revolution and its rejection of religious dogma. This New Renaissance is global and pluralistic, marked by a cultural shift away from the limits of materialism and the reductionist method of perceiving reality that has defined Western modernity. It is rejecting the dogma of the "Church of Economics" and its emissaries the finance algorithm and techno-feudalism. It reflects not merely a rebirth of humanism, but the next evolution of the human project that sees all of humanity's beautiful cultural diversity participating constructively in the ongoing fourteen-billion-year evolution of life itself, across not only Gaia, but according to the leading edge of cosmology, the entire Uni-verse—meaning literally one song! It honors the interdependence and unity in diversity of all, grounded in evidenced-based science that remarkably aligns with and at the same time radically extends our many ancient wisdom traditions. It's a true metamorphosis, but we don't yet know what the butterfly looks like. As you scan through these ten bold ambitions, notice where our Eight Principles of regenerative vitality show up. Listen for what inspires you, and what's yours to do.

CALL TO ACTION

1 Lead with education.

The Latin root of the word *education* is "educere," which means "to lead out." We are trapped in an outdated mechanistic worldview, a worldview that sees humans separate from each other and separate from nature. We are in a proverbial Plato's cave with a false reductionist perception of reality. All progress toward transformational change begins with a shift in paradigm, as Dana Meadows taught us. I invite all of us into this foundational work of learning to unlearn our confused ideas, most important, the flawed machine metaphor of a clockwork universe that dates to Newton and Descartes. It works brilliantly for what we build (machines), it fails for what we manage (complexity, from organizations to economies). Learn living systems science. Take a course on Regenerative Economics! Do a PhD in Regenerative Economics developing new measures and models. Use your creative talents to spread knowledge, from elementary school up to mid-level professionals and leaders of all kinds. If you discover it's too late for the C-suite, target their kids.

2 Begin on the ground in place.

The burgeoning interest in bioregionalism in recent years but going back decades is evidence of the regenerative economy manifesting in the real world, typically highly distrusted and under the radar. To indigenous cultures, this has always been a way of life. Hundreds if not thousands of bold initiatives working collaboratively and respectfully between modern and indigenous cultures across bioregions and across national boundaries are alive and growing throughout the world. New innovative initiatives such as the BioFi Project[179] are at work building the missing layer of financial intermediation essential to facilitate "robust circulation" of financial resources deep into the essential bioregional work, both on ecosystem health and the related community health. Every place is in varying stages of decay because of the extended and accelerating assault by modernity. Dig in at home and work to restore our vital ecosystems back to health, be they on land, in our watersheds, or at sea. Ecosystem function in all its diversity is the essential foundation of a regenerative economy, and all life. This is work for many hands. Just imagine if one-quarter of the world's population planted five trees per year for the next ten years, hardly an ambitious goal. That's one hundred billion trees to improve the water cycle, build and hold soil, provide habitat, absorb carbon, and cool the planet! It's a start.

3 Begin in the community of place.

Similarly, the local economy movement is thriving, beginning with local food systems, but extending to all essential needs both material and cultural. Join community economics visionaries including Susan Witt and the Schumacher Center, Alfa Demmolesh, Michael Shuman, Zita Cobb, Judy Wicks, and Slow Money visionary Woody Tasch and regenerate community, experimenting with innovative tools such as land trusts, community currencies, and local investment funds, all connected with relationships of trust. This work is particularly essential in underserved communities, but needed in privileged ones as well. Place provides the ideal context to work across the silos and differences of our fragmented and divided culture and economic system developed for efficiency at the expense of resiliency. Begin by using Regenesis Group's[180] development approach and their "story of place" process to truly "see" the genius and essence of place. A first simple step is organizing a community meeting of all stakeholders to begin rebuilding right relationships. Kate Raworth's doughnut framework has proven to be a useful tool for communities and entire cities to see their own challenges and identify priorities.

4 Build responsive new enterprises as regenerative ecosystems.

Build regenerative culture and supportive ownership models as well as a vast diversity of products and services that respond to the polycrisis. Seek to create the conditions to manifest unseen potential that can evolve beyond the best-laid plans. Rewire existing small businesses, especially their culture, to align with living systems. In aggregate, small business is the cellular level of the global economy, accounting for well over half of employment and most growth in employment. Its health is foundational to overall systemic health. Fight for enlightened government strategic support to small business, and small business creation. View large local businesses as coral reefs to build from.

5 Nudge large enterprise.

If you are inside a large global enterprise set up to maximize scale efficiencies, and you are patient, work on regenerative experiments where you are given freedom to create. Ideally set up skunkworks projects where you can create your own culture yet retain access to resources and the resiliency of the host as a coral reef of sorts. Some would say your role is more accurately an act of hospicing what is no longer fit for purpose. Stay objective as you assess the potential of the work. Walking away when the timing is right is always an option on the table, as more and more are discovering. But don't give up too soon, transformation is possible even in large organizations.

6 Invest thoughtfully and regeneratively.

If you have the responsibility of stewarding financial capital, determine the appropriate return and liquidity for your context as a constraint, then seek to optimize regeneration in your investment themes. Invest in regenerative businesses, but ideally regenerative ecosystems taking a systemic approach. Bring regenerative culture to your management teams just as you bring finance skills. If you manage public equities, act like a private investor. You are a sector picker and a stock picker working in long-term relationships, not a quasi-indexer and box ticker. Help your portfolio companies partner together. Hold the courage of your convictions. If you are a large investor managing surplus capital of your own, or of wealthy institutions such as sovereign wealth funds, begin to contemplate the need to compost surplus capital back into social and natural capital at scale. This is your creative moment. Create a legacy not just a portfolio.

7 Practice regenerative philanthropy.

Bring regenerative culture to philanthropic institutions, creating conditions for health within the organization and with your operating partners (I prefer not to use the term *grantee*, as it's demeaning). This is job one. Job two is composting financial capital at scale, rapidly yet thoughtfully and effectively, which means systemically. If your foundation has a perpetual legacy strategy, spend time asking why. Consider composting for your legacy, looking, for example, to Kris and Doug Tompkins as your inspiration.[181]

8 Bring paradigm shift to public policy.

Take up the challenge to educate policymakers, beginning with the paradigm shift. Seek to implement leadership and management practices in the hierarchical public sector aligned with living systems before pushing policies. Then seek to find openings to begin the shift in policy discussions. Don't underestimate how entrenched the growth paradigm is. Begin, knowing that it's a long yet vital road ahead. Begin by building deep and trusting relationships.

9 Launch the Institution of the Commons.

Take up this immense structural challenge, again beginning with the mind shift in worldviews. Begin with what exists, fisheries, for example, and extend via metaphor. On the natural commons side, work with the legal rights of nature folks where synergy exists. Set a diversity of experiments in motion and learn what works. Open a citizen-to-citizen conversation between the U.S. and China on the atmosphere, the most urgent commons of all at this moment. On the technosphere side, begin by finding some low-hanging fruit, perhaps with a library or other cultural treasure. At the same time, strategize for the financial system plumbing. And most important of all, perhaps, gather great minds to imagine how humanity could take back governance of the internet and now AI, protect it from being used for harm, and charge for its fair use so that its enormous wealth creation potential can be broadly shared. Technology networks with their network effects is where the juice lies, in terms of both regenerative impact and as a source of sharing the wealth.

10 Build islands of coherence.

This is not the work of lone heroes. This is work that can be done only in community. Join or build an island of coherence that will sustain you and others through the transformation. Link up with other islands, to form webs of genuine trust-based collaboration. Trust that you and your island have agency to shift the system. Even if you never understand how. That's now evidenced-based trust, not blind faith. It's been true all along.

THERE IS NO MASTER PLAN

We must begin. We construct the path by walking. Along this journey I'm convinced that we will rediscover our sacred purpose at this time: to participate in and co-create the next phase of the evolution of life on this magical blue marble we call Earth. We deserve to fail if we don't shift our economic system architecture into alignment with our latest evidence-based scientific understanding of reality as our most urgent priority. We must learn and embrace the regenerative process that describes how all life works. Such an approach is remarkably aligned with what our many wisdom traditions and indigenous elders have always somehow intuited. It's time we listen.

Finally, let us remain humble. Dana Meadows hastened to add one additional leverage point to her advice on how to change a system, a point that sits even above shifting the paradigm. I realize today that I must have somehow known this intuitively as I let go of my Wall-Street-ingrained beliefs upon reading *Limits to Growth* for the first time following 9/11. For some reason I'll never fully understand, this intuition to let go of my paradigm, and with it my identity, wasn't hard for me. It seemed the only option, what I had to do, once I knew. Letting go is a pattern that has defined my life purpose. It may hold that power for you as well if you summon the courage.

Dana Meadows passed away in February of 2001 at the age of 59 after a two-week battle with cerebral meningitis. A couple months later, I would walk away from JPMorgan and Wall Street for good. But I had no idea who she was and how her visionary, prescient, and controversial work with her MIT colleagues would change my life.

In a world devoid of the wise, courageous, and yes, kind and humble leaders we need, Dana was a true exemplar. I am told by one of her close colleagues that we would have loved each other dearly. With remorse for that missed opportunity, with respect for the light she shared, and with gratitude for the "entanglement" of her mind with my mind—and all of our minds as Schrödinger foresaw—I'll give Dana the final word.

> There is yet one leverage point that is even higher than changing a paradigm. That is to keep oneself unattached in the arena of paradigms, to stay flexible, to realize that no paradigm is "true," that each one, including the one that sweetly shapes your own worldview, is a tremendously limited understanding of an immense and amazing universe that is far beyond human comprehension.
>
> —DANA MEADOWS

ACKNOWLEDGMENTS

REGENERATIVE ECONOMICS remains in its infancy. Its origin is less about the discovery of some new grand theory than it is about seeing what others see, but in a revolutionary new way. As Marcel Proust famously said, "The real voyage of discovery consists not in seeking new landscapes, but in having new eyes."

My ability to perceive this new paradigm is not the result of some singular epiphany. Instead, it evolved through learning with brilliant minds, both colleagues and those I never had the privilege to know. It emerged, experientially and through a series of extraordinary synchronicities. I was particularly informed through several regenerative investment projects in agriculture and real estate. And it emerged through my insatiable hunger for answers, my tireless curiosity, and my imagination. I am therefore indebted to far too many thinkers and practitioners for opening my eyes to the ideas offered up in this book than is practical to mention here. I apologize to all those whose aid and insight I'm neglecting to mention.

My early work with Peter Brown and Bob Nadeau on "The Third Millennium Economy" project at Capital Institute was profoundly impactful, their wisdom extraordinary. In addition, my understanding of holism and the regenerative paradigm came together only through my engagement first with Allan Savory and Jim Howell in the context of the grasslands, and then with Bill Reed, Ben Haggard, Anthony Sblendorio, and Carol Sanford. I am also particularly indebted to Sally Goerner for her illumination of the empirical foundation of energy flow network science. Her contribution to my understanding and her thoughtful review of the original 2015 paper have been invaluable.

I would also like to single out some profound early influences during my post 9/11 awakening. Herman Daly, who deserved the Nobel Prize in economics that was never going to happen, Gar Alperovitz, Peter Barnes, Nora Bateson, Janine Benyus, Wendell Berry, Fritjof Capra, Bob Costanza, John Elkington, Paul Hawken, Hazel Henderson, Jessie Henshaw, Tad Homer-Dixon, Peter Victor, Tim Jackson, Wes Jackson, Susan Witt, Stuart Kauffman, Marjorie Kelly, Ashok Khosla, David Korten, Monica Sharma, Amory Lovins, David Orr, Bill Rees, Mathis Wackernagel, Rich Rosen, John Ralston Saul, Julie Schor, Gus Speth, Pavan Sukhdev, Dennis Meadows, Robert Ulanowicz, Bernard Lietaer, Woody Tasch, Mary Evelyn Tucker, Stewart Wallis, and Allen White, all of whom have contributed more to my reeducation than they are aware. Hunter Lovins has been extraordinarily supportive, and her work on natural capital is foundational.

More recently I've been privileged to learn from the truly brilliant minds of Jude Currivan, Brian Swimme, and Federico Faggin, to name just a few. Of course, there are my intellectual heroes I never had a chance to know, beginning with Dana Meadows, and including Thomas Berry, Pierre Teilhard de Chardin, Kenneth Boulding, Buckminster Fuller, Gregory Bateson, David Bohm, Carl Jung, Lin Yutang, Willis Harman, Jane Jacobs, E. F. Schumacher, Jan Smuts, and Rudolph Steiner. Geniuses all, who should be required reading at this pivotal time.

Finally, I am most grateful to all of my colleagues, board members, financial supporters, and the magnificent network of collaborators at Capital Institute over the years for their partnership, wisdom, and counsel. More recently I am indebted to Tre Cates and the team at nRhythm for putting theory into practice, and their vision and supportive partnership to manifest our shared "With Life" learning community, an example of the whole being far greater than the sum of the parts. I am particularly indebted to the thousands of students from around the world in our course community who teach me and inspire me with their ideas, courage, and action more than they will ever know.

ACKNOWLEDGMENTS

Through the process of writing this book, I learned what an immense collaborative act of giving birth it is. I'm grateful to my amazing book designer and producer, Terri Wright at Book Lotus Productions and her editing team Beret Olson and Paula Dragosh; to my publisher, Rob West, and the entire team at New Society Publishers, who jumped in to support this project without hesitation. It was a true collaborative effort.

Finally, it seems trite to say, but my dear wife, soulmate, and college sweetheart, Susan, stood by my side in unconditional loving support through my own personal transformation, my dark night of the soul, the years of searching, and the years of struggle. Collectively, it represents the blood, sweat, and tears that gave birth to the idea of Regenerative Economics. My gratitude to Sue and love for her is beyond words.

—JOHN FULLERTON, MAY 2025

ENDNOTES

PREFACE

1. Francis. *Laudato Si': On Care for Our Common Home* (encyclical letter, Libreria Editrice Vaticana: Vatican City, 2015).

CHAPTER 1

2. Capital Institute, "Ethics, Economics, Finance and Governance for the Anthropocene," 2012, http://capitalinstitute.org/our-projects/third-millennium.
3. Corey Bradsaw et al., "Underestimating the Challenges of Avoiding a Ghastly Future," https://www.frontiersin.org/journals/conservation-science/articles/10.3389/fcosc.2020.615419/full.
4. Johan Rockstrom et al., "Planetary Boundaries," *Ecology and Society* 14, no. 2 (2009, updated 2015), http://www.ecologyandsociety.org/vol14/iss2/art32.
5. This is the primary message of the "Fifth Assessment Report of the Intergovernmental Panel on Climate Change," released in March 2014, http://www.ipcc.ch/.
6. Herbert Spencer coined the phrase "survival of the fittest" after reading Darwin's *On the Origin of the Species: By Means of Natural Selection*. Darwin later used the phrase "fittest" to mean best fit, like a puzzle piece that best fits, or a species best suited to a local environment.
7. N. Stern, "Stern Review on the Economics of Climate Change" (London: HM Treasury, 2006), http:// webarchive.nationalarchives.gov.uk/+/http:/www.hm-treasury.gov.uk/sternreview_index.htm. Can be found at the Wiley online library at http://onlinelibrary.wiley.com/doi/10.1111/j.17284457.2006.00153.x/abstract.
8. Simon Rogers, "Bobby Kennedy on GDP: 'Measures Everything Except That Which Is Worthwhile,'" *The Guardian*, May 24, 2012, http://www.theguardian.com/news/datablog/2012/may/24/robert-kennedy-gdp.

9. Clinton Callahan, "Will Any Humans Become Post-Carbon?," OpEdNews, July 6, 2014, http://www.opednews.com/articles/7/Will-Any-Humans-Become-Pos-by-Clinton-Callahan-Amphibians_Civilization_Climate_Climate-Change-140706-826.html.
10. A. Wijkman and J. Rockstrom, *Bankrupting Nature: Denying Our Plenary Boundaries* (New York: Routledge, Report to the Club of Rome), 2012, http://www.anthemenviroexperts.com/?p=667.
11. See, e.g., N. Roubini, "Is Capitalism Doomed?," *Al Jazeera*, August 18, 2011, http:// english.aljazeera.net/indepth/opinion/2011/08/2011816104945411574.html.
12. R. Constanza and I. Kubiszewski, eds., *Creating a Sustainable and Desirable Future: Insights from 45 Global Thought Leaders* (New York: World Scientific, 2014).
13. E. U. von Weizsäcker et al., *Factor Five: Transforming the Global Economy Through 80% Improvements in Resource Productivity* (New York: Routledge, 2009).
14. Ellen MacArthur Foundation, "What Is a Circular Economy?," n.d., http://www.ellenmacarthurfoundation.org/circular-economy.
15. Much of the current thinking about systems change builds on the work of preeminent systems scientists like Karl Ludwig von Bertalanffy, one of the creators of general systems theory, and the work at MIT under Jay Forrester, creator of system dynamics.
16. *Limits to Growth* was ahead of its time, misunderstood, and attacked when published in 1972. However, its core thesis was prescient, as recent studies, such as that by Graham Turner, confirm.
17. D. Meadows, "Leverage Points: Places to Intervene in a System" (Hartland, VT: The Sustainability Institute, 1999).
18. J. Randers, *2052: A Global Forecast for the Next Forty Years* (White River Junction, VT: Chelsea Green Publishing, 2012); P. Gilding, *The Great Disruption* (New York: Bloomsbury Press, 2011); D. Orr, *Hope Is an Imperative: The Essential David Orr* (Washington, D.C.: Island Press, 2011). See also G. Speth, *The Bridge at the Edge of the World* (New Haven, CT: Yale University Press, 2009).
19. D. Korten, *Change the Story, Change the Future* (San Francisco: Berrett-Koehler, 2015).
20. See Savory Institute and Holistic Land Management at http://www.savoryinstitute.org.
21. See Regenesis Case studies at http://www.regenesisgroup.com/projects/.
22. See Capital Institute, *The Field Guide to a Regenerative Economy*, n.d., http://fieldguide.capitalinstitute.org/.
23. In this context, a "higher level of complexity" does not simply mean making something more complicated; rather, it refers to a higher level of evolution. Readers interested in exploring this concept further are referred to F. Heylighen, "Evolutionary Transitions: How Do Levels of Complexity Emerge?," *Complexity* 6, no. 1, http://pespmc1.vub.ac.be/Papers/Review_Complexity.pdf.
24. J. C. Kumarappa, *Economy of Permanence*, and *The Practice and Precepts of Jesus* (Rajghat, Varanasi, India: Sarva Seva Sangh Prakashan, 1945).

ENDNOTES 255

25. The "entropy law" refers to the second law of thermodynamics. Entropy is a quantitative measure of the amount of energy no longer available to do work. For example, once a log is burned, its energy is dissipated and is no longer an available energy source. Though increasing entropy actually means increasing dissipation, it is commonly thought to indicate increasing disorder.
26. J. Smuts, *Holism and Evolution* (New York: Macmillan, 1929).
27. D. Dagget, *Gardeners of Eden: Rediscovering Our Importance to Nature* (Flagstaff, AZ: Thatcher Charitable Trust, 2005).
28. Wikipedia describes the Anthropocene as "an informal geologic chronological term that serves to mark the evidence and extent of human activities that have had a significant global impact on the Earth's ecosystems."
29. Circle Economy Foundation, *The Circularity Gap Report 2024*, https://www.circularity-gap.world/2024.

CHAPTER 2
30. "Capitalism in Question" was even the theme for the Academy of Management's 2013 annual conference.
31. H. Daly and J. Farley, *Ecological Economics, Principles and Applications* (New York: Island Press, 2003); and R. Nadeau, *The Environmental Endgame: Mainstream Economics, Ecological Disaster, and Human Survival* (New Brunswick, NJ: Rutgers University Press, 2006).
32. R. Nadeau, *Rebirth of the Sacred: Science, Religion, and the New Environmental Ethos* (New York: Oxford University Press, 2012).
33. J. Smuts, *Holism and Evolution* (New York: Macmillan, 1926).
34. J. Smuts, *Holism and Evolution* (New York: Macmillan, 1926).
35. See P. Brown and G. Garver, *Right Relationship: Building a Whole Earth Economy* (San Francisco: Berrett-Koehler Publishers, 2009); and P. Victor, *Managing Without Growth: Slower by Design, Not Disaster* (Cheltenham, Gloucestershire, UK: Edward Elgar, 2008).
36. H. Daly and J. Cobb, *For the Common Good* (Boston: Beacon, 1989).
37. Author's personal communication with Janine Benyus (2012).
38. I. Prigogine, *From Being to Becoming* (New York: W. H. Freeman, 1980).
39. John Fullerton, *Regenerative Capitalism: How Universal Principles and Patterns Will Shape the New Economy* (Capital Institute, 2015).
40. Capital Institute, "Ethics, Economics, Finance and Governance for the Anthropocene," 2012.
41. Here, wisdom traditions refer to such core concepts as "oneness," which we abandoned in the name of "progress" but which underlies all major spiritual belief systems while remaining in complete alignment with our latest scientific understanding of how all living systems, energy flow networks, and indeed the entire universe actually function. See D. Korten, *Change the Story, Change the Future* (San Francisco: Berrett-Koehler, 2015); and "Third Millennium Economy Report," http://capitalinstitute.org/our-projects/third-millennium/.
42. A fractal is a natural phenomenon or a mathematical set that exhibits a repeating pattern that displays at every scale.

43. Fractals provide a foundation for local uniqueness because, like snowflakes, the same repeating pattern manifests in unique ways as determined by the unique context in which it emerges. So, while fractals seen in lungs, lightning bolts, and trees are universal patterns, no two lungs, lightning bolts, or trees are ever exactly the same.
44. S. Kauffman, *Reinventing the Sacred: A New Vision of Science, Reason, and Religion* (New York: Basic Books, 2008), 5.
45. H. Daly and J. Cobb, *For the Common Good*; T. Jackson, *Prosperity Without Growth*; and P. Victor, *Managing Without Growth*.
46. N. Stern, "Stern Review on the Economics of Climate Change" (London: HM Treasury, 2006), http:// webarchive.nationalarchives.gov.uk/+/ http:/www.hm-treasury.gov.uk/sternreview_index.htm. Can be found at the Wiley online library at http://onlinelibrary.wiley.com/doi/10.1111/j.17284457.2006.00153.x/abstract.
47. Robert Costanza, Maureen Hart, Stephen Posner, and John Talberth, "Beyond GDP: The Need for New Measures of Progress," *The Pardee Papers*, no. 4 (2009), http://www.bu.edu/pardee/files/documents/PP-004-GDP.pdf?PDF=pardee-paper-004-beyond-gdp.
48. See, e.g., J. Schor, *Plentitude: The New Economics of True Wealth* (New York: Penguin, 2010). See also the work of New Economics Foundation on well-being at http://www.neweconomics.org/issues/entry/well-being.
49. A. Maslow, "A Theory of Human Motivation," *Classics in the History of Psychology* (posted August 2000), http://psychclassics.yorku.ca/Maslow/motivation.htm. Originally published in *Psychological Review* 50 (1943): 370–96.
50. Keynes, J. M. *The General Theory of Employment, Interest and Money* (Palgrave Macmillan: United Kingdom, 1936): chapter 24.
51. Alfred Nobel understood that economics was not a natural science, so he did not create a prize for the discipline. But in 1968, the Swedish Central Bank, filled with neoclassical economists, decided that the discipline deserved a prize of comparable stature. It created the Sveriges Riksbank (central bank) Prize in Economic Sciences in Memory of Alfred Nobel. Note the words *economic sciences* in the title. The media, the public, and certainly the economics discipline now refer to this as the Nobel in Economics. But it's not a Nobel Prize.
52. Annika Kim Constantino, "ExJP Morgan CEO Says Highly Successful People Get Outside Their Comfort Zones: 'That's How You Keep Growing,'" August 8, 2022, CNBC, https://www.cnbc.com/2022/08/08/ex-jp-morgan-ceo-bill-harrison-leave-your-comfort-zone-find-success.html.
53. Donella Meadows, "Leverage Points: Places to Intervene in a System," The Donella Meadows Project, https://donellameadows.org/archives/leverage-points-places-to-intervene-in-a-system/.

CHAPTER 3

54. Capital Institute, "Ethics, Economics, Finance and Governance for the Anthropocene," 2012,
55. Joseph E. Stiglitz, Amartya Sen, and Jean-Paul Fitoussi, "Report by the Commission on the Measurement of Economic Performance and Social

ENDNOTES 257

Progress," https://web.archive.org/web/20150721025729/http://www.stiglitz-sen-fitoussi.fr/documents/rapport_anglais.pdf.
56. Carol Sanford, website, http://carolsanford.com/.
57. F. Capra, *The Web of Life: A New Scientific Understanding of Living Systems* (New York: Anchor, 1997).
58. Environmental economics, in contrast to ecological economics, is essentially the neoliberal framework with an attempt to integrate externalities into it. Such an attempt is a correct beginning but ultimately an impossible solution to the shortcomings of the neoliberal framework.
59. L. Margulis, *Symbiotic Planet: A New Look at Evolution* (New York: Basic Books, 1998).
60. P. Brown and G. Garver, *Right Relationship: Building a Whole Earth Economy* (San Francisco: Berrett-Koehler, 2009).
61. Author's personal communication with Janine Benyus. See also Benyus's talk on collaboration in nature at Google: Events at Google, "8—Nature's Collaboration System," April 13, 2010, https://www.youtube.com/watch?v=IzS7CRaCEtU.
62. L. Stout, *The Shareholder Value Myth: How Putting Shareholders First Harms Investors, Corporations, and the Public* (San Francisco: Berrett-Koehler, 2012).
63. R. Edward Freeman, *Strategic Management: A Stakeholder Approach* (Boston: Pitman, 1984).
64. C. Sanford, *The Responsible Business: Reimagining Sustainability and Success* (New York: Jossey-Bass, 2001).
65. *Externality* is a term economists use to describe costs or benefits not captured in the prices of an economy. Just as managing material and financial scarcity defined the economic problem of the twentieth century, managing the "externalities" of today's twenty-first-century economic system—both ecological and social, in the context of extreme inequality—must come to define today's economic problem. Redefining the problem we are trying to solve means we need a new conceptual framework adequate to this new job.
66. For a rigorous examination and attempt at quantification of the Earth's life-sustaining ecosystem services, see TEEB, "The Economics of Ecosystems and Biodiversity," http://www.teebweb.org/.
67. M. Z. Jacobsen and M. Delucchi, "A Plan to Power 100 Percent of the Planet with Renewables," *Scientific American* online, November 1, 2009, http://www.scientificamerican.com/article/a-path-to-sustainable-energy-by-2030/.
68. See, e.g., Rodale Institute, "Farming Systems Trial," n.d., http://rodaleinstitute.org/our-work/farming-systems-trial/; or UNCTAD, "Wake Up Before It Is Too Late," http://unctad.org/en/PublicationsLibrary/ditcted2012d3_en.pdf.
69. E. U. von Weizsäcker et al., *Factor Five: Transforming the Global Economy Through 80% Improvements in Resource Productivity* (New York: Routledge, 2009).
70. Wikipedia, "Context-Based Sustainability," https://en.wikipedia.org/wiki/Context-Based_Sustainability.
71. O. Scharmer, *Theory U: Leading from the Future as It Emerges* (San Francisco: Berrett-Koehler, 2009).

72. See, e.g., P. Hawken, A. Lovins, and L. H. Lovins, *Natural Capitalism: Creating the Next Industrial Revolution*, US Green Building Council, 1999, http://www.usgbc.org/.
73. Integrated Reporting, n.d., http://www.theiirc.org/.
74. R. Edward Freeman, Kirsten Martin, and Bidhan Parmar, "Stakeholder Capitalism," *Journal of Business Ethics* 74 (2007): 303–14, http://kirstenmartin.net/wp-content/uploads/2013/11/Stakeholder-Capitalism-.pdf.
75. L. Stout, *The Shareholder Value Myth: How Putting Shareholders First Harms Investors, Corporations, and the Public* (San Francisco: Berrett-Koehler, 2012).
76. P. Hawken, *Blessed Unrest: How the Largest Movement in the World Came into Being and Why No One Saw It Coming* (New York: Viking Penguin, 2007).
77. Global Alliance for Banking on Values, "We Put Finance at the Service of People and the Planet," n.d., http://www.gabv.org.
78. Thomas L. Friedman, "Is It Sheldon Adelson's World?," *New York Times*, March 11, 2015, http://www.nytimes.com/2015/03/11/opinion/thomas-l-friedman-is-it-sheldons-world.html.
79. I am indebted to Elisabet Sahtouris, who used this phrase in a speech, "Living Systems, the Internet, and the Human Future," in 2000.
80. K. Pickett and R. Wilkinson, *The Spirit Level: Why Greater Equality Makes Societies Stronger* (New York: Bloomsbury, 2009).
81. International Cooperative Alliance, website, http://ica.coop/en.
82. The Goldman Sachs 1MBD scandal in Malaysia coming on the heels of its central role in the Great Financial Crash all under the same CEO would cause a business enterprise to permanently lose its license to operate in any civilized society. See Office of Public Affairs, U.S. Department of Justice, "Goldman Sachs Charged in Foreign Bribery Case and Agrees to Pay over $2.9 Billion," October 22, 2020, https://www.justice.gov/archives/opa/pr/goldman-sachs-charged-foreign-bribery-case-and-agrees-pay-over-29-billion.
83. "Evergreen Direct Investing: Co-Creating the Regenerative Economy," *The Field Guide to a Regenerative Economy*, https://fieldguide.capitalinstitute.org/evergreen-direct-investing.html.
84. Denise-Marie Ordway and Leighton Walter Kille, "The Impact of Big-Box Retailers on Communities, Jobs, Crime, Wages and More: Research Roundup," *The Journalist's Resource*, December 16, 2015, http://journalistsresource.org/studies/government/municipal/impact-big-box-retailers-employmentwages-crime-health.
85. Common Future, website, https://bealocalist.org/.
86. Transition Network, "About Transition," https://www.transitionnetwork.org/.
87. *The Field Guide to a Regenerative Economy*, http://fieldguide.capitalinstitute.org/community-sourced-capital.html.
88. Joseph E. Stiglitz, "On the Wrong Side of Globalization," *The New York Times*, March 15, 2014, http://opinionator.blogs.nytimes.com/2014/03/15/on-the-wrong-side-of-globalization/?_php=true&_type=blogs&_r=0.
89. For more information, please see https://www.biofi.earth/.
90. Mondragón, website, http://www.mondragon-corporation.com/eng/.

91. "The Evergreen Cooperatives," *The Field Guide to a Regenerative Economy*, n.d., http://fieldguide.capitalinstitute.org/the-evergreen-cooperatives.html.
92. The Oberlin Project, website, http://www.oberlinproject.org.
93. John Fullerton, "The Courage to Lead," *HuffPost*, September 25, 2014, http://www.huffingtonpost.com/john-fullerton/the-courage-to-lead_1_b_5881424.
94. World Business Council for Sustainable Development, website, www.wbcsd.org.
95. W. McDonough and M. Braungart, *Cradle to Cradle: Remaking the Way We Make Things* (New York: North Point, 2002).
96. P. Hawken, A. Lovins, and L. H. Lovins, "Natural Capitalism: Creating the Next Industrial Revolution," U.S. Green Building Council, 1999, http://www.usgbc.org/; or see *Harvard Business Review*, http://www.natcap.org/images/other/HBR-RMINatCap.pdf.
97. K. E. Boulding, "The Economics of the Coming Spaceship Earth," 1966.
98. W. Stahel and G. Reday, "The Potential for Substituting Manpower for Energy," *A Research Report to the European Commission* (Battelle, Switzerland: Geneva Research Centre, 1976).
99. Ellen MacArthur Foundation, "It's Time for a Circular Economy," http://www.ellenmacarthurfoundation.org.
100. B. Lietaer, R. E. Ulanowicz, and S. Goerner, "Options for Managing a Systemic Bank Crisis," *Sapiens* 2, no. 1 (2009), http://sapiens.revues.org/index747.html.
101. RSF, website, http://rsfsocialfinance.org/.
102. J. Womack and D. Jones, *Lean Solutions: How Companies and Customers Can Create Value and Wealth Together* (New York: Free Press, 2005).
103. This is a play on the title of Richard Heinberg's important book, *Peak Everything: Waking Up to the Century of Declines* (Gabriola Island: New Society Publishers, 2005).
104. Stockholm Resilience Center, website, http://www.stockholmresilience.org/21/research/what-is-resilience.html.
105. JPMorgan's CFO Marianne Lake was responding to calls from Goldman Sachs's equity analyst to break up the bank in order to unlock shareholder value. See Gretchen Morgenson, "Smothered by a Boom in Banking," *The New York Times*, February 28, 2015, http://nyti.ms/189yd8b.
106. Global Alliance for Banking on Values, "We Put Finance at the Service of People and the Planet," https://www.gabv.org/.
107. E. O. Wilson and David Sloan Wilson, "Rethinking the Theoretical Foundation of Biology," *Quarterly Review of Biology* 82, no. 4 (2007), https://www.journals.uchicago.edu/doi/full/10.1086/522809?trk=public_post_comment-text#:~:text=Abstract,turbulent%20past%20is%20appropriately%20understood.
108. See chapter 13 of P. Hawken, A. Lovins, and L. H. Lovins, *Natural Capitalism: Creating the Next Industrial Revolution*, U.S. Green Building Council, 1999, http://www.usgbc.org.
109. L. Stout, *The Shareholder Value Myth: How Putting Shareholders First Harms Investors, Corporations, and the Public* (San Francisco: Berrett-Koehler, 2012).

110. Modern capitalist economies also include many enterprises with cooperative forms of ownership and democratic control, as well as numerous state-owned enterprises in countries ranging from China and Brazil to Germany and the United States. Governments in virtually all nations significantly influence—and, to varying degrees, control—commerce, trade, and finance through regulatory processes, tax policies, and subsidies, if not direct ownership.
111. Numerous private conversations with Savory.
112. K. Raworth, *Doughnut Economics: Seven Ways to Think Like a Twenty-First-Century Economist* (Vermont: Chelsea Green, 2017).
113. D. Bornstein, *How to Change the World: Social Entrepreneurs and the Power of New Ideas* (New York: Oxford University Press, 2007).

CHAPTER 4

114. Heerad Sabeti, "The For-Profit Enterprise," *Harvard Business Review*, November 2011, https://hbr.org/2011/11/the-for-benefit-enterprise.
115. Common Future, "We Are Building a Common Future," n.d., https://bealocalist.org/.
116. Global Alliance for Banking on Values, website, http://www.gabv.org/.
117. Living Future, "Living Building Challenge," n.d., http://living-future.org/lbc.
118. P. Hawken, *Blessed Unrest: How the Largest Movement in the World Came into Being, and Why No One Saw It Coming* (New York: Viking, 2007).
119. For more information, please see https://capitalinstitute.org/field-guide/.
120. John Fullerton, "The Courage to Lead," September 25, 2014, Capital Institute, http://capitalinstitute.org/blog/courage-lead/.
121. https://savory.global/.
122. D. Meadows et al., *Beyond the Limits: Confronting Global Collapse, Envisioning a Sustainable Future* (White River Junction, VT: Chelsea Green Publishers, 1992).
123. See J. Fullerton's speech to the Club of Rome (2014): http://capitalinstitute.org/wp-content/uploads/2014/10/Financing-the-Energy-Transition_COR_w-endnotes.pdf.
124. Carbon Tracker, "Wasted Capital and Stranded Assets," December 4, 2013, press release, http://www.carbontracker.org/report/wasted-capital-and-stranded-assets/.
125. John Fullerton, "The Big Choice," April 8, 2020, http://capitalinstitute.org/blog/big-choice-0/.
126. H. Daly and J. Cobb, *For the Common Good: Redirecting the Economy Toward Community, the Environment, and a Sustainable Future* (Boston: Beacon 1984).
127. "Evergreen Direct Investing: Co-Creating the Regenerative Economy," *The Field Guide to a Regenerative Economy*, https://fieldguide.capitalinstitute.org/evergreen-direct-investing.html.
128. RSF, "Change Finance, Finance Change," n.d., http://rsfsocialfinance.org/.
129. John B. Fullerton, "Financing the Energy Transition," Club of Rome Annual Meeting, Mexico City, October 16–17, 2014, https://capitalinstitute.org/wp-content/uploads/2014/10/Financing-the-Energy-Transition_COR_w-endnotes.pdf.

130. E. Ostrom, *Governing the Commons: The Evolution of Institutions for Collective Action* (London: Cambridge University Press, 1990).
131. IFRS Foundation, "Integrated Reporting," n.d., http://www.theiirc.org/.
132. IFRS Foundation, "SASB Standards," n.d., http://www.sasb.org/.
133. An updated version by B. Fath et al. published in 2019: https://www.researchgate.net/publication/332050528_Measuring_Regenerative_Economics_10_principles_and_measures_undergirding_systemic_economic_health.
134. S. Allesina and R. E. Ulanowicz, "Cycling in Ecological Networks: Finn's Index Revisited," *Computational Biology and Chemistry* 28, no. 3 (2004): 227–33, https://www.sciencedirect.com/science/article/abs/pii/S1476927104000404.
135. N. Bateson, "Warm Data," International Bateson Institute, https://batesoninstitute.org/warm-data-labs/.

CHAPTER 6

136. G. Boyd and J. Reardon, *The Ergodic Investor and Entrepreneur* (Evolutesix Books, 2023).
137. https://donellameadows.org/archives/leverage-points-places-to-intervene-in-a-system/.

CHAPTER 7

138. Fritjof Capra, "Principles of Life," August 27, 2024, website, https://www.fritjofcapra.net/principles-of-life/; published in *Resurgence and Ecologies*, issue 346, September/October 2024, https://www.resurgence.org/magazine/issue346-nature-our-teacher.html.
139. Readers may be pondering whether artificial intelligence or the holy (or unholy) grail of generative intelligence will make a leap from machine to living system. That is a fascinating question, but beyond the scope of this book. From what I have managed to learn so far, I'm holding on to the view that AI and even generative AI remains a machine.
140. *Scientific materialism* is a term used to describe the modern age view that the physical world defines reality, and it can be measured analytically to prove that it exists.
141. Even artificial general intelligence will require ongoing inputs of energy and be limited to only certain forms of intelligence (available on the web in digital form), so as best I can understand it, AGI will never be regenerative. But this is a fascinating question.
142. F. Faggin, *Irreducible: Consciousness, Life, Computers, and Human Nature* (Essentia, 2024).
143. See, e.g., Stuart Kauffman, Jude Currivan, Andreas Webber, and Brian Swimme.
144. S. A. Kauffman and A. Roli, "A Third Transition in Science?" (Royal Society Publishing, 2023).
145. "First Principles," fs blog, n.d., https://fs.blog/first-principles/.

CHAPTER 8

146. P. Polman and A. Winston, *Net Positive*.

CHAPTER 9

147. There is no actual Nobel Prize in Economics. Alfred Nobel did not consider economics a science. So the Swedish Central Bank decided to create a prize "in honor of Alfred Nobel." It is referred to erroneously as the Nobel Prize in Economics.
148. The rebound effect was first proposed by economist William Stanley Jevons in the nineteenth century in the context of coal. More broadly, what became known as "Jevons' Paradox" explains that when a new technology improves efficiency, the resulting reduced cost stimulates demand for more and new uses. So the efficiency gains are never translated into reduced consumption. For example, more efficient combustion engines have let to bigger cars and more driving rather than reduced emissions. Researchers have estimated the rebound effect between 10 percent and 50 percent depending on the industry.
149. David Ricardo was a contemporary of Adam Smith, and his "law" assumed that capital would not flow across national borders, which made sense in his day. Why would the Brits ever trust their capital to be invested in France, or vice versa? The law of comparative advantage said that the British should continue making sweaters with their plentiful flocks of sheep, while the French should continue making champagne rather than diversify into sweaters. The two nations should trade instead, leveraging their "comparative advantage" to mutual benefit. Neoclassical economics never updated that fatal flaw about capital not crossing national borders, even as the "Nobel Prize" was handed to Paul Krugman for his work on international trade. This profound flaw remained the basis for economists on both sides of the political divide to champion free trade, in the belief that comparative advantage would lead to win-win. It turned out in a world of capital mobility that we live in today, comparative advantage turned to competitive advantage. The unprecedented pace of the rise of China while the U.S. middle class was hollowed out was the direct consequence of this error in trade theory.
150. Ecosystem services is a concept designed to put a value on the services provided by nature. For example, what is the value of pollination by bees, or cloud creation by rainforests? It is a controversial concept in that it reduces the value of nature to a monetary value of what it provides to humans. Defenders of the concept argue that economics already has put a value on it—zero. So any estimate is better than what economics is currently doing. While the author acknowledges this argument, we take a different approach to both by protecting ecosystem *function*—this is the key. And we offer an entirely fresh mechanism to share the wealth of the commons democratically at the same time.
151. See Global Wealth Report 2025, UBS, https://www.ubs.com/us/en/wealth-management/insights/global-wealth-report.html.
152. Girardet, H. "Biosphere and Technosphere," *Ecologist*, December 1, 2022.
153. Lovelock, J. *Gaia: A New Look at Life on Earth* (Oxford University Press, 1979).
154. WWF, "Catastrophic 73% Decline in the Average Size of Global Wildlife Populations in Just 50 Years Reveals a 'System in Peril,'" October 9, 2024, https://www.worldwildlife.org/press-releases/catastrophic-73-decline-in-

the-average-size-of-global-wildlife-populations-in-just-50-years-reveals-a-system-in-peril.
155. R. Wilkenson and K. Pickett, *The Spirit Level: Why Greater Equality Makes Societies Stronger* (Bloomsbury Press, 2010).
156. The topic of universal basic income is beyond the scope of this chapter. In the context of a regenerative economy, the concept would serve to subsidize the dignity of a chosen form of work aligned for us all with our unique calling. It should not be seen as an alternative to work, nor should work be understood as "disutility," as it was assumed to be in legendary economist Irving Fisher's equations that provide the foundation of neoclassical economics.

CHAPTER 10

157. Regenerative Technology white paper can be found on the Regenerative Technology Project website: https://www.regentech.co/.
158. Our cognition is far more complex than the left brain/right brain division suggests. See I. McGilchrist, *The Master and His Emissary*.

CHAPTER 11

159. For more information, please see https://www.levyinstitute.org/pubs/wp74.pdf.
160. Kolbert, E. *The Sixth Extinction: An Unnatural History* (Henry Holt and Co., 2014).
161. Bioregional Finance for a Planetary Regeneration, website, https://www.biofi.earth/.
162. For more information, please see https://www.nobelprize.org/prizes/physics/2022/press-release/.
163. J. Fullerton, *Finance for a Regenerative World* (Capital Institute, 2018).
164. To oversimplify, ESG is premised on the idea that the "invisible hands" of markets are a far better tool than government regulation, so by improving markets with better information, somehow the "invisible hand" will address our most pressing systemic challenges.
165. Office of Public Affairs, "Goldman Sachs Charged in Foreign Bribery Case and Agrees to Pay over $2.9 Billion," October 22, 2020, https://www.justice.gov/opa/pr/goldman-sachs-charged-foreign-bribery-case-and-agrees-pay-over-29-billion.
166. Bill Baue, "#SustyGoals 2: A Dialogue with Allen White of GISR, the Godfather of Sustainability Context (Part 2)," November 8, 2013, https://sustainablebrands.com/read/sustygoals-2-a-dialogue-with-allen-white-of-gisr-the-godfather-of-sustainability-context-part-2.

CHAPTER 12

167. Beyond Bretton Woods, "An Invitation to a Radical Paradigm Shift," n.d., https://www.beyondbrettonwoods.org/.
168. Land Trust Alliance, "What Is a Land Trust?," n.d., https://landtrustalliance.org/why-land-matters/land-conservation/about-land-trusts.
169. Garrett Hardin, "The Tragedy of the Commons," Econlib, n.d., https://www.econlib.org/library/Enc/TragedyoftheCommons.html.

170. https://capitalinstitute.org/blog/why-we-need-financial-transactions-tax/.
171. Robert H. Frank, "Heads, You Win. Tails, You Win, Too," *New York Times*, January 6, 2013, http://www.nytimes.com/2013/01/06/business/pigovian-taxes-may-offer-economic-hope.html?_r=0.
172. Excessive Wealth Disorder Institute, "What Is Excessive Wealth Disorder?," n.d., https://www.excessivewealth.org/excessive-wealth-disorder.
173. I realize this is a highly controversial proposal, in conflict with the narrative we tell ourselves in our capitalist economy. We live in a world where the board of Tesla tells us it must grant the richest man in the world $30 billion in fresh equity as incentive to get out of bed. This is utter nonsense, evidence of a system and a culture gone mad. But nonetheless, restraining the market for talent is a difficult challenge. This is why I favor prioritizing the establishment of an Institution of the Commons over a wealth tax blunt enough to address inequality. As we have discussed, such an Institution of the Commons would structurally insert feedback loops into the system that act as automatic, self-governing stabilizers for both a healthy commons sector and for out-of-control inequality.
174. S. Goerner, B. Lietaer, and R. Ulanowicz, "Quantifying Economic Sustainability: Implications for Free Enterprise, Theory, Policy and Practice," *Ecological Economics* 69, no. 1 (2009): 76–81. See also http://people.biology.ufl.edu/ulan/pubs/Goerner.pdf.
175. John Fullerton, "Limits to Investment: Finance in the Anthropocene," Great Transition Initiative, April 2014, https://greattransition.org/publication/limits-to-investment?kuid=25b2a55b-c58e-4030-bdfc-c6ebbe37fbbe-1745248320&kref=https%3A%2F%2Fcapitalinstitute.org%2Fthought-pieces%2F.
176. John Fullerton, "High-Frequency Trading Is a Blight on Markets. Tobin Tax Can Help," April 4, 2014, https://capitalinstitute.org/blog/high-frequency-trading-blight-markets-tobin-tax-can-help/; Fullerton, "Why We Need a Financial Transactions Tax," Capital Institute, August 21, 2011, https://capitalinstitute.org/blog/why-we-need-financial-transactions-tax/.
177. U.S. housing policy that incentivized homeowners to take on high levels of debt relative to income seemed efficient but harmed resiliency, in conflict with the principle of balance. Equity subsidies in right relationship with new homeowner needs coupled with new supply incentives would be wiser policy.
178. For more information, please see https://en.wikipedia.org/wiki/The_Cultural_Creatives.
179. For more information, please see https://www.biofi.earth/.
180. For more information, please see https://regenesisgroup.com/.
181. Tompkins Conservation, website, https://www.tompkinsconservation.org/our-team/.

ABOUT THE AUTHOR

JOHN FULLERTON is an unconventional economist, writer, educator, and impact investor. He is considered the architect of Regenerative Economics and its companion Regenerative Finance.

John is the founder of the Capital Institute, dedicated to the bold reimagination of economics and finance. Previously he was a managing director of JPMorgan until walking away from Wall Street in 2001. John is also the co-founder of Grasslands, LLC, a board member of the Savory Institute, and a member of the Club of Rome. He was featured in the 2021 award-winning documentary *Going Circular*.

John and his wife Susan live in coastal Stonington, Connecticut.

ABOUT CAPITAL INSTITUTE

Our mission is to develop the theoretical foundation and policy implications of Regenerative Economics and Regenerative Finance, illuminate and facilitate their emergence in the real world, and educate leaders of all kinds about the promise of Regenerative Economics as a serious response to the polycrisis that defines our age.

Please visit us at www.capitalinstitute.org

ABOUT NEW SOCIETY PUBLISHERS

New Society Publishers is an activist, solutions-oriented publisher focused on publishing books to build a more just and sustainable future. Our books offer tips, tools, and insights from leading experts in a wide range of areas.

We're proud to hold to the highest environmental and social standards of any publisher in North America. When you buy New Society books, you are part of the solution!

At New Society Publishers, we care deeply about *what* we publish—but also about *how* we do business.

- Our corporate structure is an innovative employee shareholder agreement, so we're one-third employee-owned (since 2015)
- We've created a Statement of Ethics (2021). The intent of this Statement is to act as a framework to guide our actions and facilitate feedback for continuous improvement of our work
- We're carbon-neutral (since 2006)
- We're certified as a B Corporation (since 2016)
- We're Signatories to the UN's Sustainable Development Goals (SDG) Publishers Compact (2020–2030, the Decade of Action)

To download our full catalog, sign up for our quarterly newsletter, and to learn more about New Society Publishers, please visit newsociety.com.

www.ingramcontent.com/pod-product-compliance
Lightning Source LLC
Chambersburg PA
CBHW071954070526
44583CB00015B/1188